News Coverage of Global Disasters

News Coverage of Global Disasters

Journalism's Power to Aid Healing and Recovery

Michael McCluskey

LEXINGTON BOOKS
Lanham • Boulder • New York • London

Published by Lexington Books
An imprint of The Rowman & Littlefield Publishing Group, Inc.
4501 Forbes Boulevard, Suite 200, Lanham, Maryland 20706
www.rowman.com

6 Tinworth Street, London SE11 5AL, United Kingdom

Copyright © 2021 The Rowman & Littlefield Publishing Group, Inc.

All rights reserved. No part of this book may be reproduced in any form or by any electronic or mechanical means, including information storage and retrieval systems, without written permission from the publisher, except by a reviewer who may quote passages in a review.

British Library Cataloguing in Publication Information Available

Library of Congress Cataloging-in-Publication Data Available

ISBN 9781793625342 (cloth)
ISBN 9781793625366 (pbk)
Library of Congress Control Number: 2020944244

Contents

Acknowledgments		vii
1	Introduction	1
2	Tragedies and Journalism	5
3	Journalism Culture	27
4	Patterns and Influences on News about Natural Disasters	41
5	Survivor Stories	57
6	Death Stories	71
7	Selfless Behavior	77
8	Recovery Efforts	85
9	Community, Cohesion, and Intimacy	97
10	Faith, Belief, and Salvation	105
11	Reassurance, Purpose, or Meaning	109
12	Actions	113
13	Blame, Responsibility	137
14	External Validation	159
15	Analysis By Country	165
16	Conclusions	175

References	187
Index	213
About the Author	217

Acknowledgments

Putting this book together has been a lifelong journey that started when I was introduced to journalism at West Seattle High School and continued through studies at the University of Washington. Then came professional work in newspapers, mostly at the *Snoqualmie Valley Record* and the *Wenatchee World*. By the time I headed to graduate school, again at the University of Washington, I was already thinking about the connections between trauma and journalism. Many wonderful colleagues, especially at the *Wenatchee World*, guided my interest and thinking about this topic as we sorted through difficult stories that triggered traumas in our communities of North Central Washington.

I had many inspiring mentors in graduate school at the University of Washington and the University of Wisconsin who helped flesh out and direct my scholarly work. Trauma and journalism was a topic that I started exploring upon entering grad school, then set aside, only to return to in recent years. It was upon completion of my previous book, *News Framing of School Shootings: Journalism and American Social Problems*, that the ideas for this book came together. By that time, I was at my fourth academic institution and each had wonderful colleagues who kept me on track. Many thanks need to go out for the help I received from my friends at Fresno State University, Ohio State University, American University, and the University of Tennessee at Chattanooga. Additional thanks goes out to colleagues in academia around the world who listened to my ideas and gave me needed feedback.

One undergraduate student at the University of Tennessee at Chattanooga was instrumental in this project—Lacey Keefer. For her help, I'm forever thankful. Lacey played critical roles in developing the ten themes of healing, coping, hope, and recovery that dominate this book; working through intercoder reliability testing; and conducting much of the quantitative coding. Mark Drinkard, another undergraduate student at the University of Tennessee at Chattanooga, also helped out on this project.

Finally, none of this would have been possible without the love and support of my terrific wife, Sharen Fisher.

Chapter 1

Introduction

Trauma is a common element in the lives of humans. So is recovery, as those affected begin the process of healing and coping. The movement from trauma to recovery is part of humanity, transcending time or location. While literature about the human condition during times of trauma populates historic and recent works in a wide variety of contexts, from popular fiction to clinical books, the role of news in this healing process has been underacknowledged. This book contends that a human need to recover is shared within the news content that follows traumas. Further, this book argues that news serves an important societal role by articulating ideas that aid the transition from shock and loss to hope, healing, coping, and recovery.

This news role in recovery seems more instinctual than learned. As a former journalist, during my years as a student or as a working professional, I cannot recall being taught or told about journalism's contribution to healing. Yet during serious traumas, events that shatter a community's sense of safety or stability, such themes emerge within the news stories. My experience in a newsroom is that we seemed to know that perspectives related to healing, hope, and coping in the community were not only acceptable, but necessary. Most memorable for me were covering a wildfire and reporting on a double homicide of a fourteen-year-old girl and her mother while working at the *Wenatchee World* newspaper in the United States. Both caused significant trauma to people in our area of Washington State. Themes of healing, coping, hope, and recovery were key elements of stories we published. Maybe subtle newsroom socialization made such stories seem natural and inevitable, maybe the justification came from elsewhere. Regardless of its source, the role of journalism to aid in the healing process following a trauma seems natural and logical.

My motivation for writing this book was spurred while finishing a previous book (McCluskey, 2017) about news and school shootings. Something profound about the journalistic performance was missing from the book—the newspaper and television reports about school shootings played roles in bringing communities together and help them heal, recover, and cope. This resonated, not just as a communication scholar, but as a former journalist. This tendency seemed to transcend context—it appeared to exist in historic examples and cross borders.

While much of the cited work is from the last twenty years, some evidence of this journalistic role comes from the first half of the twentieth century (e.g., Pantti & Wahl-Jorgensen, 2007). Additionally, this author (McCluskey, 2018) found similar patterns of healing, coping, hope, and recovery within news coverage of a traumatic event in the United States from 1865. Healing, coping, hope, and recovery in the news after a traumatic event may be centered in a human trait rather than a product of contemporary contexts or news practices. Further, this book was written during the COVID-19 pandemic of the winter and spring of 2020, in which similar themes were prominent in the news coverage of that worldwide trauma. The conclusions section will make comparisons between the natural disasters analyzed in this book and patterns of news about the pandemic.

Additionally, there is some evidence of this being international in scope (Pantti & Wieten, 2005; Tenenboim-Weinblatt, 2008), but those are primarily drawn from Western democracies. Do similar trends exist in non-Western countries, even countries with limited freedom of expression? That could help clarify whether this is a product of human nature or is developed through education and socialization. Analysis of three countries—Sweden, Bangladesh, and Tunisia—found many shared values among journalists and students (Frey et al., 2017). Additionally, Galtung and Holmboe Ruge (1965) noted, consonance of values such as culture and language would lead to similarities in news presentations. Evaluating eight traumas around the world help identify patterns in common across news outlets and those a product of contextual and structural factors. In addition, news around the world about the COVID-19 pandemic featured themes of healing, coping, hope, and recovery, a further indication of its international scope.

The focus of this book is a comparison of news content about significant traumas that took place around the world in 2018. Each trauma was a natural disaster and each included news content about how people dealt with the disaster. The disasters studied were an earthquake in Papua New Guinea, an earthquake and tsunami in Indonesia, flooding in Japan and Nigeria, a heat wave in Pakistan, a volcanic eruption in Guatemala, and wildfires in Greece and the United States. Each disaster resulted in numerous deaths and most caused damage to homes and other structures. The news coverage was analyzed to evaluate patterns that matched themes of coping, healing, hope, and recovery.

Why does this matter? Trauma may be an abnormal condition, but is also unavoidable for many people and societies. If news provides ideas and emotions that aid healing, coping, hope, and recovery after significant and broad traumatic events, then journalism can be acknowledged as playing an almost clinic role in recovery. These journalistic characteristics can be added to the everyday functions of the news industry. Considering generally declining trust in journalism since the late 1970s in the United States (Mayer, 2019) and low levels of trust in other countries, including Greece and Japan (Watson, 2019), understanding the broader role of journalism could give the public a more balanced perspective on the news and what it contributes to the world. Additionally, this proposed journalistic role highlights news workers as people first who bring that sensitivity and perspective into their professions. So it may more broadly point toward how humans respond to trauma in ways that aids the healing of themselves and society overall.

The plan of this book is to provide conceptual understandings and quantitative analysis, followed by qualitative evaluation. Chapter 2 evaluates the linkage between tragedies and journalism, suggesting the potential connection between themes of healing, coping, hope, and recovery with news values and values held by journalists. The chapter explores connections between healing and journalism, introduces ten themes of journalistic healing, explains the study approach, and details on the eight natural disasters explored in this book. Chapter 3 examines the journalistic culture within each country, including comparative multicountry attributes. Chapter 4 provides quantitative evidence for the analysis of news content from each of the eight natural disasters about the ten themes of healing, coping, hope, and recovery. Analysis includes five contextual elements inherent to each disaster and five structural elements within each country as potential influences on news coverage.

Chapters 5–14 use details in the news coverage as qualitative evidence for each of the ten themes of coping, healing, hope, and recovery. For each theme, several subthemes emerged within the news content. Since sources used in stories are a product of journalistic choice that can direct the focus of each story, the sources are described within each of the ten themes. Survivor stories are the focus of chapter 5, uplifting tales of people who escaped imminent danger. Chapter 6 articulates death stories, in which the deceased become well-rounded people rather than mere statistics. Tales of selfless behavior form chapter 7, as heroes, volunteers, and donations reflect the best of society. In chapter 8, news content examines recovery themes, dealing with the immediate and long-range needs of people and infrastructure.

Community, cohesion, and intimacy, demonstrating ways in which people are able to come together in coping with the disaster, comprise chapter 9.

In chapter 10, faith, belief, and salvation are highlighted as news articulated spiritual aspects of hope and healing. Themes of reassurance, purpose, or meaning are evaluated in chapter 11, as the news highlighted people finding perspective following the trauma. Chapter 12 is devoted to actions, both physical and verbal, as government and other entities addressed the current disaster and planned for the future. Blame or responsibility, mostly targeting government, was the focus of chapter 13, as concerns being aired in the news helped the audience cope. In chapter 14, external validation in the news featured sympathy and solidarity coming from outside the affected country.

Chapter 15 evaluates news themes by country, including comparative analysis across the countries to identify potential patterns of news practices. Chapter 16 examines the themes and patterns that emerged from this analysis, including contextual and structural factors. It also evaluates elements that can be generalized and offered suggestions for future scholarly work on news content related to healing, coping, hope, and recovery.

Chapter 2

Tragedies and Journalism

Tragedies are a common part of human existence, from natural disasters to destruction perpetrated by people to accidents. Survivors move on in their lives, remembering the losses and beginning the road to recovery. This process of healing is universal to humans as social creatures. Tragedies not only affect victims and those closely tied to victims, but the rapid spread of information through modern communication means that communities, those with shared attributes, and even entire nations may also suffer.

Natural disasters are one type of tragedy, which are a common occurrence around the world and trauma-inducing events that can seriously affect victims, survivors, and entire countries. Natural disasters often arise suddenly and can cause widespread harm to people, through deaths and injuries, and to property, damaging homes and infrastructure that can leave communities and even nations facing lengthy recovery. These physical, emotional, and psychological traumas provide an opportunity for news organizations to help the public cope with the sudden loss, raise hope, and provide a path toward healing and recovery.

News attention to natural disasters and other tragedies fits several characteristics of what Dayan and Katz (1993) refer to as media events—they are not routine, they monopolize television, often feature live broadcasting and often celebrate reconciliation rather than conflict. According to Dayan and Katz (1993, p. 12): "The message is one of reconciliation, in which participants and audiences are invited to unite in the overcoming of conflict or at least in its postponement or miniaturization." News organizations not only spread information about tragedies, but focus on recovery as well. This can range from pragmatic steps an audience can take, such as donating blood, goods, or money; uplifting stories of those who have persevered after losing homes or loved ones; acts of heroism, as people put their own lives in harm to aid others; and highlighting group gatherings like memorial services to honor those lost and come together as a community.

But where do these themes originate? Scholarly understanding of what prompts news attention and focus falls within labels such as news values (Galtung & Holmboe Ruge, 1965; Harcup & O'Neill, 2001; McGregor, 2002), journalists' values (Deuze, 2005; Gans, 1979; Paletz & Entman, 1981), and news functions (Park, 1941, 1967/1925). Regardless of the label, each represents an attempt to generalize the complex mix of contextual and individual factors that influence news coverage choices. Within that list of explanations, found more within the gaps among values than explicitly articulated, is a journalistic role to promote healing after a trauma. Journalism textbooks refer to tragedies more often as ethics case studies of how journalists should behave than an explicit responsibility of news to aid healing. Yet it seems to be a normal journalistic practice that may address a universal human need. Further, this news practice may transcend borders and time. By exploring news coverage of different types of natural disasters occurring in countries of varied size, location, and cultural norms, this study helps evaluate common approaches and differences among news organizations around the world.

Natural disasters often arise suddenly and pose many challenges to affected citizens that news coverage can aid. Wildfires, floods, earthquakes, volcanic eruptions, tornadoes, and other shattering events cause death, physical injuries, damage to infrastructure, and emotional trauma. Whether the disasters occur across minutes, hours, days, or longer, the effects linger for survivors, rescuers, the local community, and even nations. Recovery—both physical and emotional—takes time. The range of possible injuries and responses is quite large, with the resulting news coverage perhaps moderated by contextual and structural factors. Each news organization belongs to its own worldwide professional cultural group and its principles—the responsibilities of journalism to inform and serve its audiences. This study uses this professional orientation as a starting point to consider potential patterns in how news organizations covered natural disasters.

IMPACT OF TRAUMA

When a trauma occurs, the effects on family and friends of victims are built upon personal connections and how their lives have changed. But traumas can have larger impacts, engulfing entire communities, nations, or the world. Trauma, according to Ostertag and Ortiz (2013, p. 188), is "an extraordinary and potentially dangerous life-changing event linked to reacting and coping." Trauma can be experienced individually or collectively; individual trauma includes physical or emotional shock of psychological damage (Ostertag & Ortiz, 2013), while collective trauma affects bonds of social life, including communality (Erikson, 1976). When individuals sense their trauma is shared, an individual trauma can turn into a collective trauma (Ostertag & Ortiz, 2013). Elements of a collective trauma include a tear in the social order, threat to a group's collective identity, and a threat to shared values (Ostertag & Ortiz, 2013). Similar to collective trauma is cultural trauma (Sztompka, 2000), which is sudden and surprising, with deep substance and scope, is perceived as coming from the outside and is seen as repulsive. Cultural trauma creates a large effect (Alexander, 2004, p. 1), which "occurs when members of a collectivity feel they have been subjected to a horrendous event that leaves indelible marks upon their group consciousness, marking their memories forever and changing their future identity in fundamental and irrevocable ways."

The process by which suffering extends to those not directly victimized by trauma carries labels such as vicarious traumatization (McCann & Pearlman, 1990), secondary traumatic stress (Creamer & Liddle, 2005), and compassion fatigue (Backholm & Björkqvist, 2010). Each explains the spread of psychological distress to those not directly affected by the trauma, with symptoms similar to post-traumatic stress disorder. This includes reexperiencing the trauma through intrusive thoughts or images, avoiding reminders of the trauma, general numbing, and physiological hyperarousal symptoms (Ben-Zur & Shamshins, 2012).

Vicarious trauma is especially likely when members share characteristics with victims (Noelle, 2002), tied to social identity (Tajfel & Turner, 1979). When reminded of a shared characteristic, such as similar demographics, experiences, perceptions, or values, including social groups like religion, ideology, or lifestyle (Slater, 2007), that social identity becomes salient. For instance, sexual minorities suffered trauma from the Matthew Shepard murder (Noelle, 2002), Israeli students experienced secondary trauma when exposed to information about a terror attack (Ben-Zur et al., 2012), and members of a minority group in Turkey were affected years later by a massacre (Yildiz & Verkuyten, 2011).

News coverage is a common means for people to be exposed to trauma without personally witnessing the event. Identity reminders can come from news and other media (Slater, 2007). For most people, according to Joye (2014), disasters and suffering are mainly presented to them through media, stressing the importance of news as a key signifying agent in studying effects of disasters. Tester (2001) stated that it is common for people to have an experience of reading or watching news and being deeply moved by the horrors we read about or see. Media play a critical role in extending individual trauma to a collective trauma by turning incidents into significant, meaning-laden events (Ostertag & Ortiz, 2013). In a national survey after the 9/11 terror attack in the United States, 44% of TV viewers developed one or more secondary post-traumatic stress disorder symptom (Schuster et al., 2001). National tragedies through media, especially television, affected children exposed to the space shuttle Challenger explosion (Wright et al., 1989) and the Oklahoma City bombing (Pfefferbaum et al., 2000) in the United States. Political violence through media resulted in negative psychological impacts like anxiety, anger, pity, and fury (Slone et al., 2008). Effects were associated with high levels of posttraumatic symptoms, acute distress, and feelings of insecurity and vulnerability (Slone et al., 2008).

According to Alexander (2004, p. 18), "When the trauma process enters the mass media, it gains opportunities and at the same time becomes subject to distinctive kinds of restrictions. Mediated mass communication allows traumas to be expressively dramatized and permits some of the competing interpretations to gain enormous persuasive power over others." Ostertag and Ortiz (2013, p. 189) contend that the communication and framing of tragedies "are fundamental to the construction of cultural trauma." Chouliaraki (2006) suggested that witnessing events of suffering via television evokes emotions, a sense of care, and responsibility for the distant suffered and what to do about the suffering. According to Monahan and Ettinger (2018, p. 479), "Media coverage can serve as a galvanizing force in a community by providing an outlet for those experiencing loss and trauma or bringing needed attention to the challenges that emerge in the aftermath of a disaster." News content (especially visuals) can spread information about the disaster, solicit assistance from outside the affected area, provide information about relief efforts and rescue missions, and alert communities about risks (Monahan & Ettinger, 2018).

HEALING, COPING, HOPE, AND RECOVERY AS A VALUE IN NEWS

Values affecting journalistic performance fall into two broad categories, one focused on practices that identify characteristics of events or issues as more or less newsworthy, the other related to the values held by journalists. However, healing or recovery from trauma is not explicitly mentioned among the news values or journalistic values.

News Values

Journalism textbooks suggest higher levels of newsworthiness when more news values are present. Audience attention is also predicted by news values

(Lee, 2009). The focus of news stories may be affected by the values, as stories often are constructed by emphasizing news values. Galtung and Holmboe Ruge (1965) proposed twelve characteristics of foreign news selection—frequency, threshold, unambiguity, meaningfulness, consonance, unexpectedness, continuity, composition, reference to elite nations, reference to elite people, reference to persons, and reference to something negative. While several of these values can be tied to tragedies—such as threshold, meaningfulness, unexpectedness, reference to persons, and reference to something negative—there is no explicit mention of a journalistic role to aid healing.

The limited context of Galtung and Holmboe Ruge (1965) and passage of time led future scholars to revisit those twelve news values. Harcup and O'Neill (2001) looked at the most prominent stories in three daily United Kingdom newspapers and found evaluation using the Galtung and Holmboe Ruge typology required extensive interpretation. Their analysis found unambiguity, reference to elite people, frequency, and reference to something negative to be the most common among the news values. Harcup and O'Neill (2001) created a revised set of ten news values: the power elite, celebrity, entertainment, surprise, bad news, good news, magnitude, relevance, follow-up, and newspaper agenda. Similarly, McGregor (2002) added four television-driven attributes to the list—visualness, emotion, conflict, and celebrification of the journalist. Harcup and O'Neill (2017) revisited news values with a larger and broader sample, arriving at a longer list than in their 2001 work. The updated version added five values—exclusivity, conflict, audiovisuals, shareability, and drama. Analysis of the original ten news values in newspapers showed bad news, surprise, and entertainment were the most common, while social media content had entertainment as the most common, followed by surprise and bad news (Harcup & O'Neill, 2017).

Altogether, these additional factors provide little clarification to healing as a news value—perhaps the visualness and emotion listed by McGregor (2002), along with the audiovisuals from Harcup and O'Neill (2017), may be a partial fit when considering memorials and similar public events. Additionally, the drama mentioned by Harcup and O'Neill (2017) encompasses anecdotes about rescues and survivors.

While scholarly approaches evaluated news content to extract news values, textbooks used to train journalists approach it as a guide. News values in the classroom become a checklist to help prospective journalists evaluate events and issues, and help craft the emphasis of news stories. Journalism textbooks suggest that the presence of more news values increases the chance that an event or issue is considered newsworthy or will be prominently located within the news product. Journalism textbooks often contain similar lists of news values—timeliness, impact/magnitude, prominence, proximity, unusualness/oddness, and conflict/controversy (Bender et al., 2016, pp. 13–16);

impact, timeliness, prominence, proximity, conflict, bizarre/unusual, and currency (Stovall, 2006, pp. 85–88); impact, conflict, novelty, prominence, proximity, and timeliness (Brooks et al., 2005, pp. 5–6); and timeliness, proximity, unusual nature, celebrities, human interest, conflict, impact, helpfulness, entertainment, issues, or problems in the community and trends (Rich, 2005, pp. 25–30). Healing or recovery is not explicitly a part of published news values, but can be found within the margins, such as Rich's helpfulness or somewhat by proximity (especially the psychological perspective, see Bender et al., 2016).

Journalists' Values

Another approach to evaluating the linkage between values and news rests within the values held by journalists. The perspective suggests that the norms and ethics of journalism are internal and guide an understanding of the profession and of the world. Similar to news values, scholarly evaluation of the values held by journalists is mainly developed retrospectively and contain overlapping themes.

Gans (1979), in his ethnography of elite news organizations, lists six values in the news—ethnocentrism (a tendency to value American practices), altruistic democracy (an understanding that democracy should work for the public interest), responsible capitalism (an expectation that businesses should operate fairly), small-town pastoralism (presenting rural areas as idyllic), individualism (praising individuals as heroes), and moderatism (discouraging excess or extremism)—as central to explaining how journalists define news. Gans (1979, p. 41) explained that enduring values "are values that can be found in many different types of news stories over a long period of time; often, they affect what events become news, for some are part and parcel of the definition of news." To those, Paletz and Entman (1981) add social order (which helps define acceptable and unacceptable behavior) and leadership (especially as operating for social good). Gans (1979) also saw order in the news to be a function of journalism, including natural disasters in which journalism acted as moral guardians. Deuze (2005) proposes five core journalistic values: public service, objectivity, autonomy, immediacy, and ethics. Frey et al. (2017) list nine common values—truth, providing information to the public, immediacy, autonomy/freedom/independence, watchdog/Fourth Estate, objectivity/neutrality, accuracy, verification, and balance.

News stories about healing or recovery are not explicit within values of journalists—individualism (Gans, 1979) tied to heroism may fit, along with social order (Paletz & Entman, 1981) if seen as restoring community norms. Public service (Deuze, 2005) may fit, along with providing information to the public (Frey et al., 2017).

Another nonspecific value of journalists that ties into healing and recovery is creating and maintaining community, a perspective articulated in the Chicago School in the 1930s and 1940s. A community interest function of the news (Park, 1941) implicitly suggests that journalism caters to audience needs. According to Park (1967), newspapers serve as an institution of social control in a community. Park (1967) saw a purpose of news to raise public morale and will to persevere during times of stress. Park (1967, p. 50): "The function of news is to orient man and society in an actual world. In so far as it succeeds it tends to preserve the sanity of the individual and the permanence of society."

This orientation and preservation thrust within a community interest function of news is reflected in subsequent scholarship. Editors and publishers of nondaily newspapers, in a nationwide survey, listed sustaining community as the fifth-highest rated function of the community press (Jeffres & Kumar, 2014). Paletz and Entman (1981) include leadership, especially operating for social good, as a news media value. Schudson (1995) lists caring for others among his seven goals of a media system dedicated to democracy. According to Schudson (1995, p. 29): "The news media should evoke empathy and provide deep understanding so that citizens at large can appreciate the situation of other human beings in the world and so elites can come to know and understand the situation of other human beings, notably nonelites, and learn compassion for them." Similarly, Kitch and Hume (2007, p. 151) wrote: "Although a crisis event initially happens in one place to particular people, when those people are explained as being 'just like us,' a narrative transformation takes place through which the event itself becomes a shared American experience—and larger, lasting lessons emerge in journalism."

Constructive Journalism

A relatively new perspective on journalism and its purposes somewhat overlaps with the themes of healing, coping, hope, and recovery addressed in this book. Under labels such as constructive journalism and humanitarian journalism, reflecting older perspectives on news such as peace journalism and narrative journalism, each is an effort to reconceptualize journalism in the twenty-first century based upon positive aspects of news, often as an intentional process in the creation of news.

Constructive journalism is both old and new; the term was used by Walter Williams in early twentieth-century college course syllabi and also reflected in actions by American journalism figures like Joseph Pulitzer and William Randolph Hearst (Bro, 2019). The newer perspective emerged in a 2008 Danish newspaper column by Ulrik Haagerup, then head of the news division of the national broadcasting company (Bro, 2019), advocating for constructive news. It also has roots in civic journalism, which attempts to strengthen the bonds between professional journalism and citizens (Hermans & Drok, 2018). Cathrine Gyldensted (2011) linked techniques from positive psychology to news works "in an effort to create more productive, engaging news stories while remaining committed to journalism's core functions" (McIntyre, 2015, p. iii). It adopts a social responsibility approach to journalism that includes a commitment to society's well-being, including solutions to societal problems. As defined by McIntyre and Gyldensted (2017, p. 23), constructive journalism is "an emerging form of journalism that involves applying positive psychology techniques to news processes and production in an effort to create productive and engaging coverage, while holding true to journalism's core functions." Constructive journalism builds upon positive emotions and solutions, which can undo negative emotions, build resilience, and promote positive meanings (McIntyre & Gyldensted, 2017), plus build positive emotions like hope (a key theme of this book), trust, resilience, and grit (Hermans & Gyldensted, 2019).

Humanitarian journalism incorporates advocacy into news to improve outcomes, especially in stories about crises, including rescue efforts (Bunce et al., 2019). A survey in four Western countries found that some forms of humanitarian journalism were popular among readers (Scott et al., 2018).

HEALING AND JOURNALISM

Traumatic events, as mentioned previously, can trigger psychological distress to a broader group of individuals than those directly affected by the trauma. This can extend to communities and even nations, especially among those who share characteristics with the affected population. Death can disturb the social order of society, suggested Hertz (1960/1907), with survivors suffering from helplessness, guilt, and a need to blame someone for the crisis (Fast, 2003). Gatherings of the afflicted, such as memorial services, aid recovery. Mourning, according to Van Gennep (1909/1960, p. 147), "is a transitional period for the survivors, and they enter it through rites of separation and emerge from it through rites of reintegration into society (rites of the lifting of mourning)." According to Alexander (2004), public acts of commemoration or cultural representation help restore collective psychological health.

Media attention amplifies public acts of memorialization to a broader population. Not only is news the primary means by which many people experience traumatic events, but news may also be the means of exposure to responses. According to Doss (2002, p. 7): "Television has become the witness and conduit for the public expression of grief and the collective enactment of ritual. Victims and visitors eagerly talk with reporters and openly describe their loss and suffering on camera, and viewers become naturalized to these expressive displays of grief." Doss (2002) suggested that the main stories of the Oklahoma City bombing and the Columbine High School shooting were public expressions of grief, with a focus on healing and surviving.

Mourning via media may serve as a proxy for public grieving and help a community manage tension. Journalism helps communities return to normal (Berkowitz, 2010), reaffirms group values and identities (Kitch, 2003), or brings mobilizing information (Lemert, 1981) to guide individual action. According to Berkowitz (2010), news can offer healing, consolation, and inspiration. News coverage of events honoring the dead merges the private (funerals) with the public (via news attention). While mourning has traditionally been a private function, individuals increasingly are culturally dislocated and journalism provides a community-wide forum (Kitch, 2000) for actions like memorialization and recovery. News focused on funerals and other memorial services are part of the community's self-evaluation of core values and eventual reaffirmation of values tied to faith and healing (see Kitch, 2000; Turner, 1977). Similarly, Berkowitz (2010) proposes that journalism enters "a pastoral role" in which it facilitates public mourning and engages in a sphere of consensus. Pantti and Wahl-Jorgensen (2011), in their evaluation of disaster coverage, offer a parallel argument for community, in which journalism focuses on emotions that bring people together.

This role of journalism in healing has been found in local communities and at a national level. Scholars contend that journalism about recovery and healing plays a therapeutic role for the affected community (Pantti & Wahl-Jorgensen, 2007; Tenenboim-Weinblatt, 2008); help guide and create community consensus (Kitch, 2003; Kitch & Hume, 2007; Pantti & Wieten, 2005; Zandberg et al., 2012), and reflection and hope (Berkowitz, 2010, 2011; Kitch & Hume, 2007). According to Tenenboim-Weinblatt (2008), who evaluated coverage of Israel's 2005 disengagement from the Gaza Strip, journalism took up five therapeutic tasks—establishing a healing relationship, establishing safety, constructing a therapeutic narrative, remembrance and mourning, and reconnection. Remembrance and mourning in the visual coverage helped the collective move on, while reconnection involved return to ordinary news (Tenenboim-Weinblatt, 2008). Pantti and Wahl-Jorgensen (2007) suggest that disaster reporting has always possessed properties of therapy news, often in coverage that gives voice, counsel, and comfort to victims. Their examination of six man-made disasters in the United Kingdom showed that therapy news is not a product of 24-hour news, but rather a sustained genre of journalism. Journalists can lead toward a sense of normality by reaffirming group values and identities (Kitch, 2003). Healing comes in narratives that journalists know how to tell and the audience knows how to interpret (Berkowitz, 2010).

TEN THEMES OF JOURNALISTIC HEALING

Previous scholarly work, mixed with analysis of news coverage of eleven school shootings (some of which was published previously in McCluskey, 2017) and several contemporary examples, led to a working list of ten themes of journalistic healing in news content. Not all themes may be relevant to every trauma. Additionally, this list is not mutually exclusive, that is, some story elements potentially could fit into more than one theme. Each theme contributed to one or more of four dimensions—healing, coping, hope, and recovery. Healing involves ways to improve physical and psychological conditions. Coping represents content that guides people to effectively deal with the trauma, such as providing insights. Hope establishes reasons for the audience to believe that something good may happen. Hope, according to Lazarus (1999), is a vital coping resource. Recovery represents a return to normalcy.

Survivor Stories

Anecdotes about those who survived trauma help others by reflecting continuity and hope. Survivors demonstrate continuity by showing that life goes on despite tragedy and suggests hope and optimism for the future. Stories of mine disaster survivors were uplifting, according to Kitch and Hume (2007). Tales of narrow escapes and dramatic rescues may be especially inspiring. Events in 2017, including an earthquake in Mexico City and a concert shooting in Las Vegas, prompted survivor stories. Especially dramatic were two tales from the earthquake, one a survivor pulled out of the rubble two days after the earthquake (Patterson et al., 2017) and the other a mechanic who escaped a collapsing building by grabbing a tree branch (Stevenson, 2017). One concert shooting survivor's story focused on the shoes she wore to run away (Las Vegas shooter discusses life after shooting, 2017). Another common example was profiles of survivors, such as a story focused on Maddy Wilford, a student who survived after being shot multiple times in a February 2018 shooting at a high school in Florida (Batchelor, 2018).

Death Stories

Turning a victim into a whole person can be uplifting by allowing memories of that person to live on. Profiles or anecdotes about those who were victims, along with particularly poignant deaths, can trigger empathy and can be especially uplifting to demonstrate the personality and accomplishments of victim. Such publicity gives meaning to the deceased person's life, helping others cope with the trauma. The portraits in grief that the *New York Times* published after the 9/11 terrorist attack provided a public memory of the victims, resonated with readers and put those victims into public consciousness (Hume, 2003). News coverage of school shootings in the United States, especially Columbine and Newtown, contained numerous profiles of young victims. Of 1,326 articles evaluated in McCluskey (2017), 30% included a name of one or more victim. Many were poignant descriptions, focused on their personalities, beliefs, and goals in lives cut short. Several of the Columbine victims who voiced their Christian faith in the face of death were memorialized by their friends and religious leaders (McCluskey, 2017). Stories about the first-grade victims at Sandy Hook Elementary focused on their loving personalities and youthful interests. Peace journalism advocates for identifying victims in conflict coverage (Tenenboim-Weinblatt et al., 2016).

Selfless Behavior

Tales of people acting selflessly can serve as aspirational models that represent the best of humanity, providing hope. This includes anecdotes of people helping others escape from trauma, with hero stories the most dramatic examples. Additionally, it can include people volunteering to help after a trauma. Stories of selfless behavior show that people beyond those directly affected are contributing to ease the pain of others, giving hope. Heroes create collective identities and national myths that people aspire to attain (Yair et al., 2014). Additionally, heroes create and preserve the moral basis for social cohesion (Yair et al., 2014); they surpass normal people by demonstrating values that people find worthy to follow. Heroism stories are uplifting, reminding the audience of sacrifice and triumph of good over evil, creating a positive message of healing (Berkowitz, 2010; Kitch & Hume, 2007).

The hero, according to Berkowitz (2010), is a standard news narrative that builds on collective memory to heal society, bringing people together through stories. Berkowitz (2010) analyzed the actions of a professor whose self-sacrifice helped others during the Virginia Tech University campus shooting. The hero narrative is familiar and the hero archetype is efficient and accessible to journalists (McCluskey, 2017). Analysis of news coverage of eleven school shootings (McCluskey, 2017) found dimensions of morality, selflessness/sacrifice, physical prowess, power/leadership, empathy/compassion, skills/training, decisiveness/confidence, humility, and character within the news coverage. Acts of heroism or explicit use of the term hero was found in ten of the eleven school shootings, with thirty-four individuals described as heroes (McCluskey, 2017).

Selfless acts abounded in news coverage of traumas. A story from a 2017 Las Vegas concert shooting (Carcamo et al., 2017) read: "Strangers ripped off their clothes to apply makeshift tourniquets to gunshot wounds. At least one was grazed by a bullet while giving someone CPR. Others drove through the gunfire, filling the beds of their trucks with bloodied victims they took to hospitals. Some threw themselves in front of loved ones, trying to save their lives and, in at least one case, losing their own." A story recounted how "neighbors, co-workers and passers-by pulled people from the jaws of death" during a 2017 Mexico City earthquake (Stevenson, 2017), with patients delivered to hospitals in private cars. From a 2018 Florida school shooting, stories included profiles of individuals explicitly identified as heroes, including CNN's article on seven heroes (Chavez, 2018) and *Redbook*'s profile of ten heroes (Friedman, 2018).

Recovery Efforts

Efforts that restore normalcy help others see progress and a path forward. Recovery efforts can be physical or psychological—from goods and services to counseling and emotional stability. Physical recovery includes examples of those who have received assistance after losing homes or property to trauma, as well as providing goods toward recovery. The presence or opportunity to work with trauma specialists or counselors can aid in emotional or psychological recovery efforts.

News coverage of school shootings included numerous examples of psychological recovery—of victims' families, shooting survivors, or witnesses who took steps to aid their recovery (McCluskey, 2017). Schools and community leaders provided mental health experts to heal the emotional trauma after school shootings (McCluskey, 2017). Stories after a 2018 shooting in Florida focused on students returning to high school as part of the recovery process as they learned to cope with "haunting memories" (Rosenblatt, 2018). Physical recovery was found in the days after Hurricane Maria hit Puerto Rico in 2017, in stories about people trying to restore normalcy, including a café that reopened despite no running water or electricity (Stories from the aftermath of Hurricane Maria in Puerto Rico, 2017). That story also included examples of people volunteering to clear fallen trees and mountain roads.

Community, Cohesion, and Intimacy

This represents both physical and virtual examples of people coming together, to share support, thoughts, and emotions. It aids healing by displaying continuity, demonstrating that the whole will go on despite the hurt to some. Memorials followed significant traumas such as the 1995 Oklahoma City bombing (Kitch, 2003) and 9/11 terrorist attack, in which stories focused on local acts of public gatherings and memorialization, what their deaths meant to the nation and collective remembering (Laderman, 2002; Walsh, 2001). The news coverage suggested that mourners were seeking solidarity, something larger than themselves and spiritual strength (Walsh, 2001). As Laderman (2002) explained: "America has always relied on invocations of the dead to define itself and its mission in the cosmos. For Bush and numerous journalists attuned to the value of promoting social unity and common cause, our understandings of the dead and interactions with them bind us together and reflect national commitments to act appropriately in the face of atrocities."

In the aftermath of the 2017 Mexico City earthquake, hospital director Dr. Fryda Medina described the willingness of people to aid victims (Stevenson, 2017): "It was in those moments that one feels the spirit we have in Mexico, the solidarity." During hurricanes, media provided emotional support and companionship, creating a sense of community and connected isolated individuals (Perez-Lugo, 2004). More examples were revealed in the aftermath of U.S. school shootings, including gatherings tied to religion and coping (McCluskey, 2017). Memorials were mentioned following all eleven of the school shootings (McCluskey, 2017), with stories emphasizing community cohesion during both religious and secular events. This included examples of solidarity, such as a candle-lighting ceremony (Dummit, 1999), students gathering in a prayer circle (Reel, 1997), and memorial services that drew hundreds of mourners (Lipsher & Finley, 1999; Wills & Boyle, 2012). Intimacy appeared within the gatherings, by providing details about the interaction and emotion among mourners (Edwards, 2012; Robbins, 1999; Williams, 1997; Young, 1999). Community was created when gatherings transcended group solidarity, especially following the Columbine and Newtown shootings (e.g., Hendrick, 1999; Mitchell, 2012).

Community and consensus in trauma reporting can extend to a national level, such as the national consensus that Pantti and Wieten (2005) found in Dutch coverage of a politician's murder and Kitch (2003) found in the aftermath of the 9/11 terrorist attack in the United States. According to Pantti and Wieten (2005), disasters trigger a uniform frame represented as integrative events, moments of national consensus, and unity out of collective mourning, with news conveying a temporary national consensus and as the protector of societal values and cultural identities.

News after the 9/11 terror attack constructed consensus by conducting a national funeral ceremony that provided catharsis and consolation (Kitch, 2003). Consensus may be rooted in news as shaping collective memory (Zandberg et al., 2012, p. 66), with news items commemorating "the traumatic past by narrating the triumphal present and thus cultivates the understanding of past events as continuous ones, constantly extending into the present." Additionally, Kitch and Hume (2007, p. 150) wrote: "Narratives about death contribute to society by strengthening it collectively and by highlighting the importance of its individual members." Students in Florida were portrayed as relying on each other and having a sense of hope in the aftermath of the campus shooting (Farinas, 2018).

Faith, Belief, and Salvation

Religion is often the foundation for spiritual beliefs. This may be found in declarations of faith, especially from the survivors, or surrendering to a higher authority. School shooting news coverage contained several examples, focused around themes of seeking spiritual support, religious conversion, and religious forgiving (McCluskey, 2017). Stories included religious institutions providing spiritual support and people offering support for others, often in mention of services, prayer, and counseling. Mourner Kiersten Kirkman after the 2012 Sandy Hook school shooting (Wills & Boyle, 2012) said: "We're here to pray for peace, and also the souls of these children and certainly peace and comfort for their families." Fellow members of a church youth group found solace in talking about a 1999 Columbine school shooting victim who affirmed her faith when confronted by one of the shooters (Martin & Bingham, 1999). Those attending a Columbine service recited together (Lowe, 1999): "God has not abandoned us, and we turn to God to find safety in this community God has called together."

The 2018 Florida school shooting brought stories focused on responses from religious leaders, such as a portrayal of a rabbi comforting families (Valys, 2018). The story featured Rabbi Mendy Gutnick, who said: "The truth is, if everyone talks the same language of fairness and justice, that's how our community will grow from this." Religious forgiving was represented by witnesses, mourners, and religious leaders who looked to religion for shifting anger and hurt to peace. Themes of forgiveness were prominent in a 1997 Paducah school shooting, in which students forgave the shooter (Bowles, 1997; Reel, 1997). Forgiveness in a 2006 Nickel Mines shooting was focused on explaining the Amish religious philosophy, in which the Amish community readily forgave the shooter (Goodstein, 2006).

Reassurance, Purpose, and Meaning

This category encompasses themes of people finding a larger goal or desire in life in response to trauma, helping them cope. This includes seeking or finding meaning, perspective, or understanding, which can be about themselves, the world, or life itself. After disasters, news helps society reflect and join together for healing, according to Berkowitz (2011). News after trauma deals with the meanings of loss, mourning, and sacrifice, suggested Kitch and Hume (2007). According to Kitch and Hume (2007, p. 195): "On the whole, news stories about death reassure us about both the past and the present. . . .

These kinds of stories do function to reassure local communities after a traumatic event." When faced with public trauma, people work toward recovery by drawing upon personal aspects of their identity, including remembrance and mourning (Zelizer, 2002).

News after school shootings offered perspective and purpose (McCluskey, 2017). After the Sandy Hook shooting, the Very Rev. Gary Hall of the Washington National Cathedral (Hunter & Harris, 2012) said: "God has a purpose for everything, but I don't know what this purpose is. I don't think He's punishing us, but maybe He's trying to get our attention." Young Christian mourners, primarily among friends of Columbine victims, portrayed their deaths as part of God's plan. For instance (Goldstein, 1999): "Now, in sermons and youth groups and quiet moments of personal reflection, these students are being heralded in saintlike terms. For some teenagers and adults, the deaths are strengthening individual belief."

Actions

Plans or steps designed to mitigate the present trauma or prevent future similar traumas can include physical acts, public officials or others addressing the tragedy, and promises of future change in policies or practices. Actions aid coping, healing, hope, and recovery through physical acts of doing something and the psychological impact on the audience of actual or intended consequences. Physical acts provide goods or services to deal with the immediate need following a natural disaster. Actions—both actual and promised—aid those affected by the disaster by suggesting authorities recognize the problems and are doing something to help. Analysis of news coverage of school shootings (McCluskey, 2017) identified potential actions for authorities to prevent future school violence. The 2018 Parkland shooting sparked collective action to push for gun control at both the state and national level, led by Marjory Stoneman Douglas students but joined by supporters across the country. Several students gained national fame for their ideas and willingness to speak out. Another common theme is stories listing places where people could donate money, goods, or services to aid trauma victims. Peace journalism supports context to explain and justify courses of action needed by society (Tenenboim-Weinblatt et al., 2016).

Blame and Responsibility

Individuals find relief by venting about who to blame for the trauma, including government, helping them cope. People assessing responsibility for the disaster or otherwise seeking an explanation fit as blame. Further, any questioning of acts or failures to act by authorities establishes responsibility.

Blame and responsibility give both the accusers and others a target to express their frustration about the trauma and suggest that it could have been prevented or mitigated. The alternative perspective is that people have no control over disasters, which can be psychologically difficult to handle.

Attributing responsibility fits within peace journalism as a means to address conflict (Tenenboim-Weinblatt et al., 2016). The school shootings triggered news content speculating on the reasons behind the trauma. Among the common themes (McCluskey, 2017) were guns (both gun control measures and promoting more guns in society), media and pop culture, school security measures, mental health, the criminal justice system, teen life (especially bullying), and drugs and alcohol. Many of the stories blamed shortcomings among authorities for allowing violence to occur, for instance, the lack of policies limiting firearms, media industries creating content that coarsened society, or poor school security policies.

External Validation

Governments, organizations, and prominent individuals may acknowledge the affected area's trauma, creating a hope by showing others care about the afflicted. This includes expressions of remorse or solidarity, along with financial and other assistance, coming from outside the affected area. This reassures the affected that they are not alone, which may bring a sense of relief. External validation occurred throughout the school shootings, which were events occurring in one location with impacts beyond those communities. National and internal leaders expressed sympathy or prayers for those affected (McCluskey, 2017), counselors from outside the region came to help, and occasionally support came from outside the country.

STUDY APPROACH AND NATURAL DISASTERS ANALYZED

News coverage was analyzed from eight natural disasters that took place in 2018. The study selected severe natural disasters (high levels of deaths, injuries, and/or property damage) from diverse locations—by continent, by country size, by economic status. The eight disasters analyzed in this study were an earthquake in Papua New Guinea (Australia/Oceania), an earthquake and tsunami in Indonesia (Asia), floods in Nigeria (Africa) and Japan (Asia), a heat wave in Pakistan (Asia), a volcanic eruption in Guatemala (Central America), and wildfires in Greece (Europe) and the United States (North America).

For each natural disaster, a single worldwide news organization (the BBC) and a local news organization aimed at a broad audience were selected for the news sample. BBC adopts a worldwide focus in its news coverage and has been utilized as such in previous research (e.g., Tian & Stewart, 2005). In seven of the eight cases, the in-country news organization was an English-language publication available online, thus accessible to many people around the world. No similar news source was found for Guatemala, so a Spanish-language publication available online was selected and translated into English for analysis. Content was drawn from archives of news websites, with search terms unique to each incident. Four weeks of news content was downloaded into text files for analysis.

Descriptions of each natural disaster (in chronological order), with the starting date of the news sample, number of casualties, and the identity of the local publication:

Papua New Guinea Earthquake

An estimated 132 people died and 500 were injured following a 7.5-magnitude earthquake that hit Papua New Guinea on February 26, 2018. The initial earthquake triggered more than 100 aftershocks and landslides across several provinces. Hela, Southern Highlands, Western Province, and Enga were hit the hardest. Effects of the disaster were felt for several months. As of April 13, 2018, 540,000 people had been affected by the disaster and 270,000 people needed life-saving assistance, including 125,000 children. Providing clean water, food, sanitation, and health services was still a concern as the earthquake had wiped out water sources, health facilities, and farms (Papua New Guinea: Humanitarian Situation, 2018). In April, more than one-fourth of roads were damaged (Papua New Guinea: Humanitarian Situation, 2018), making the delivery of aid difficult. Access to shelter was also a concern as approximately 43,000 people had been displaced (Violence and landslides block aid access, 2018). The United Nations International Children's Emergency Fund sought $13.8 million in aid (Papua New Guinea: Humanitarian Situation, 2018), focused on access to food, water, and sanitation, and providing children with proper medical care and vaccines. Several international organizations helped with the humanitarian response to the disaster.

Local newspaper is *The National*. According to the newspaper's website, *the National* is the top-selling newspaper in the country and is headquartered in Port Moresby. It is owned by the Malaysian logging company Rimbunan Hijau.

Pakistan Heat Wave

An estimated seventy people died when temperatures rose as high as 44 degrees Celsius (111 Fahrenheit) during May 2018 in Karachi (UK aid gives emergency medical treatment, 2018). News sampling started on May 20. As early as March, people in Karachi were experiencing high temperatures they would normally see during the peak of summer (Pakistan's "shocking" spring heat, 2018). All thirty-four meteorological stations across the country showed temperatures more than 10 degrees above normal in March (Pakistan's "shocking" spring heat, 2018). Many worried that temperatures would rival the heat wave of 2015 that killed approximately 2,000. City-wide power outages made the disaster worse (Saifi & Yeung, 2018) and it coincided with Ramadan, when Muslims fast from eating and drinking anything during daylight. The lack of green spaces and shade in Karachi made the heat wave difficult to navigate (Saifi & Yeung, 2018). To mitigate the heat, precautions such as banning outdoor work were put into effect. Little outside relief was given, but the United Kingdom pledged support to the victims (UK aid gives emergency medical treatment, 2018), helping 30,000 people, most from the poorest and most vulnerable parts of the city. They supported thirty relief camps, providing fans, water, shelter, and trained medical staff.

Local newspaper is *The News International*, which is owned by the Jang Group of Newspapers, the largest group of newspapers in Pakistan. Paper versions are printed in Lahore, Karachi, and Islamabad/Rawalpindi, and it has circulation of 140,000.

Guatemala Volcanic Eruption

The Fuego volcano in southern Guatemala erupted on June 3, 2018, sending molten lava, pyroclastic flows, ash, and smoke into villages around the mountain. Eruptions continued for several days, eventually killing an estimated 169 people (UNICEF Guatemala Humanitarian Situation, 2018) and causing about 300 injuries. A month after the first eruption, more than 200 people were still missing and as many as 1.7 million were affected (Guatemala Volcano: These families, 2018), including more than 12,000 who had to be evacuated. Among the villages hit by the volcanic eruptions were El Rodeo, La Reunión, Las Lajas, and San Miguel Los Lotes. Fine ash covered half of the country, contaminating water supplies, impacting crops and livestock, and damaging medical facilities and infrastructure (Guatemala Volcano: These families, 2018). Ash closed the airport in Guatemala City, 44 kilometers from the volcano. Search and rescue operations were conducted in the provinces of Escuintla, Sacatepéquez, and Chimaltenango. About 1,600 volunteers searched for survivors in the weeks following the eruption (Guatemala Volcano: Helping Communities, 2018). The Red Cross distributed more than 130 tons of relief supplies such as food, hygiene kits, and breathing masks (Guatemala Volcano: These families, 2018), along with shelters and psychological care. Government authorities built temporary houses for displaced families.

Local newspaper is *La Hora* (The Hour), a Spanish-language publication based in Guatemala City with a circulation of about 10,000. Its general director is Oscar Clemente Marroquín.

Japan Flooding

Flooding from rainstorms killed 237 people, with eight people still missing in January 2019 and 433 people injured (Report—The Japanese Red Cross Society's Response, 2019). Torrential rain in southern Japan began in late June 2018 and continued into July, with news sampling starting on July 5. On July 8, evacuation orders were issued to 1.9 million people and advisory notices to 2.3 million people in eastern and western prefectures (Japan Floods and Landslides, 2019). Property damage was severe, with 50,470 houses destroyed (Report—The Japanese Red Cross Society's Response, 2019) and an estimated cost for rebuilding roads, levees, bridges, and other public works, plus restore farmlands, exceeding 270 billion yen ($2.39 billion U.S. dollars) as of late July 2018 (Japan faces $2bn price tag, 2019). Small and midsized businesses were estimated to need an additional 407 billion yen for damages (Japan faces $2bn price tag, 2019). Heavy rain in mountains triggered flash flooding and landslides (Berlinger, 2018). Hiroshima, Okayama, and Hyogo were among the areas most affected by the rain as they received more than 20 inches of rain initially (Berlinger, 2018). The Japanese Red Cross Society provided immediate relief to the affected areas and people. Teams distributed blankets, torchlights, sleeping kits, and emergency radios, plus deployed medical help (Report—The Japanese Red Cross Society's Response, 2019).

Local newspaper was *Japan Times*, published in Tokyo by the Japan Times Ltd., a subsidiary of News2u Holdings, Inc. Its circulation is estimated as 44,000.

Greece Wildfires

More than a dozen fires swept across Greece in July 2018 and news sampling began on July 23. Months later, the tally included 102 dead, more than 200 injured, 5,600 hectares of land burned, and thousands of buildings destroyed (Sideridis, 2019). The first fire was reported on July 23 in Kineta, a village in the Gerania Mountains of west Attica. Thick pine forests in the area quickly burned and spread the fire to nearby villages. Soon after Kineta caught fire, the town of Rafina had a breakout of flames. Mati, a village in eastern Attica on the Aegean Sea, was extensively burned and the location where most of the deaths occurred. About 700 people were saved by the coast guard, the navy, and other boaters when people waded into the Aegean Sea near Mati to escape the flames (Greece: Wildfires Information bulletin, 2018). Northern Greece and several islands also burned. Overall, the fires were difficult to handle given the dense forests, high winds, and high temperatures (Greece: Wildfires Information bulletin, 2018). About 4,000 residents were affected by the fires. When the fires broke out, Red Cross volunteers immediately aided in the search and rescue efforts (Red Cross responds, 2018). Hellenic Red Cross lent its support by sending resources, providing first aid, relief supplies, and psychological help.

Local newspaper is *Kathimerini* (The Daily), owned by Kathimerini Publishing S.A and published in Athens. It publishes editions in Greek and English, with a print circulation of about 95,000. Not only is *Kathimerini* one of the largest newspapers in Greece, but it also has been analyzed in previous research about wildfire coverage in Greece (Hovardas, 2014).

Nigeria Flooding

Continued rainfall, which began in July 2018, reached a dangerous peak in mid-September, killing about 200 people and injuring 1,310 (Nigeria: Large-scale floods affect close to two million people, 2018). News sampling started on September 14. Overall, 1.9 million people were affected, 210,000 people were displaced by the floods, 82,000 homes were destroyed, and 150,000 hectares of farmland were flooded. The Niger and the Benue rivers overflowed and caused massive destruction as they spread into nearby communities (Nigeria: Large-scale floods affect close to two million people, 2018). Thirty-four of Nigeria's thirty-six states were affected and a state of emergency was declared for nine states (Nigeria Floods 2018: Work Report 1, 2018). The World Food Program and its partners provided food and nutrition to about 1.2 million people (Nigeria Flood Response Preparedness, 2018). The World Health Organization also provided help to affected people (WHO works with government agencies, 2018).

Local newspaper is *The Nation*, which is owned by Asiwaju Bola Ahmed Tinubu and published by Vintage Press Limited. It is based in Mushin, Lagos State. The newspaper's website describes it as "A quality, national, newspaper with credible and dependable information. Not beholden to any interest group. Loyalty is to the nation."

Indonesia Earthquake and Tsunami

An estimated 2,200 people died and 4,400 were injured (2018 Indonesia quakes and tsunamis, 2018) when a 7.5-magnitude earthquake struck on September 28, 2018, triggering a tsunami, seventy-six aftershocks, and landslides. The tsunami reached up to 3 meters in some areas, striking Talise beach in Palu and Donggala in the Central Sulawesi province (Central Sulawesi Earthquake Response Plan, 2018). Searchers pulled victims from collapsed buildings immediately after the disaster (Central Sulawesi

Earthquake Response Plan, 2018) and some villages were submerged when the land liquefied (Indonesia, 2019). Approximately 1.5 million people in Central Sulawesi alone were affected and 68,000 homes were either damaged or destroyed (2018 Indonesia quakes and tsunamis, 2018). The Central Sulawesi earthquake was part of a string of earthquakes affecting Indonesia within a few months. International aid arrived shortly after the disaster. The Indonesia Humanitarian Country Team sought $50.5 million in aid (Indonesia Earthquake and Tsunami Response, 2018). As of December 29, 2018, the plan was 36% funded. Other organizations pledged support and helped as well, including Act For Peace (emergency shelter, tools, hygiene kits, water), the Australian Red Cross (search-and-rescue efforts on the ground and provided medical care, food, water, and shelter), and the United Nations International Children's Emergency Fund of Australia (provided psychosocial support to children and families, and helped reconnect kids with their families).

Local newspaper is *Antara News*. Based in Central Jakarta, Antara is a news agency organized as a private company under the Ministry of State-owned Enterprises. It has been independent of government since 2007. It publishes in multiple languages.

U.S. Wildfires

Three major wildfires in November 2018 burned forests and residential areas in Northern and Southern California. The news sample began on November 8. Overall, the fires killed eighty-eight people, caused $11.4 billion in damages (Gonzales, 2019), and destroyed about 20,000 structures. Most severe was the Camp Fire in Butte County (Northern California), which erupted on November 8. Fed by gusty winds in a forested area occupied by numerous houses, the Camp Fire eventually killed eighty-five people and destroyed nearly 14,000 homes (Gonzales, 2019). The town of Paradise suffered the brunt of damage from the Camp Fire, which will require a multiyear rebuilding effort. Months later, thousands were still living in emergency shelters (Siegler, 2019). The largest of the other two fires in the Los Angeles area of Southern California was the Woolsey fire, in which three people died and about 1,600 structures were destroyed. A mix of governmental and nongovernmental organizations helped those who lost homes and goods. As of May 2019, the Federal Emergency Management Agency had paid out $85 million in emergency aid and the United States Small Business Administration $370 million in loans (Siegler, 2019). FEMA gave direct assistance to homeowners and renters, along with grants for household repairs and the replacement of household items. The Small Business Administration offered low-interest loans to cover residential losses to supplement insurance. The American Red

Cross provided meals, shelters, health care, and financial assistance (2018 California Wildfires, 2019).

Local newspaper is *New York Times International Edition*, which was accessed via the ProQuest database. Owned by the New York Times Company, the International Edition is printed in thirty-eight sites around the world. Its worldwide circulation is about 240,000.

Chapter 3

Journalism Culture

The eight countries analyzed in this book present a large contrast in national cultures, which influence the backgrounds of the journalists. Those backgrounds, along with socialization processes, education, economics, religion, and demographics, all potentially influence the stories pursued and how those stories were presented, including themes of healing, coping, hope, and recovery.

A central question of comparative studies into journalism is whether universal journalistic values or a common journalistic culture transcends national boundaries (Pintak & Nazier, 2013) or whether journalistic practices are primarily influenced by the local culture (Hanitzsch et al., 2011). According to Hanitzsch et al. (2019b, p. 4), "Journalism is a complex and multifaceted concept when explored against a global background." While this study cannot directly compare a universal journalistic culture with a societal-bound journalistic system, it can examine characteristics of the journalism environment in the eight countries used in this study and incorporate themes found in the news analysis. Comparative studies have examined many of the countries used in this study, but no study was found that encompasses all eight countries, making any direct comparisons impossible. Another shortcoming is that some journalistic systems have been extensively studied (such as the United States) while others have received less scrutiny.

Do journalists around the world possess a similar perspective on their roles or aspire to share professional goals (e.g., Deuze, 2005; Herrscher, 2002)? Scholars have found much uniformity in journalists' role conceptions, ethical views, editorial procedures, and socialization processes in a diverse range of countries, including Brazil (Herscovitz, 2004), Egypt (Ramaprasad & Hamdy, 2006), Nepal (Ramaprasad & Kelly, 2003), Tanzania (Ramaprasad, 2001), and Uganda (Mwesige, 2004). While values of objectivity and impartiality were born in Western and developed countries, those values are broadly accepted in newsrooms around the world (Hanitzsch et al., 2011).

Alternately, journalistic practices could be primarily influenced by the local culture, since journalists were socialized by the culture in which they were raised and live, including education systems. Comparative studies found differences among journalists across countries in role perceptions and practices (Hanitzsch et al., 2011). Journalistic cultures (Hanitzsch et al., 2019, p. 34) "become discernable in the way journalists think and act; they can be defined as particular sets of ideas and practices by which journalists legitimate their role in society and render their work meaningful for themselves and wider society." This may vary by nation, such that a critical style of reporting common in Western societies may appear disrespectful within an Asian values system that stresses collective harmony and social stability (Hanitzsch et al., 2019). For instance (Hanitzsch et al., 2019), an Asian values system encompasses freedom with responsibility, communalism and consensus, social harmony and self-restraint, and respect for order and authority, which may not accept a critical type of journalism.

One of the largest comparative studies, the *Global Journalist in the 21st Century: News People around the World* (Weaver & Willnat, 2012), evaluated surveys from more than 29,000 journalists working in thirty-one countries. Their analysis found differences in demographics, working conditions, and journalistic roles across the sample. According to the authors (Weaver & Willnat, 2012, p. 545), "most of the research reviewed in this book shows that journalistic norms and values depend heavily on social, political and cultural contexts." A comparative study of journalists from eighteen countries (Hanitzsch et al., 2011) found variety in journalistic roles such as being a watchdog over government and business elites, and providing political information, along with commonalities like impartiality and ethics of reporting.

Another large investigation into journalistic cultures drew survey data from more than 27,500 journalists in sixty-seven countries (Hanitzsch et al., 2019b). While journalists from the sixty-seven countries had widespread agreement on traditional professional values like informer and watchdog, cross-national differences were found across four role dimensions labeled as monitorial, collaborative, interventionist, and accommodative (Hanitzsch et al., 2019). Interventionist roles were more supported in less developed countries, monitorial roles in democratic countries, collaborative roles in countries with lower levels of democracy, and accommodative roles in developed and stable countries. Of the eight countries included in this study, four were part of the sixty-seven-country analysis—Japan and Greece were similar in a primarily monitorial role, the United States alone in (high) monitorial and accommodative roles, and Indonesia in a mostly collaborative role (Hanitzsch et al., 2019). Correlations with press freedom scores from Freedom House (the source of press freedom scores in this study) found positive correlations with monitorial and accommodative roles, and negative relationships with collaborative roles.

The context of this study, on journalistic content devoted to healing, coping, hope, and recovery, has enough room to reflect both a common journalistic mission and variety among the journalists by country. Differences among journalists and their stories about natural disasters could reflect cultural influences or could arise from contextual factors. The structural conditions examined in chapter 4—including level of press freedom, political freedom, wealth, and population—offer examples of potential influences on journalistic practices. Press freedom included three countries rated as free (the United States, Japan, and Papua New Guinea), four as partly free (Greece, Indonesia, Nigeria, and Guatemala), and one as not free (Pakistan). As for political freedom, three countries were rated as free (Japan, Greece, and the United States), and the other five as partly free. Wealth ranged from two of the richest countries in the world (the United States and Japan) to some of the poorest (Nigeria, Pakistan, and Papua New Guinea). The eight countries included five of the ten largest countries in the world by population (led by the United States and Indonesia) and one of the smallest (Papua New Guinea). Each of these factors, singly or in combinations, could affect journalists' views about their professional responsibilities and limits, their personal perception about their place in the world, and opportunities to influence others. As noted in chapter 4, each structural factor correlated with one or more themes of healing, coping, hope, and recovery.

One overarching cultural difference across countries is based upon individualistic or collectivistic societies, which has long been a topic in cross-cultural psychology. Individualistic attributes include independence, autonomy, self-reliance, and competition, while collectivism includes duty toward one's group, interdependence with others, a desire for social harmony, and conformity with group norms (Green et al., 2005). Societal values influence members—potentially including journalists—through conforming to norms to gain social approval or avoid disapproval (Blau, 1960). Much groundwork was established by Geert Hofstede (1980, 2001) in his surveys of IBM employees from seventy-one countries, in which the contrast between individualism and collectivism was one of four dimensions. Among the eight countries evaluated in this study, Hofstede (2001) found the United States to be the most individualistic and Guatemala the most collective, with Japan and Greece on the individualistic side and Indonesia, Pakistan, and Nigeria more collectivist. Subsequent scholarship found collectivism and individualism to be separate; a meta-analysis from Oyserman et al. (2002) showed no correlation between the two. Their meta-analysis showed that the United States was more individualistic and less collectivistic than most other countries, but also that collectivism was higher in the United States than in Japan. In addition, Americans were more individualistic than Japan and no different than Indonesia, and less collective than Nigeria and Indonesia. North Americans were more individualistic and less collectivistic than most others but nowhere near the end of either range (Fiske, 2002).

A few studies have placed cultural differences within a news orientation. U.S. television interviews with U.S. gold medal winners in the 2008 Olympics had more emphasis on individual characteristics like athletic ability, personality, and desire to win, while Chinese TV interviews with Chinese gold medalists attributed success to rigorous training, expectation of others, and national pride (Hua & Tan, 2012). This reflected cultural differences between collectivist Chinese and individualistic Americans, either a product of news perspectives or the athletes' perspectives (Hua & Tan, 2012). Sylvie and Huang (2008) found that the value system of newspaper editors correlated with their decision styles.

The media structure of the eight countries in this study is outlined below, based upon available evidence from scholarly and other sources. Media structure includes elements of the country's political, social, cultural, and economic conditions, combined with the values, practices, and policies of news organizations and individual journalists. Thus, the media structure encompasses a wide range of micro, mesa, and macro characteristics.

GREECE'S JOURNALISM CULTURE

Greece is a member of the European Union, but also among countries with lower economic standing within the EU. The press is considered partly free by Freedom House (Greece report, 2017), with a score of 44 out of 100 (lower score is freer), fourth most free among the eight countries in this study. It has more press freedom than surrounding countries, but in turn it has less press freedom than most other EU members. Freedom of expression has been protected by the country's constitution since 1975. Compared with the eight countries evaluated in this study, Greece is relatively high in political freedom and wealth, and low in population.

News media are either state-owned or for-profit companies, with news organizations dependent upon advertising, subscriptions, and other sales-related revenue. State advertising in the media is common, raising questions about political influences on content. *Kathimerini*, the news organization used in this study, is one of the country's largest newspapers by readership with 14,190 daily and 56,880 Sundays as of March 2018 (Kathimerini report, nd). According to EuroTopics (Kathimerini report, nd), *Kathimerini*'s political orientation is conservative, but more recently often publishes left-leaning commentaries. Newspaper readership in Greece is just 53 per 1,000 people, despite high levels of literacy (Iosifidis & Boucas, 2015). Newspaper circulation figures dropped from thirty-five million copies in 1989 to less than ten million in 2011 (Siapera et al., 2015). By contrast, the frequency of Internet news users in Greece (72%) is close to the EU average (Michailidou, 2012). The financial crisis of the 2010s strained the resources and capabilities of private media outlets (Greece report, 2015).

The history of Greek newspapers featured divisions along party lines; not only have newspapers been highly partisan, but were also used by their owners to pressure government (Papathanassopoulos, 1999). Historically, the Greek state has intervened in news media through censorship, ownership (tight state control), and subsidization through the overt and covert use of public money to support preferred media outlets (Iosifidis & Boucas, 2015). Michailidou (2012) described media owners as dominated by industrialists with interests in shipping, travel, construction, telecommunications, and oil industries, businesses often involved in lucrative contracts with the state. Further, the intertwining of political elites and media has led to practices based upon clientelism (Touri et al., 2017), as patrons control access to social resources in exchange for deference and other types of support (Iosifidis & Boucas, 2015). According to Iosifidis and Boucas (2015, p. 12), "In effect, this has led to a journalistic culture cautious about reporting news that could be embarrassing to state officials."

The net effect of the country's history of political and economic influence on news organizations is that journalists in Greece differ from those globally. According to Papathanassopoulos (2001, p. 507), "One can say that due to the political particularities of Greek society, it is difficult to develop a culture of journalistic professionalism faithful to the Anglo-American model." Further, Papathanassopoulos (2001, p. 513) wrote, "It seems that for Greek journalists neutrality or objectivity are closely linked to freedom of expression and accountability in news reporting rather than to factuality. In other words, while neutrality or objectivity is supposed to refer to political pluralism and fair play, in daily practice political neutrality is (or is forced to be) abandoned for the political position of their news organization." According to Dimitrakopoulou (2017, p. 1), survey results showed that "Greek journalists found it most important to report things as they are, to let people express their views, to provide analysis of current affairs, to promote tolerance and cultural diversity, and to provide information people need to make political decisions." Further, they were ambivalent toward guiding roles of journalists toward the audience, perceived a high degree of professional autonomy, and had limited faith in public institutions (Dimitrakopoulou, 2017).

GUATEMALA'S JOURNALISM CULTURE

Guatemala is the largest economy in Central America, yet it has one of the highest rates of inequalities in Latin America (The World Bank in Guatemala, 2019). Its press system is rated as partly free with a total score of 58 (Guatemala Report, 2017), seventh among eight countries in this study, and Guatemala has slightly more press freedom than its neighboring countries. Roughly two-thirds of the country is literate, with 60% speaking Spanish and the remaining 40% one of the Amerind tongues (Sheasby, nd). However, the weekly reach of newspapers in Guatemala is a robust 74% of the population (World Press Trends, 2016).

Freedom of the press is protected under the country's constitution and is generally respected by the government, although some legal restrictions are in place (Guatemala report, 2015). Among eight countries evaluated in this study, Guatemala is relatively low in political freedom, wealth, and population. *La Hora*, the newspaper used in this study, is one of six major daily Spanish-language newspapers in Guatemala (Avila & Gutierrez, 2013). The Carpio and Marroquin families control *La Hora* and two other Spanish-language daily newspapers in Guatemala (Avila & Gutierrez, 2013). Guatemala's national newspapers are owned by two competing news groups affiliated with elite Guatemalan families who control the country's major sources of income and wield considerable political influence (Suchenwirth & Keeble, 2011).

Guatemala's first newspaper, *Gazeta de Guatemala* in 1729, became only the second in the New World (Sheasby, nd), beginning a history of cooperation between the state and press in the country. The modern Guatemalan media ecology is described as underdeveloped (Avila & Gutierrez, 2013), with little quality investigative journalism, a gap in developing advanced journalism skills, and low pay forcing working journalists to take other jobs. For instance, Suchenwirth and Keeble (2011) described journalists working part-time in public relations for local authorities. Newspapers, despite low levels of readership fueled by low rates of literacy, are influential among the country's elites (Suchenwirth & Keeble, 2011). Major independent newspapers in Guatemala regularly criticize the government and military, along with other powerful segments of society (Sheasby, nd). Despite constituting a demographic majority, indigenous people are excluded politically, socially, economically, and culturally (Suchenwirth & Keeble, 2011).

INDONESIA'S JOURNALISM CULTURE

Although Indonesia's history is marked with periods of tight state control over the press, a continued era of reformation has led to a recent status of partly free, with a total score of 49 (Indonesia report, 2017), fifth among eight countries in this study. The media ecology of Indonesia is described as vibrant and diverse, although editorial positions are often tied to the owners' interests (Indonesia report, 2017). Freedom of the press is supported in the country's constitution, although freedom is sometimes obstructed by both government and private actors (Indonesia report, 2017). Major media ownership is concentrated, with the major television stations and newspapers owned by a handful of media companies, most tied to a political party (Indonesia report, 2017). Among the eight countries in this study, Indonesia is the second-largest by population and in the middle for political freedom and wealth.

Journalism in Indonesia originated in the fifteenth century with Dutch-language newspapers (History of Journalism in Indonesia, nd), followed by newspapers in indigenous and Chinese languages. By the middle of the nineteenth century, about thirty Dutch-language newspapers, twenty-seven Indonesian-language newspapers, and one Javanese-language newspapers were available (History of Journalism in Indonesia, nd). Freedom of the press emerged in the twentieth century. Studies of Indonesian journalists found practices in line with Western values like objectivity, truth, and independence. In evaluating responses from 385 journalists in Indonesia, Hanitzsch (2005) typified Indonesian journalists as young, male, well educated, and earning above-average salary who saw themselves as neutral and objective disseminators of news and as watchdogs. Nearly half had not completed any professional education related to journalism. Rather than adopting what Hanitzsch (2005) labeled as fundamental values of Asian journalism, which are separate from Western journalism, especially being supportive of national development, his survey found fewer than one in five saw themselves as an agent of nation building. Instead, the Indonesian journalists looked similar to others around the world in seeing themselves as neutral disseminators of news. Cross-national comparisons found Indonesia to have fewer female journalists and higher education levels, but also relatively less value for objective reporting (Weaver & Willnat, 2012).

In an eighteen-country comparative study, journalists in Indonesia were relatively high in audience orientation, placed high importance on objective and factual reporting, and disapproved of news being influenced by journalists' beliefs and convictions (Hanitzsch et al., 2011). As the country with the largest Muslim population in the world, the influence of the dominant religion on journalistic practices was a focus of semistructured interviews by Steele (2011). The study found that truth resonated with Islam, skepticism was in line with Islamic values, and independence fit well with Islam in challenging authoritarianism. Survey findings showed that journalists in Indonesia (Muchtar & Masduki, 2016, p. 2) "found it most important to report things as they are, educate their audience, promote tolerance and cultural diversity, let people express their opinions and advocate for social change." They saw themselves as having limited professional autonomy and reasonable faith in some institutions (Muchtar & Masduki, 2016).

JAPAN'S JOURNALISM CULTURE

Japan is rated as having a free press status with a score of 27 (Japan report, 2017), second among eight countries in this study and the freest system in Asia. Freedom of the press is protected by the country's constitution and generally respected by authorities (Japan Report, 2015). While the Japanese mass media system is essentially Libertarian, it tends to deviate from the Libertarian ideal type (Akhavan-Majid, 1990). The press in Japan, according to Akhavan-Majid (1990), is viewed as an elite power group. Among eight countries evaluated in this study, Japan has the most political freedom and second-most wealth, plus fifth in population.

Japan has one of the highest levels of newspaper readership in the world, with 77% of the population consuming newspapers each day and 95% of readers are regular subscribers (World Press Trends, 2016). National newspapers play a prominent role in contemporary Japan, with *Yomiuri Shimbun* and *Asahi Shimbun* possessing the two highest circulation figures in the world (World Press Trends, 2016) and *Mainichi Shimbun* sixth. According to Freedom House (Japan Report, 2015), "There is considerable homogeneity in coverage due to the conservative nature of these newspapers." The largest national daily English-language newspaper is the *Japan Times*, the newspaper used in this study. Cross-national comparisons portray journalists in Japan as older, more educated, and comparatively fewer women, plus lower value on analyzing events and watchdog over government (Weaver & Willnat, 2012).

Japanese newspapers emerged in the seventeenth century and modern newspapers in the mid-nineteenth century. After press censorship during and after World War II, freedom of the press was returned to the country in 1951 and included in Japan's constitution. According to Hayashi and Kopper (2014), Japan was strongly guided by the United States immediately after World War II to erase journalism that supported the totalitarian military regime and introduce liberal journalism. The Japanese press history has characteristics that separate it from Western countries, including press clubs dating to the late nineteenth century. Press clubs were integral for journalists seeking access to Japan's parliament and are still required for entry to major governmental ministries and many commercial organizations (Dickinson & Memon, 2012). Strict reporting rules guide their efforts, limiting investigative journalism and independent reporting. In addition, Winfield, Mizuno and

Beaudoin (2000) contend that the free press system in Japan is influenced by an Asian culture that emphasizes the group over the individual, resulting in dramatic differences from the West on their political role. A strong focus on collectivism stems largely from Confucianism and to a lesser extent from Buddhism, leading to a collectivity with roots in an authority that defines truth and reality separate from individual thought. Truth from Confucianism is a collective truth in which the hierarchy is supreme, so the masses accept truth from above (Winfield et al., 2000). In the modern Japanese press system, journalism became a tool to help reform social ills and serve as a government watchdog, yet hierarchy and harmony remain highly valued (Winfield et al., 2000). According to survey data, Japanese journalists (Oi & Sako, 2017, p. 1) "found it most important to monitor and scrutinize political leaders, to provide analysis of current affairs, and to provide information people need to make political decisions." Journalists in Japan reported a moderate level of professional autonomy (Oi & Sako, 2017).

The primary task of journalism in Japan has been disseminating practical, everyday-life information, rather than political information and commentaries as is understood in the West (Hayashi & Kopper, 2014). Yet the Japanese press tradition includes a genre of social journalism that deals with actual problems and questions of ordinary citizens, documenting human drama in original voices (Hayashi & Kopper, 2014). A study of first-year journalism students around the world placed Japan into the "paternal" group with developing and socialist countries, as the students identify the role of the state and political parties as more important (Sparks & Splichal, 1989).

NIGERIA'S JOURNALISM CULTURE

Nigeria's press is classified as partly free, with a total score of 51 (Nigeria report, 2017), sixth among eight countries in this study. Nigeria is described as having a vibrant and varied media landscape, with outlets that openly criticize government policies (Nigeria report, 2017). While the constitution protects freedom of expression and the press, journalists risk prosecution under restrictive laws, including sedition, criminal defamation, and publication of false news (Nigeria report, 2017). In addition, Sharia (Islamic law) statutes in twelve northern states can impose severe penalties for press offenses (Nigeria report, 2017). Nigeria has low levels of political freedom and wealth compared with other countries in this study.

The news media ecology of Nigeria includes more than 100 national and local news publications, with privately owned entities among the most influential (Nigeria report, 2017). State and local governments, along with individuals directly involved in politics, also own news outlets (Nigeria report,

2017). Among the most popular news outlets (Agboke, 2019) are *Punch*, *Vanguard*, the *Guardian*, *This Day*, and the *Nation* (the newspaper used in this study). Newspapers first appeared in Nigeria in the mid-nineteenth century. Although most of Nigeria's educational approaches were adopted from Great Britain, its mass communication education systems were modeled after American approaches (Odunlami, 2014). According to Eze (2019), a lack of funding is a widespread problem for Nigerian news media. The media are forced to accept advertising from powerful individuals or companies to stay in business, leading to perceptions of misleading readers by covering up apparent corruption (Eze, 2019). Omenugha and Oji (2008) trace the commercialization of news media to the withdrawal of subsidies from government starting in 1986. The influence of money can be direct, such as the "brown envelope" practice of journalists in Nigeria who demand a bribe or other form of gratification before covering an event (Okoro & Chinweobo-Onuoha, 2013). Similarly, Omenugha and Oji (2008, np) describe a practice in which "individuals, communities, private and public organizations, local governments, state governments and ministries, gain access to the mass media during news time for a prescribed fee."

According to Babalola (2002, p. 407),

> "In Nigeria today, the vibrancy, fearlessness and steadfastness of a newspaper are usually conditioned by the ownership status of the newspaper. The privately owned newspaper outfits are usually more direct in their reports, they are usually not given to unbridled propaganda and acting as government mouthpiece like the government-owned outfits. They usually tell the story as it is without fear or favour. . . . Also, privately owned newspaper outfits rarely get advertisements from the government, its agencies or individuals that happen to be pro-government. But government-owned newspapers are usually used as propaganda machinery to popularize government policies and portray them in good light."

Mass media in sub-Saharan Africa share a common history of colonialism that contrasts with precolonial values that stressed group orientation, continuity, harmony, and balance (Bourgault, 1995). According to Bourgault (1995, p. 5), "Strong group orientation sustained the importance of continuity." Bourgault (1995) argues that the oral tradition of sub-Saharan Africans is reflected in their mass media, with news stressing narratives based upon logical and chronological order. Bourgault (1995, p. 181) explained: "The press in Africa displays 'preempirical' stylistics typical of oral discourse." Similarly, Schaefer (2003) found more oral-narrative story forms in the African press as compared to press in the United States in stories about terrorism.

PAKISTAN'S JOURNALISM CULTURE

Pakistan's press system is rated as not free by Freedom House with 65 points (Pakistan report, 2017), last among the eight countries in this study, with little freedom found in any of the three dimensions of legal, political, and economic conditions. Reasons for the not free designation are restrictive laws, including those penalizing defamation and blasphemy; threats directed at journalists from military and intelligence agencies; and the threat of violence (Pakistan report, 2017). Authorities can legally censor online content in the name of national security and the constitution allows government to curb freedom of speech (Pakistan report, 2017).

The media ecology includes more than 1,500 newspapers published in Urdu, English, Sindhi, and regional languages (Dickinson & Memon, 2012). Pakistan's monthly audience reach, at 10% of the population, is among the lowest in the world (World Press Trends, 2016), as is the country's circulation per capita (Siraj, 2009). The English-language press cater to the urban elite readers, have limited circulation, and are considered more professional and accurate (Prakash, 2013), while the Urdu-language press have higher circulation; dominate rural areas; and are religious, conservative, and sensationalistic. Prakash (2013) lists three prominent news organizations. The Jang Group, the country's largest media group, publishes major Urdu newspapers and adopts a moderate-conservative perspective. The Jang Group publishes the *News International*, the largest English-language newspaper in Pakistan and the newspaper used in this study. The Dawn Group is Pakistan's second largest and is considered a liberal, secular paper with moderate views. Nawaiwaqt publishes in Urdu and has large readership, with right-wing, conservative, and democracy as central viewpoints.

Pakistani journalism has evolved through years of autocratic government followed by less restrictive policies. Pintak and Nazir (2013) described journalism in Pakistan as historically restricted due to censorship by a series of autocratic rulers, with more latitude for press freedom in the twenty-first century. Print news media are not subject to the same degree of overt governmental controls as electronic media, but are still dominated by the country's political and economic elite (Dickinson & Memon, 2012). Owners' interests set editorial stances (Dickinson & Memon, 2012) and journalists are expected to follow the company's editorial lines (Pakistan report, 2017). Most political influence on news is indirect, such as threats to cut off advertising, as government accounts for 30% of the advertising in Pakistan and the government periodically cuts the supply of newsprint or restricts access to official information (Dickinson & Memon, 2012). Additionally, government; police; political parties; representatives of commercial interests; and ethnic, sectarian, and religious groups pressure journalists through intimidation, harassment, and other tactics (Dickinson & Memon, 2012).

A survey of 395 Pakistani journalists by Pintak and Nazir (2013) found nationalism, religious identity, defending national sovereignty, and facilitating societal development as key values and goals, along with an emerging professional identity. They saw a lack of professionalism and corporate pressures as the biggest threats to journalism.

PAPUA NEW GUINEA'S JOURNALISM CULTURE

Papua New Guinea has a free press status and a total score of 29 (Papua New Guinea report, 2017), third among eight countries in this study. News media in Papua New Guinea have been among the strongest and most independent in the South Pacific, with freedom of speech, the press and information guaranteed under the country's constitution (Papua New Guinea report, 2015). In recent years, however, journalists have been harassed and blocked from investigating wrongdoing by officials (Papua New Guinea report, 2015). Although the media are free, they are still heavily reliant on government advertising as a source of revenue (Robie, 2008). Papua New Guinea has the least wealth and lowest population among countries in this study, plus ranks in the middle for political freedom.

The Papua New Guinea news media primarily serve the country's elites, making the press important due to their ability to reach decision makers (Rooney, 2003). The country's two daily newspapers are both under foreign ownership—the *Post-Courier* is owned by an Australian subsidiary of the U.S.-based News Corporation, while the *National* is owned by the Malaysian logging company Rimbunan Hijau (Papua New Guinea report, 2015), which runs Papua New Guinea's biggest forestry and timber processing operation (Khosla & Rowlands, 2014). The *National*, the newspaper used in this study, has the larger circulation of the two dailies. Although the *National* publishes little on the controversial subjects of logging and forestry, it is generally independent and unbiased on other issues (Press Reference: Papua New Guinea, nd). Since independence in 1975, several provinces have started their own newspapers (Press Reference: Papua New Guinea, nd).

Papua New Guinea has primarily a rural population and a literacy rate of less than 50%, reasons why radio is the primary source of news (Press Reference: Papua New Guinea, nd): "The nature of media coverage in Papua New Guinea is strongly linked to the isolation of many of its peoples. The country's population is divided; some 85 percent live in remote villages, retaining ancient cultures and tongues, with little contact with the modern world. Few publications or televisions signals reach its rugged interior, where a multiplicity of tribal languages fragments communication. In addition to the absence of a common language, Papua New Guinea's literacy rate complicates the country's publishing climate."

According to Khosla and Rowlands (2014), many Papua New Guinean journalists are conscientious, educated, and free. Journalism in Papua New Guinea follows a Western model favoring objectivity (Matbob, 2007). However, the country's ongoing social, political, and economic problems, fueled by corruption and misuse of resources, have led news organizations to work toward restoring good governance and stability in the country (Matbob, 2007). In evaluating the news practices of the *Post-Courier*, Matbob (2007) found the paper adopting advocacy journalism on major national issues, placing journalists in a role as representatives of the people. A survey of news organizations by Robie (1999) found that journalists saw a direct relationship between watchdog and nation-building roles. However, Rooney (2003) calls journalistic endeavor in the country as weak, with one-source stories, little attempt to find additional information, and limited background information.

U.S. JOURNALISM CULTURE

The United States has one of the world's largest and most dynamic media sectors. It is rated as free, with a total score of 23 (United States report, 2017), first among the eight countries in this study. The United States is rated as having strong economic and legal status, with the country's constitution protecting high levels of press freedom (United States report, 2017). Additionally, the United States is first in wealth and population among countries in this study, along with third in political freedom. Most news media in the United States are under private ownership, with a smaller role for public news organizations funded by government allocations and private contributions. Advertising remains a significant source of funding for private news media. However, the revenue distribution has changed in the twenty-first century; the ad-to-subscription ratio was 4.6 to 1 in 2005 and shifted to 1.5 to 1 by 2015, and the U.S. newspaper industry lost more than $40 billion in advertising revenue during the past fifteen years (World Press Trends, 2016). In 2018, the total estimated advertising revenue was $14.3 billion and the circulation revenue was $11.0 billion (Newspaper fact sheet, 2019). Newspaper circulation in 2018 was the lowest since 1940, the first year with available data, at 28.6 million for weekday and 30.8 million for Sunday publications (Barthel, 2019). Those figures were down 8 and 9%, respectively, from the previous year (Newspaper fact sheet, 2019).

No significant restrictions are placed on news production or distribution, and fees or taxes on media operations are not excessive (United States report,

2017). Increased competition and availability of news media has led to fragmentation of the audience, with some news organizations (especially in television) targeting specific ideological groups. According to the United States report (2017). "While self-censorship among journalists remains relatively rare in the United States and official censorship is virtually nonexistent, an increasing number of news outlets are aggressively partisan in their coverage of political affairs. The press itself is frequently a source of contention, with conservatives and liberals alike accusing the media of bias."

The news media ecology in the United States is rich and varied. The *New York Times* (publisher of the *New York Times International*, the news source used in this study) and *Washington Post* are considered influential on policy makers and other news media. Both bring a national focus to reporting and coverage. Three newspapers are among the largest in the world by circulation (World Press Trends, 2016)—*USA Today* (third), the *Wall Street Journal* (15th) and the *New York Times* (17th). The country has dozens of newspapers that are significant regional presences and are joined by hundreds of smaller daily and weekly newspapers. Television news includes four over-the-air national networks, several cable networks, and regional/local stations around the country. In addition, several significant radio networks and online news publications add to the complex and varied news landscape.

Compared to journalists around the world, U.S. journalists have more education, fewer women, more perceived autonomy, higher job satisfaction, and higher perception as watchdogs over government (Weaver & Willnat, 2012). In general, however, journalists in the United States are similar to those from other developed countries. In a survey among journalists from the Netherlands, Germany, Great Britain, Australia, and the United States by Deuze (2002), U.S. journalists were the most educated and least interested in trying to exert influence on public/political agenda, but otherwise were similar to those from the other countries. Journalism students also showed common perspectives. Surveys showed that journalists in the United States (Vos & Craft, 2016, p. 2), "most embraced the roles of reporting things as they are, educating the audience, and providing information people need to make political decisions" and had little support for the status quo. They reported a high degree of professional autonomy and had little trust in political and societal institutions (Vos & Craft, 2016). Sparks and Splichal (1989) clustered U.S. students adjacent to Canada and close to Japan, India, and Australia on strength of influences upon media policies. A comparative study of journalism students in Australia, Brazil, Chile, Mexico, Spain, Switzerland, and the United States (Mellado et al., 2013), the U.S. students favored a consumer-oriented approach to journalism, similar to Swiss and Australian students.

Chapter 4

Patterns and Influences on News about Natural Disasters

Evaluation of news content generally falls into two distinct approaches—quantitative and qualitative. Quantitative approaches use numbers to understand themes within news stories, allowing for numerical tests of comparisons. Qualitative approaches rely on details and examples within the content being analyzed to reveal and illustrate key themes. This chapter is focused on quantitative analysis of the news content; subsequent chapters provide qualitative and detailed examples of themes within the news coverage.

One advantage of quantitative analysis is a high degree of reliability—variables can be established as arising from common understandings of meaning. Quantitative analysis brings statistical tests to establish intercoder reliability, that is, two or more people agree upon the presence of each relevant characteristic within the content being analyzed. Reliability suggests that the content variables are so distinct that potential coders, using the same approach, will arrive at similar findings.

ANALYZING TEN THEMES OF JOURNALISTIC HEALING

As mentioned in Chapter Two, ten themes of news content that typify healing, coping, hope, or recovery were analyzed. Those ten themes are (1) survivor stories, primarily anecdotes about those who survived trauma; (2) death stories, which highlight personal characteristics of victims; (3) selfless behavior, including acts of heroism and other efforts to help others; (4) recovery efforts, focused on acts that restore normalcy; (5) community, cohesion, and intimacy, including physical and virtual examples of people coming together; (6) faith, belief, and salvation, primarily religious and spiritual actions; (7) reassurance, purpose, or meaning, reflecting people finding a larger goal or desire in life; (8) actions, including plans or steps dealing with the present or future traumas; (9) blame or responsibility, focused on people establishing blame for the trauma; and (10) external validation, which covers entities outside the affected area providing assistance.

Intercoder Reliability

Each news article was examined for content that fit within categories of healing, coping, hope, or recovery. After several weeks of training and practice coding, the two coders evaluated fifty-four articles (10.2%) for intercoder reliability using Cohen's kappa, which takes chance agreement into account. Each measure had a reliability kappa of 0.90 or higher, which Lombard et al. (2002) suggest is nearly always acceptable—survivor stories ($k = 0.91$); death stories ($k = 0.90$); selfless behavior ($k = 0.91$); recovery efforts ($k = 1.00$); community, cohesion, and intimacy ($k = 0.91$); faith, belief, and salvation ($k = 1.00$); reassurance, purpose, or meaning ($k = 1.00$); actions ($k = 0.91$); blame ($k = 0.90$); and external validation ($k = 0.91$).

POTENTIAL INFLUENCES ON COVERAGE

The range of influences on news coverage selected for this study falls into two categories: those intricately tied to each disaster and broader social, political, and journalistic ecologies. Potential influences on coverage were analyzed for frequency of each theme of healing.

Contextual Elements

Elements directly tied to each disaster may have influenced coverage patterns, including the specific event, the type of disaster, its geographic reach, passage of time since the disaster, and the number of casualties. Each of the eight natural disasters was evaluated as an independent variable.

Reach

Descriptions of each disaster, from articles analyzed and other material about the disasters, helped determine reach. Five disasters were considered centralized—earthquakes in Papua New Guinea and Indonesia, wildfires in Greece and the United States, and a volcanic eruption in Guatemala, as in each case the natural disasters were mostly confined to a specific area of the country. The other three (a heat wave in Pakistan and flooding in Nigeria and Japan) were decentralized, as each affected a relatively large geographic area. Centralized disasters could make it easier for journalists to locate people directly affected by the disaster, making them perhaps more likely to be included as sources for stories. Decentralized disasters, by affecting a broader geographic area, may lead to more people in the country feeling affected by the disaster.

Time

This was determined by the week after the disaster in which the story appeared. Since the sample was drawn from a four-week period, this allowed longitudinal comparisons, with week 1 starting on the day of the disaster and the time period concluding at the end of the fourth week (twenty-eight days total). Time may influence coverage, for instance, recovery efforts may occur later, due to the need to bring in supplies, while survivor stories may occur immediately after an event.

Casualties

The numbers of deceased were compiled from data released after each disaster; some figures are estimated due to people missing or never accounted for (the figures used in this study are listed in chapter 2). Casualties, the number of people who died, may reflect news attention focused on the human toll, perhaps leading to more attention toward death stories or blame themes.

Type of Disaster

This was based upon the cause (two floods, two earthquakes, two wildfires, and two other). Thus, Japan and Nigeria (floods), Papua New Guinea and Indonesia (earthquakes), Greece and the United States (wildfires), and Guatemala and Pakistan (volcano and heat wave) were grouped for analysis.

STRUCTURAL ELEMENTS

Broader structural elements may influence coverage (e.g., Wu, 2003). Five structural elements were analyzed; each is described separately below.

Press Freedom

How free the press system is in each country potentially has a direct and significant influence on what journalists can write about. Each country was assigned a score of 1–100 by Freedom House (2017), with the lower number representing more freedom. Scores by country, starting with the most press freedom—the United States (23), Japan (27), Papua New Guinea (29), Greece (44), Indonesia (49), Nigeria (51), Guatemala (58), and Pakistan (65).

Political Freedom

The amount of political freedom within a country could influence the coverage, such as less-free nations avoiding criticism of government. Rankings were drawn from Freedom House (2019), in which a higher number meant more political freedom in the country—Japan (96), Greece (87), the United States (86), Papua New Guinea (64), Indonesia (62), Guatemala (53), Nigeria (50), and Pakistan (39).

Wealth

This was based upon each country's gross domestic product per person from the International Monetary Fund (2018). Listed by the wealthiest (in thousands)—the United States (65.06), Japan (46.07), Greece (30.52), Indonesia (13.97), Guatemala (8.71), Nigeria (6.13), Pakistan (5.96), and Papua New Guinea (3.76). Wealth could influence both individuals' and the country's financial ability to recover from a natural disaster.

Population

The amount of people in each country was drawn from Nations Online (2019), with figures drawn from each country's latest official estimate (the oldest was 2012 and the newest February 2019). Population reflects the size of each country, suggesting the relative impact of each disaster. Five of the ten largest countries in the world were in the study—three, the United States (328.5 million); four, Indonesia (265 million); six, Pakistan (207.8 million); seven, Nigeria (191.8 million); and ten, Japan (126.7 million)—along with Guatemala (68th, 15.8 million), Greece (76th, 11.5 million), and Papua New Guinea (101st, 7.3 million).

Type of Publication

This could influence coverage patterns, especially the distinction between those focused on an international audience and local publications. Comparisons were made between BBC and the local publications.

EVALUATION AND ANALYSIS

Descriptive Data

All ten of the anticipated themes of journalistic healing were found in news coverage (n = 528) of the eight natural disasters. In order of volume of news coverage, the Greece wildfires had the most stories, 206, followed by Indonesia (109), Guatemala (51), the United States (50), Japan (33), Pakistan (32), Papua New Guinea (31), and Nigeria (16). Ninety-four of the stories were in the BBC (17.8%), with the remainder in the local news outlets. Stories were more common in the first week after the disaster (57.2%), then steadily decreased over time—week 2 (23.9%), week 3 (12.7%), and week 4 (6.3%).

Sixty-five of the articles (12.3%) contained no relevant themes, with 40.5% featuring one theme and 27.7% two themes; seven themes were found in three articles, the most in any one article. A theme appeared in 52.1% of the lead (first) paragraphs, but only two disasters (Greece, 72.3%) and Guatemala (51.0%) had the majority of its articles including a theme of healing in the lead paragraph.

Descriptions of each of the ten themes of journalistic healing, in order of frequency:

Actions (52.8%)

Examples were primarily focused on a governmental entity or the country's leader doing something or promising to do something, Throughout all the events, stories mentioned government steps to address trauma by declaring a state of emergency or promises to do something to mitigate future disasters.

Blame and Responsibility (33.9%)

Most expressions of blame or responsibility came from individuals or political opponents criticizing government for failure to prevent the disaster, inadequate warning, or poor response to the disaster. Examples included poor tsunami detection technology (Indonesia tsunami: Palu hit by "worst case scenario," 2018) and mismanagement of the forests (California wildfires: Town of Paradise will need "total rebuild," 2018).

External Validation (17.8%)

Examples contained messages inferring the affected area was not alone, that others outside the community and nation were offering support, both tangible and intangible. For instance, several stories listed help to Indonesia, ranging from material assistance to condolences, from countries in Asia, Europe, and

North America, plus the International Monetary Fund, the World Bank, an affiliation of 14 UK charities and other relief organizations.

Recovery Efforts (15.3%)

Most recovery efforts involved individuals or authorities taking steps to bring normalcy and stability to the lives of victims. This included concrete steps from government and aid groups to address the immediate needs of victims, including temporary shelters, clothing, and food, along with long-term needs like constructing new housing, installing warning devices, and improving flood control. It also included efforts by individuals, such as an Indonesian family that trekked more than 10 hours through the mountains with no food or clean water to reach safety (Indonesia tsunami: Death toll rises to nearly 1,350, 2018 Oct. 3) and a team of volunteers who saved cats and dogs in the aftermath of the wildfires in Greece (Pemble & Hadjicostis, 2018).

Community, Cohesion, and Intimacy (13.1%)

Stories described cohesion, togetherness, and gatherings in intimate groups to remember the victims. Stories focused on funerals and memorials, especially those honoring victims. Other stories took a broader focus, such as describing the event as affecting the entire country; one example came when Prime Minister Alexis Tsipras said "Greece is going through an unspeakable tragedy" as he appeared on television to declare three days of national mourning (Triandafyllou & Konstantinidis, 2018). An example of collective remembrance (Tamindael, 2018) focused on the country's grieving from a disaster that "caused deep sorrow and trauma for Indonesians."

Survivors (12.3%)

Disasters often put people directly in the path of danger and news stories focused on people surviving life-threatening situations. The quick-moving wildfires in the United States left many people in imminent harm as they fled hilly, forested areas. People told of driving along thin strips of road surrounded with flames (Hughes, 2018) until finally they were in the clear of the "fire tornado." In Greece, fires around Mati trapped people on narrow strips of land next to the Aegean Sea, leaving people little choice but to enter the sea (Gatoploulos, 2018). In Nigeria, survivor stories included sad tales of lost property and goods, Guatemalans told of narrowly escaped pyroclastic flows, and Japanese survivors waded through flood waters to safety.

Selfless Behavior (9.8%)

Examples of selfless behavior included people who aided others in distress, in some case putting their own lives in danger, along with volunteer efforts.

An Indonesian air traffic controller was a "national hero" (Indonesia tsunami: Pilot calls air traffic controller his "guardian angel," 2018) for helping an airplane and its passengers safely take off during an earthquake after colleagues left the control tower; the air traffic controller died shortly after the plane took off. Wildfires in Greece and the United States prompted harrowing examples of people who aided others when the fires approached, including several cases of strangers rescuing elderly and/or immobile people.

Death Stories (7.4%)

At times, victims of natural disasters were transformed from names into people with depth. Sometimes this was done through mentioning details of the victim in life. In other situations, it was the reaction of family or friends that gave the victim depth. For instance, BBC ran a profile (Greek fires: "Hearts empty" over death of Irishman Brian O'Callaghan-Westropp, 2018) of a newly married Irishman who died in Greece. In Nigeria, two victims were described by name (Ololade, 2018) as "hard working, tenacious, responsible and ready to take on any task."

Faith, Belief, and Salvation (5.1%)

The most common mentions were use of prayer or religion to cope with the disaster, expressions of religious themes to deal with individual needs, or fatalism. For instance, the heat wave in Pakistan prompted a special prayer for rain (Karachiites gather to offer special prayer for rain, 2018). Stories in several disasters included calls to pray for victims, including a special prayer to the Greeks from Pope Francis (Pope prays for victims of Greek fires, 2018).

Reassurance, Purpose, and Meaning (1.9%)

While explicit mentions of reassurance, purpose, or meaning were rare, implicit examples included words to the Indonesian public to remain calm (President orders government agencies to prepare for quake effects, 2018) and a Greek father of two missing girls expressing hope that they were alive after viewing television footage (Desperate Greeks search for missing after fires, 2018).

ANALYSIS OF CONTEXTUAL FACTORS

Event

Each dependent variable showed significant differences (at $p < 0.05$) across the eight events on chi-square analysis (see table 4.1). Survivor stories

Table 4.1 Frequency, in Percentage, of Themes of Healing, Hope, Coping, and Recovery by Each Natural Disaster, along with Chi-Square Figures (n = 528)

	Greece	Guatemala	Indonesia	Japan
Survivor stories	6.8	11.8	11.9	12.1
Death stories	12.6	11.8	0.9	0
Selfless behavior	5.8	19.6	8.3	15.2
Recovery efforts	11.7	11.8	20.2	39.4
Community, cohesion, and intimacy	15.5	27.5	5.5	0
Faith, belief, and salvation	3.4	7.8	4.6	3.0
Reassurance, purpose, or meaning	0.5	2.0	2.8	0
Actions	57.8	29.4	54.1	54.5
Blame, responsibility	47.1	21.6	9.2	33.3
External validation	21.8	19.6	27.5	3.0
N =	206	51	109	33

	Nigeria	Pakistan	Papua N. Guinea	United States
Survivor stories	12.5	0	9.7	46.0
Death stories	25	0	0	4.0
Selfless behavior	12.5	3.1	9.7	20.0
Recovery efforts	25	0	19.4	12.0
Community, cohesion, and intimacy	31.3	6.3	12.9	12.0
Faith, belief, and salvation	0	3.1	19.4	6.0
Reassurance, purpose, or meaning	0	0	3.2	8.0
Actions	87.5	62.5	32.3	48.0
Blame, responsibility	68.8	46.9	16.1	38.0
External validation	25	0	12.9	0
N =	16	32	31	50

Chi square:

Survivor stories	$\chi^2 = 63.09$	$p < 0.001$
Death stories	$\chi^2 = 31.10$	$p < 0.001$
Selfless behavior	$\chi^2 = 18.14$	$p < 0.01$
Recovery efforts	$\chi^2 = 27.09$	$p < 0.001$
Community, cohesion, and intimacy	$\chi^2 = 26.85$	$p < 0.001$
Faith, belief, and salvation	$\chi^2 = 16.55$	$p < 0.05$
Reassurance, purpose, or meaning	$\chi^2 = 14.53$	$p < 0.05$
Actions	$\chi^2 = 28.00$	$p < 0.001$
Blame, responsibility	$\chi^2 = 65.01$	$p < 0.001$
External validation	$\chi^2 = 33.21$	$p < 0.001$

were more common in the United States and less common in Pakistan and Greece. Death stories were more common in Nigeria and less common in Pakistan, Papua New Guinea, and Japan. Selfless behavior was more common in the United States and Guatemala, less common in Pakistan. Recovery stories were more common in Japan and Nigeria, less common in Pakistan. Community, cohesion, and intimacy were more common in Nigeria and Guatemala, less likely in Japan. Faith, belief, and salvation were more frequently found in Papua New Guinea and not found in Nigeria. Reassurance, purpose, and meaning were more common in the United States and not found in Nigeria, Pakistan, and Japan. Action stories were more common in Nigeria and Pakistan, less common in Guatemala and Papua New Guinea. Blame and responsibility stories were more common in Nigeria, Greece, and Pakistan, less likely in Indonesia and Papua New Guinea. External validation was more common in Indonesia and Nigeria, with none in the United States.

Type of Disaster

Six of the ten themes of journalistic healing showed significant differences across the four types of disasters in chi-square analysis—recovery stories ($\chi^2 = 23.62$, $p < 0.001$); blame or responsibility ($\chi^2 = 51.36$, $p < 0.001$); death stories ($\chi^2 = 13.88$, $p < 0.01$); actions ($\chi^2 = 8.50$, $p < 0.05$); community, cohesion, and intimacy ($\chi^2 = 8.21$, $p < 0.05$); and external validation ($\chi^2 = 7.84$, $p < 0.05$). Overall, floods led to higher levels of recovery, action, and blame stories; earthquakes to more recovery stories; wildfires to more death, action, and blame stories; and heat wave/volcanic eruption to more community, cohesion, and intimacy stories.

Reach

Chi-square analysis showed significant differences (at $p < 0.05$) on three themes based upon the centralization of the disaster. Actions ($\chi^2 = 4.95$, $p < 0.05$) were more likely in disasters affecting a large geographic area (64.2%) than in centralized disasters (50.8%). External validation ($\chi^2 = 8.84$, $p < 0.001$) was found more often in centralized disasters (19.9%) than broad-based events (6.2%). Blame or responsibility stories ($\chi^2 = 5.92$, $p < 0.05$) were more common in centralized disasters (45.7%) than in events affecting a broader area (31.8%).

Time

ANOVA tests for each theme (table 4.2) showed significant across-time differences on survivor ($F = 5.81$, $p < 0.001$), recovery ($F = 2.66$, $p < 0.05$), and

Table 4.2 Analysis of Variance for Each Theme of Healing, Hope, Coping, and Recovery by Time

	Week 1	Week 2	Week 3	Week 4	F
Survivor stories	17.2	7.9	3.0	3.0	5.81***
Death stories	7.0	7.0	6.0	15.2	1.07
Selfless behavior	10.6	6.4	9.0	18.2	1.53
Recovery efforts	12.9	15.1	19.4	30.3	2.66*
Community, cohesion, and intimacy	15.6	8.7	11.9	9.1	1.43
Faith, belief, and salvation	5.6	4.8	4.5	4.5	0.18
Reassurance, purpose, or meaning	1.7	0.8	6.0	0	2.53#
Actions	57.0	50.0	43.3	45.5	1.89
Blame, responsibility	28.8	45.2	37.3	30.3	3.81**
External validation	21.5	12.7	11.9	15.2	2.29#
N = 528	302	126	67	33	

*** = $p < 0.001$.
** = $p < 0.01$.
* = $p < 0.05$.
\# = $p < 0.10$.

blame/responsibility ($F = 3.81$, $p < 0.01$) stories. Post-hoc testing (Scheffe, at $p < 0.05$) showed significant differences on survivor stories between week 1 (17%) and week 3 (3%). Blame stories were significantly more likely in week 2 (45%) than week 1 (29%).

Casualties

Significant Pearson's correlations were found on four variables. A high number of casualties correlated with more external validation stories ($r = 0.13$, $p < 0.01$), while lower casualties correlated with higher levels of death stories ($r = -0.13$, $p < 0.01$); community, cohesion, and intimacy ($r = -0.11$, $p < 0.05$); and blame/responsibility stories ($r = -0.28$, $p < 0.001$).

ANALYSIS OF STRUCTURAL FACTORS

Press Freedom

Significant Pearson's correlations were found on four variables. Countries with higher levels of press freedom correlated with more survivor ($r = -0.22$, $p < 0.001$); recovery ($r = -0.10$, $p < 0.05$); and reassurance, purpose, and meaning stories ($r = -0.09$, $p < 0.05$). Lower levels of press freedom correlated with more external validation stories ($r = 0.11$, $p < 0.01$).

Political Freedom

Just one variable showed a significant Pearson's correlation—high political freedom with more blame and responsibility stories ($r = 0.15$, $p < 0.001$).

Wealth

Three significant Pearson's correlations were found, as higher per capita GDP correlated with more survivor ($r = 0.24$, $p < 0.001$) and blame or responsibility stories ($r = 0.13$, $p < 0.01$), and lower wealth with more external validation stories ($r = -0.12$, $p < 0.01$).

Population

Higher population correlated with more survivor ($r = 0.21$, $p < 0.001$) and reassurance, purpose and meaning ($r = 0.11$, $p < 0.01$) stories. Lower population was tied to more death ($r = -0.15$, $p < 0.001$); community, cohesion, and intimacy ($r = -0.12$, $p < 0.01$); and blame or responsibility ($r = -0.14$, $p < 0.001$) stories.

Type of Publication

Chi-square analysis showed significant differences on the frequency of two of the ten themes. BBC had significantly higher frequencies of both survivor (42.6% vs. 5.8%, $\chi^2 = 96.89$, $p < 0.001$) and selfless behavior stories (17% vs. 8.3%, $\chi^2 = 6.63$, $p < 0.01$) compared with the local news outlets.

OVERALL ANALYSIS BY THEME

The wide range of independent variable analyses allowed for profiles for each of the ten themes, listed in order of frequency.

Actions

Contextual influences tied to more action stories were decentralized disasters, floods, and wildfires, typified by disasters in Nigeria and Pakistan. No structural variables were significant. In essence, journalists were driven by a wide range of contextual factors that called for responses to infrastructure needs, as floods and wildfires were relatively more destructive toward homes, businesses, and roads than other types of disasters.

Blame and Responsibility

The contextual influences were similar to those for actions—decentralized disasters, floods and wildfires, and disasters in Nigeria and Pakistan (plus Greece), along with fewer casualties. As with actions, these disasters were particularly damaging to infrastructure, requiring extensive reinvestment. Three structural variables were tied to stories about blame and responsibility—high political freedom, high wealth, and low population. Perhaps criticism and blame are something that a rich and politically open country is more likely to tolerate. That is, blame is more likely in a country that can afford to change, especially when political freedom is the norm. In a less-populated country, people may have a stronger personal sense of duty to speak out as compared to a larger country.

External Validation

Two contextual factors were tied to stories about external validation—centralized disasters and high numbers of casualties—along with disasters in Nigeria and Indonesia. Structural conditions of low press freedom and low wealth led to more stories of external validation. The combination of factors provides an interesting perspective—countries with low press freedom may have been compelled to demonstrate the home country has the respect of other countries, reinforcing the government's desires to be seen as legitimate by outside countries. Meanwhile, conditions of many casualties and low wealth may have triggered more help from outside the country to address humanitarian crises. Countries with low wealth have a more obvious need for outside help than wealthier countries.

Recovery Efforts

Three contextual variables—time (later in the four-week sample), floods, and earthquakes—were connected to more stories about recovery efforts, along with disasters in Nigeria and Japan. Of the structural conditions, recovery stories were more common in countries with high press freedom. Since marshaling recovery efforts can take time, it's no surprise that such stories were more common later in the time period. Recovery efforts suggest a negative condition exists that needs attention, so countries with low press freedom may be reluctant to publicize efforts signaling a shortcoming in the country to deal with the disaster.

Community, Cohesion, and Intimacy

Stories about community, cohesion, and intimacy were more common under the contextual conditions of fewer casualties and the volcanic eruption/heat wave, along with disasters in Nigeria and Guatemala. The only significant structural condition tied to more stories was lower population. Closer ties are more likely in less populated areas, especially true in Guatemala since the volcano primarily affected small, rural villages.

Survivors

The only contextual condition linked to more survivor stories was earlier in the time period. Four structural factors were linked to more survivor stories—high press freedom, high wealth, high population, and BBC stories. The structural conditions are an interesting combination, as press freedom may allow for greater focus on individuals rather than state action, while high wealth may bring a more individualistic perspective. The difference by news organizations suggests BBC focused more on individual stories than did local publications.

Selfless Behavior

No contextual factor was connected to selfless behavior stories, which were more common in Guatemala, the United States, and Japan. BBC was the only significant structural variable. Similar to the explanation on survivors, the BBC emphasis may demonstrate more focus on individual values.

Death Stories

Two contextual factors (fewer casualties and wildfires) were connected to more death stories, typified by coverage of events in Nigeria, Greece, and Guatemala. Just one structural factor, low population, was linked to more death stories. Lower population and fewer casualties may make each death relatively more important, while the centralized conditions around wildfires made it easier for journalists to find people who knew victims.

Faith, Belief, and Salvation

No contextual or structural variable was connected with frequency of stories about faith, belief, and salvation. More stories of this theme were found in Papua New Guinea, which has a high level of religiosity.

Reassurance, Purpose, or Meaning

Two structural conditions were connected with stories about reassurance, purpose, or meaning—high press freedom and high population. No contextual condition was significant, although higher numbers were found in Papua New Guinea and the United States.

DISCUSSION

News coverage of eight natural disasters around the world revealed many examples of content that could help others heal, cope, and recover from the traumatic blow of death and destruction. All ten themes proposed to represent common news approaches following traumatic events were present in the news coverage. While not every theme was found in each of the eight disasters, overall there were many examples of common patterns in news approaches. The presence of these themes strengthens the argument that healing, coping, hope, and recovery should be considered a news value, norm, or practice that transcends borders and cultures. Distinct patterns of influences were found on each type of healing, coping, hope, and recovery, suggesting each was conceptually different and had unique combinations of influence.

The first contribution of this analysis is evidence that the ten themes are not only present, but can be readily identified. Intercoder reliability testing, using a measure that takes chance agreement into account, demonstrated high levels of reliability on each measure. Second, this analysis contributes to a scarcity of scholarly attention to international comparative studies, answering critiques from other scholars (e.g., Chaudhary, 2001). By analyzing news attention to natural disasters in eight distinct nations with varied contextual and structural conditions, it allowed for insights based upon the social, cultural, and political conditions of each nation.

Among contextual factors, centralized disasters were tied to higher external validation and decentralized to more action and blame stories; more casualties to higher external validation and fewer casualties to death, community, and blame stories; and time to survivor stories (early) and blame/responsibility (middle). Types of disasters showed a stark contrast between earthquakes (high on recovery, low on blame, actions, and death) and wildfires (high on blame, actions, and death, low on recovery), while floods were high on recovery and action and blame stories, and volcanic eruption/heat wave high on community. Among the structural conditions, high levels of press freedom led to more stories on survivors, recovery, and meaning, and fewer on external validation. High political freedom was connected with more blame/responsibility stories. Wealth led to survivor and blame stories (each high wealth) and external validation (low wealth). High population was tied with more survivor and meaning stories, and fewer blame, death, and community stories. BBC coverage led to more survivor and selflessness stories.

While this collection of independent variables was carefully considered, it may have excluded other contributing factors. For instance, individualistic or collective values within each country's culture may influence news coverage (e.g., Chaudhary, 2001), a topic that is explored further in Chapter Three. Other potential structural influences could include political conditions, news organizations' characteristics (ownership, size, competition), and demographics of journalists (education, experience, values). Future research can help tease out a lengthy list of structural and contextual influences.

Third, analysis across eight disasters around the world adds to the generalizability of these findings. A case-study approach may well have arrived at much different conclusions; in fact, a quick look at any of the eight nations used in this study shows each to be an outlier in some ways and typical in other ways. The compilation increases the generalizability of these news patterns, although further research would be necessary to increase confidence of generalizability. For instance, the dependence on English-language publications may mask local news points of emphasis—they may well be telling different stories to aid the healing of local news users who speak local languages.

These limitations, however, do not seriously take away from the overall findings. A close reading of 528 news articles by two trained researchers demonstrated the presence and viability of healing, coping, hope, and recovery within news coverage of natural disasters. Considering the range of events and locations, this analysis suggests that journalists around the world in their daily practice recognize the value of stories highlighting healing, coping, hope, and recovery.

Chapter 5

Survivor Stories

The natural disasters often put people directly in the path of danger and many news stories focused on people escaping life-threatening situations or giving eyewitness reports. These anecdotes showed that life can go on despite tragedy, offering continuity and hope. Such stories were especially common in the two wildfires, but also found often in the volcanic eruption in Guatemala and earthquake/tsunami in Indonesia. Survivor stories were found in seven of the eight disasters (all but the Pakistan heat wave).

Seven subthemes fit characteristics of survival stories. Most common were stories about people who escaped danger and witnesses to disaster. Other subthemes were trauma, fear, and anxiety; loss of home or property; unknown fate of family or friends; and injuries. Among the sources used who were quoted or paraphrased in survivor stories, the vast majority (97%) were victims, witnesses, or survivors.

ESCAPED DANGER

Quick-moving wildfires left many people in imminent and often unsuspecting harm in both Greece and the United States, with nearly all of the sources fitting as survivors or witnesses. In Greece, the fires around Mati trapped people on narrow strips of land next to the Aegean Sea. Many people had little choice but to enter the sea, such as Nikos Stavrinidis and five friends, who quickly became disoriented from the strong winds and the current (Gatoploulos, 2018). A fishing boat saved four of them. According to Stavrinidis, "We fell into the sea and tried to distance ourselves, to get away from the carbon dioxide. We went as far in as we could. . . . But as we went further, there was a lot of wind and a lot of current and it started taking us away from the coast.

We were not able to see where we were." Survivor Kostas Laganos (Greece wildfires: Dozens dead in Attica region, 2018) said: "Thankfully the sea was there and we went into the sea, because the flames were chasing us all the way to the water.... It burned our backs and we dived into the water ... I said: 'My God, we must run to save ourselves.'" George Vokos in Mati said he is lucky to be alive after two people died in his arms (Greece wildfires: 'Hundreds went into the sea', 2018): "Thank God my family are safe, we ran down to the sea for safety." Mati resident Agni Gantona estimated 250–300 people were on the beach to escape the flames (Georgiopoulos & Kambas, 2018). Gantona said: "Groups of us, we were holding each other by the hand and shouting each other's names, because we could not see from the smoke." An 82-year-old woman named Vassiliki, her 83-year-old sister, a niece, and her husband escaped, too. Vassiliki, said (Maltezou, 2018a): "They stayed in the sea for four and a half hours.... They tried to escape in the car but when they saw the traffic jam, they just left the car, ran and jumped into the water."

On land, people were in dire danger in homes and automobiles. Susan Margaret Stephos, who escaped from the fire in Mati, said (Greece wildfires: British man in hospital with burns, 2018): "When I was in the house and the fire was going over I thought 'I'm not going to make it, this is the end'. But prayers were answered and I managed." Katerina Pantelidis (Lee, 2018) narrowly escaped; the story explained: "She picked up her two cats, and attempted to pick up her dog, but had to leave him when he ran into a smoke-filled part of the house. She ran with her parents to the beach, along with hundreds of others escaping the flames and smoke. Her house was destroyed. Many swam into the sea, but Katerina remained on shore with her cats and elderly parents, breathing through their clothes and waiting five hours for the coastguard. Incredibly, the dog survived—Katerina later found him hiding in a back room underneath a broken window."

Those in cars were trapped by the heat, flames, and smoke. As two cars exploded from the flames, Vassiliki Psevedourou, fifty-four, escaped on foot despite a limp from a birth defect and aided her cousin's wife (Maltezou, 2018a): "We tried to lift her but it was impossible. My cousin then dragged her on the ground, trying to take her away to safety." Thanassis Moraitis, fifty-three, drove away with his mother, wife, and nineteen-year-old son until fire caught them and they had to run into the water (Greek officials see 'serious indications' arson led to fire, 2018), where they were picked up by boats about 3 hours later. "In the sea, there was a rain of fire, there was smoke, there was a Force 12 wind," Moraitis said.

Nikos Stavrinidis, before escaping into the sea, narrowly avoided disaster on the road. Stavrinidis (Greece wildfires: At least 74 dead as blaze 'struck like flamethrower', 2018), who felt heat from flames as he drove on a highway, said: "We were driving along the road going into smoke, then all-of-a-sudden the flames were at the side of the car. . . . All the houses on the hill beside the highway were completely burnt out." Giannis Labropoulos drove through the flames (Greece wildfires: 'Hundreds went into the sea', 2018): "We didn't know if we would make it through, we just did not know what to expect. Branches and debris were hitting the car. The power of the fire and the intense heat made it something we would not want to experience ever again." Vassiliki Psevedourou escaped with relatives (Maltezou, 2018a), including a cousin whose "shoes melted from the heat, the ground was burning. He was trying to hug (an aunt), to shield her from the flames, and his legs, his hands, his face were burned."

Survivors of wildfires in the United States also experienced close calls as they fled the hilly areas around Paradise, California. Stories featured anecdotes about survivors overcoming treacherous conditions to reach safety. People told of driving along thin strips of road with flames everywhere else until finally they were in the clear (Hughes, 2018). A group of more than a dozen people escaped the flames by jumping into Lake Concow, in the mountains above Paradise (California wildfires: Survivors share stories of heroic rescues, 2018). Individual stories were featured prominently in the stories. Karen Davis' vehicle broke down and she said (Hughes, 2018). "Fire was coming on both sides. It was a fire tornado." Davis called her daughter Wendy, who heard heavy items falling on the car, then she hitched a ride back to the hospital in Paradise where she worked (Hughes, 2018).

Brynn Parrott Chatfield was sitting in the back seat and praying as her husband drove through flames on a narrow, unburned strip of road (Hughes, 2018). The story described embers striking the windshield. "By now, no road was visible, and only a dense orange cloud could be seen in front of the car. Then suddenly, it cleared, and the fires seemed to scatter. Clear skies opened up, the last embers bounced off the windscreen and the fire was finally behind them." Sorrell Bobrink of Paradise put her son, cat, and dog in the car before escaping along a slow-moving highway (Hughes, 2018). According to the story, "Sorrell knows that each decision she makes could be fatal. She knows there is a section in the road up ahead that is not surrounded by trees. But with little around her to help her get her bearings, she doesn't know how close it is. So she fears she may be driving herself and her passengers to their deaths. Instead, she makes it out." Bobrink described the scene (California fires: At least 42 die in state's deadliest wildfire, 2018) as "exactly like any apocalyptic movie I have ever seen. . . . I had to drive through the fire—it was awful. It was probably the most awful experience I will have in my life."

Nurse Tamara Ferguson described putting the hospital's sixty-seven patients into any vehicle they could find to escape. After one of the ambulances caught fire, Ferguson and colleagues moved the patients into a nearby house. She said (Hughes, 2018): "I looked out the back window at the devastation, while I conversed with the sweetest 95-year-old woman.... We watched the flames beside us, burnt cars in the road, power lines down and fresh homes burning. It went on for miles. I honestly couldn't believe I was alive, that I would see my family, kids and boyfriend again." Lauri Kester took 1 hour to travel 3 miles in gridlock surrounded by flames (Nicas et al., 2018). She said: "It was hot, it was smoky and—this sounds like such an exaggeration, but—it was apocalyptic." Allyn Pierce, who was trapped by flames and even recorded a farewell message (Del Real & Nicas, 2018), and said: "I just kept thinking, 'I'm going to die in melting plastic.'"

William Hart picked up a passenger and two abandoned dogs as he drove away from the fire (Hughes, 2018). Hart documented his evacuation in a video he posted on Facebook, but found some of the footage to be too harrowing to post (California wildfires: 'I saw cars become metal and bones', 2018). Joseph Metcalfe woke his children around midnight to evacuate (California wildfires: 'I saw cars become metal and bones', 2018). "We tried to make it an exciting adventure so as to not worry the kids too much but on our exit we drove past 30ft (9m) high flames and could clearly see the raging fires burning down the hills." Anita Waters of Paradise was ordered by police into a truck bed and rode for a mile before jumping out and walking back to her car (Del Real & Nicas, 2018). She said: "I took a chance on my life. Yes, I did.... But I felt I needed to." Erin McLaughlin and her 81-year-old neighbor, Elisabeth Mesones, left their homes in Magalia, north of Paradise, but were diverted to a restaurant parking lot for 6 hours (Del Real & Nicas, 2018). McLaughlin said: "Everything was on fire all around you.... It was the most scary thing I've ever seen."

Even celebrities needed to escape fires around Malibu in Southern California (California wildfires: 250,000 flee monster flames ravaging state, 2018). Singer Lady Gaga posted a video on Instagram that showed dark smoke billowing overhead while evacuating her home and Oscar-winning director Guillermo del Toro tweeted that he left behind fantasy and horror memorabilia while leaving his home. Also escaping from Malibu was Rebecca Hackett, who was surrounded by flames as she drove, documenting her escape in videos (Del Real & Nicas, 2018). Hackett said: "I just have to keep going, that's all I could think. I just have to keep driving because if I don't, no one is going to come in here and save me."

In Guatemala, survivors and even rescuers escaped volcanic rock, ash, and mudflows. Jorge Luis Altuve, a member of Guatemala's mountain rescue brigade, experienced the danger on the mountain. Altuve said (Guatemala volcano: Dozens die as Fuego volcano erupts, 2018):

> At first, we thought it had started to rain but then I heard something hitting my safety helmet and I said to one of my colleagues: "This is not rain, these are

stones!" The stones raining down on us started getting bigger and bigger. Some were as big as 5cm (2in) in diameter. We'd already started our descent from the mountain when the ash cloud reached us and day turned into night. From daylight it went to being as dark as at 10pm. Luckily we were carrying all of our equipment which includes torches and helmets and we also know the volcano very well.... We started to move a lot more quickly. We were also in constant communication with our colleagues at the mountain rescue command post and they kept telling us: "Get out of there! Get down, quick!" In total it took us three or four hours to reach the command post. Luckily we got away unscathed, just with some bruises from the falling stones.

La Hora shared tales of five survivors in one story (The survivors of the Fire Volcano safe, but with uncertainty about the future, 2018), most explaining that they left with just what they had. Maria Nelly Segura said: "We left with what we had in hand, we could not take anything, we just went with what we had, my house there is alone that in Los Lotes there is no more. From my family we all left alive." Aura Garcia said: "All the people came bathed in ashes, it's amazing how we managed to get out. I thought that it would reach us, they all shouted, it was a nightmare." Boris Rodriguez, twenty-five, survived because he was working lower on the mountain (Grant, 2018). He said: "After the eruption I managed to cross over the coffee plantations on the hillsides and found the tin homes completely buried."

The other disasters had fewer tales of survivors. Indonesians faced both an earthquake and tsunami. Palu resident Rusidanto said (Indonesia earthquake: Huge surge in death toll, 2018), "I just ran when I saw the waves hitting homes on the coastline." Adi was hugging his wife when the tsunami struck (Indonesia earthquake and tsunami: Dead buried in mass grave, 2018): "When the wave came, I lost her.... I was carried about 50 metres. I couldn't hold anything." An unidentified man described how he grabbed a child and clung to a tree as the tsunami approached (Indonesia tsunami: Palu hit by 'worst case scenario', 2018).

WITNESSES

Eyewitness accounts about survivors were especially common in the two wildfires and Guatemala's eruption and all of the sources were witnesses, survivors, or their relatives. In the wildfires in the United States, witnesses saw odd light before the fires reached Paradise. Sorrell Bobrink saw a glow before the flames (Hughes, 2018): "It looked like the sunrise was coming up.... But we were far past sunrise. There was this moment of 'Oh, that's odd...that's not good.'" William Hart saw a darkening gray-brown sky and first thought it was from fireplaces. Hart said (Hughes, 2018): "But when we saw black, brown smoke coming, we knew it wasn't chimney smoke.... No, it is not six o'clock or seven o'clock at night, people."

Other witnesses in the United States remarked on the power of the fires. Joseph Metcalfe, who saw flames burning down the hills, said (California wildfires: 'I saw cars become metal and bones', 2018): "This was a whole different level. The fire carried no prejudice." Gloria Selby, who evacuated from Paradise, said (Nicas et al., 2018): "It sounded like a war.... It was very scary, very intense." Witnesses in Southern California received a nice surprise. Jed St. Henry, whose home survived, said (Nicas et al., 2018) the fire had been "incomparable to any fire I have lived through on this side of Malibu." Chris Gonzalez (Del Real & Nicas, 2018)

> stayed at his house in Agoura Hills despite evacuation orders. He began to second-guess how long he should stay as the air grew increasingly black. Fire engulfed the hills around his community and ripped through several neighborhoods. One house nearby spontaneously erupted in flames from stray embers. 'Basically there was like a ring of fire all around. There was this thick, thick smoke, and just a bunch of ashes everywhere.... The freeways are closed north and southbound, the canyons, there was no way in or out.'

Witnesses in Guatemala were used to volcanic activities, but not to the degree of June 2018. Hilda Lopez in Guatemala (Perez, 2018): "We were at a party, celebrating the arrival of a baby, when a neighbor shouted us to come and see that the lava was coming, we did not believe him, and when we went out to see the hot mud was coming down the street." Rutilia Garcia, also from El Rodeo, saw dramatic video of people fleeing the tragedy and said (The survivors of the Fire Volcano safe, but with uncertainty about the future, 2018): "I say we saw it and we do not believe this." Arnulfo Santos of El Rodeo said (the survivors of the Fire Volcano safe, but with uncertainty about the future, 2018): "We have always lived here, we have grandchildren and we learned to live with the noise of the volcano, but it was like ugly because I never saw it that way, I got scared when my son told me and then I saw on Facebook what people went up and in a while we saw a big cloud."

Faye Dunstan described lava ash falling from the sky (Guatemala volcano: Lava ash like 'black rain', 2018): "The volcano has erupted before so no one thought it was a big deal. But then we were driving and the police were stopping everyone from driving.... Everyone has lava ash in their hair." Jorge Luis Altuve, member of Guatemala's mountain rescue brigade (Guatemala volcano: Dozens die as Fuego volcano erupts, 2018), said: "This really came as a surprise, there had been no alert when we'd set out to search for this missing person. . . . We only really realised the magnitude of this when we got back down and saw everything covered in ash and bridges destroyed."

Eyewitnesses to the fires in Greece included three personal tales in one story that reflected how quickly the fires spread (Greece wildfires: 'Hundreds went into the sea', 2018). Olivia Exarchakou, nineteen, said: "There was a lot of wind as well, the winds were so strong cushions and mops were blown from balconies onto the street below." Argyro Moustaka Brettou saw fire spread from the mountains to engulf Mati in just 5 minutes. Brettou said:

> It was like something in a Hollywood movie. I've never witnessed anything like that. My mother then called again and said our garden was on fire. She and my aunt were screaming that they were going to be burned alive. They were afraid to go out through the garden because whole area was on fire. But the roads were jammed. Nothing could get in—so I told them to get out of the house and scream for help.

Witnesses saw fires that were otherworldly. Catherine Hooper (Greece wildfires: 'Hundreds went into the sea', 2018) said: "This is a biblical catastrophe." Survivor Kostas Laganos echoed that view (Greece wildfires: Dozens dead in Attica region), "We're talking about a biblical catastrophe in this wonderful area of Mati." British tourist Ronan Grant, nineteen, was in Athens when the fire began. Grant said (Greece wildfires: British man in hospital with burns, 2018): "We looked up and we saw the sky was grey and red, almost as if there was a border between being stuck in [the fire] and reality." The impact of the fires was vivid to some witnesses. Vassiliki Psevedourou (Maltezou, 2018a) "heard a loud bang and in horror saw flames dancing menacingly outside her living room window at Neos Voutzas, east of Athens. 'I could only see a blur, sparks and cars driving aimlessly.'" Nikos Stavrinidis (Gatopoulos, 2018) said: "It happened very fast. The fire was in the distance, then sparks from the fire reached us. Then the fire was all around us. . . . The wind was indescribable—it was incredible. I've never seen anything like this before in my life."

TRAUMA, FEAR, AND ANXIETY

Most of the content that fits as trauma, fear, and anxiety came in the wildfires in the United States, with a handful of examples from the Indonesia, Guatemala, Papua New Guinea, and Greece natural disasters. Victims, survivors, and witnesses contributed all of the sources on trauma, fear, or anxiety. Harrowing escapes from the flames produced high levels of fear, trauma, and anxiety among survivors of the wildfires in the United States. In the Paradise area, Hughes (2018) captured the potentially final words between a frightened nurse trapped in the fire and a loved one. Nurse Karen Davis spoke with her daughter: "'It's getting really hot. I can't breathe,' Karen says. 'Well guess what?' Wendy says, urging her mother to leave. 'I'm not going to be here on this line listening to you die.'" Tamara Ferguson was talking with a boyfriend, who tries to calm her and she replied: "Babe, there's no way I'm going to survive this."

Another nurse, Allyn Pierce, was trapped in traffic and even recorded a goodbye message to his family (Del Real & Nicas, 2018). Pierce said: "I was like, 'I think I'm done. . . . I just kept thinking, 'I'm going to die in melting plastic.'" Pierce recalls saying into his phone "Just in case this doesn't work out, I want you to know I really tried to make it out." According to the story, Pierce held his coat against the window as a shield from the intense heat and put on Peter Gabriel's song "In Your Eyes" to calm himself. Even after reaching safety, Pierce said: "It's completely traumatic. . . . When I close my eyes at night, I see fire." Anabel Lois, fifteen, and her mother Mee Forbes, who lived near Paradise, were fearful and anxious shortly after escaping a dangerous situation (California wildfires: 'I saw cars become metal and bones', 2018). Lois told the BBC that "the situation 'is still frightening' and that she is struggling to comprehend what has happened. . . . 'I don't think I am going to believe it until I go back [home].'" Her mother also found the situation unreal. Forbes said: "You see it on the news and you just don't think it'll happen to you. You don't feel like you would ever be affected. We don't have any idea [when we can go home], there are fires still burning in our area. We are just waiting to see if our home is still standing."

Others experienced anxiety as well. Sorrell Bobrink, a Paradise resident (California fires: At least 42 die in state's deadliest wildfire, 2018) said: "It was traumatising, we will be traumatised for a long time. My whole community was traumatised—I can't watch the videos anymore because I actually went through it." Reality TV star Kim Kardashian (California wildfires: 250,000 flee monster flames ravaging state, 2018) wrote on Twitter: "Trying to get my mind off this fire . . . We are all safe and that's all that matters." Reliving the experience was another type of anxiety and fear. Rebecca Hackett (Del Real & Nicas, 2018) said: "The fire came so quickly. One minute it was calm and then suddenly they were on top of us. . . . I thought I was going to die." James Reed, sixty-five, a retired tow-truck driver from Magalia (Romero, 2018) said: "Getting out of that fire was like a B-rated horror movie. I never thought I'd see something like this in this country." William Hart (California wildfires: 'I saw cars become metal and bones', 2018) said: "Three minutes separated me from death."

Indonesian hospitals recorded cases of depression and other trauma, including a teenage girl named Risna, who was traumatized after being buried more than 12 hours before being rescued (Depression cases surface at hospitals following earthquake, tsunami, 2018). Nirwansyah Parampasi, the director of Madani Hospital in Palu, said (Depression cases surface at hospitals following earthquake, tsunami, 2018): "When she woke up, she could not recall who her father and mother were. The mother was experiencing anxiety while merely sitting still in a room." Fleeing the volcanic danger was treacherous in Guatemala. According to BBC (the survivors of the Fire Volcano safe, but with uncertainty about the future, 2018), Aura Garcia "did not hesitate to recount the minutes of terror that she lived that day. When they were told to leave, they all ran everywhere, shouted and cried. Although they are fine, she does not stop shedding tears because she knows that nothing will be the same." The article quoted survivor Mardoqueo González as saying "What ended up scare us was the mud that began to fall, it was like a drizzle . . . my dad has not yet appeared, he stayed there. I still went on the motorcycle to see how it was left but it was already destroyed."

Anxiety in Papua New Guinea involved coping with the trauma and ongoing fear. Hela police commander Thomas Levongo said the province was "still trying to come to terms" with the earthquake, because it was the first earthquake of such magnitude to hit the provincial capital (Nalu, 2018a). Agnes Kep, a resident of Mendi, said (Papua New Guinea earthquake: at least fourteen killed amid landslides, 2018) "she feared 'the ground might open up and swallow us' when her thatched roof collapsed." Fear and anxiety were prominent for one survivor of the Greece wildfires. Giannis Labropoulos said (Greece wildfires: 'Hundreds went into the sea', 2018): "We were pretty scared. We didn't know if we would make it through, we just did not know what to expect. The power of the fire and the intense heat made it something we would not want to experience ever again."

LOSS OF HOME OR PROPERTY

Survivors reacting to their losses were especially common in the U.S. wildfires, but also in Nigeria's flooding, Guatemala's volcanic eruption, Japan's flooding, Papua New Guinea's earthquake, and the wildfires in Greece. Many residential and commercial structures burned in the U.S. wildfires. Frank Kerze, fifty-eight, lost his 1982 Ford pickup truck, but he saved his Malibu-area home, because he stayed behind and fought the fire (Nicas et al., 2018) with "no water pressure" but "a couple of garden hoses." In Southern California, actor Gerard Butler and musician Neil Young lost houses. Butler shared a picture of a charred house on Twitter, writing (California wildfires: Death toll reaches grim milestone, 2018): "Returned to my house in Malibu after evacuating. Heartbreaking time across California." Young wrote on his website (California wildfires: Death toll reaches grim milestone, 2018): "I have lost my home before to a California wildfire, now another." Anjeanette Ramey, thirty, from the Malibu area (Romero, 2018), said: "All I made it out with were the clothes on my back. . . . My house, my car, gone. No money, no job. I have no idea what happens next." The response to one loss was humor. Nurse Allyn Pierce's charred ambulance was shown in a viral Instagram photo (California wildfires: Survivors share stories of heroic rescues, 2018), which he jokingly said gave it the color of "Custom Campfire Marshmallow."

In Nigeria, flood survivor stories included sad tales of lost property and goods. An "elderly man" named Ilu Mato said (Adeyemi et al., 2018): "I am relatively privileged in this village but with this flood I have become poor as the flood damaged all my farm produce. As I'm talking to you I have nothing; I've lost all my stored food and cash crops, and I am not alone. Many others lost as much as I did." Malam Yunusa Adamu had a similar tale (Adeyemi et al., 2018): "I had gone out for a family meeting. When it started threatening to rain, I rushed home, but on getting close to my house under the heavy downpour, I sensed danger. As I struggled to gain entrance into the house, the next thing I heard was a heavy sound as flood already covered everywhere." A community leader in Aduralere community, Alhaji Abdurasheed Jimoh (Akinrinade, 2018) said: "This is not the first time we are experiencing flood in our community, but this one came with an ugly and bitter experience as the drainage channels got filled up and submerged houses suddenly." The effects of loss hit hard for Malam Ibrahim Dankaka a ninety-year-old man, sitting sorrowfully at a corner. He said (Adeyemi et al., 2018), "I no longer have a home. I sleep here, I wake up here."

Effects of the volcanic eruption hit residents of Guatemala hard, as little was left from some homes. Ricardo Reyes, who was forced to quickly abandon his home, said (Guatemala volcano: Dozens die as Fuego volcano erupts, 2018): "The only thing we could do was run with my family and we left our possessions in the house. Now that all the danger has passed, I came to see how our house was—everything is a disaster." José Manuel Sacol lost nearly everything from his home in El Rodeo, other than one bed and some dishes. Sacol said (The survivors of the Fire Volcano safe, but with uncertainty about the future, 2018): "By being here we learned that Los Lotes had been destroyed and that the lava stayed close to where we lived." Joel González (Perez, 2018) said: "That was like a beach, everything full of sand, nothing was left. The houses, the animals, the people, everything burned, we have nothing."

Mentions of property loss were rare in Japan, Papua New Guinea, and Greece. In Japan, Teruo Sasai, whose house in Mabicho was flooded, said (Johnston, 2018b): "The floodwaters were up over my house, probably reaching 4 or 5 meters, up past the roof all the way to the TV antenna.

Thankfully, I was OK and nobody in this neighborhood was severely injured." In Papua New Guinea, Agnes Kep said (Papua New Guinea earthquake: At least 14 killed amid landslides, 2018): "When we came out we barely recognised everything around us, nothing was familiar to us. . . . The house or tree that was there wasn't there anymore." In Greece, Mati's George Vokos (Greece wildfires: 'Hundreds went into the sea', 2018) said: "I have lost two cars in the fire as they are burnt out, and my house has been semi-burnt too."

UNKNOWN FATE OF FAMILY OR FRIENDS

Nearly half of the examples of missing family or friends were in Indonesia, where the earthquake and tsunami separated family members. All sources addressing unknown fate came from survivors or those connected to survivors. When the earthquake hit, Dwi Haris was in Palu for a wedding with his wife and daughter. Haris said (Indonesia earthquake: Huge surge in death toll, 2018): "I was squeezed into the ruins of the wall . . . I heard my wife cry for help but then silence. I don't know what happened to her and my child. I hope they are safe." The tsunami separated a man named Adi from a loved one. Adi (Indonesia earthquake and tsunami: Dead buried in mass grave, 2018) "was hugging his wife by the beach in Palu when the tsunami struck, and has not seen her since. 'When the wave came, I lost her,' he said. 'I was carried about 50 metres. I couldn't hold anything.'" At a health clinic in Palu, a five-year-old girl was treated for a broken leg after being found alone. Dr. Sasono said (Henschke, 2018a): "We don't know where her family is and she doesn't remember where they live."

Wildfires in Greece led to the separation of loved ones, including a desperate mother trying to reach her children. Argyro Moustaka Brettou was 3 kilometers away from home, where her two young children were with her mother and aunt. Brettou said (Greece wildfires: 'Hundreds went into the sea', 2018): "Whilst trying to drive back home, I was yelling, 'My mother is being burned alive, please let me back!' I had no battery on my phone after a while and didn't know if my mother had made it or if my children were safe. The several hours of waiting were a living hell. I got to see them the next morning." Maria Saridou's sister disappeared while swimming with a friend in Mati. Saridou, sixty, who looked for her sister at the morgue, said (Greek officials see 'serious indications' arson led to fire, 2018): "I believe she's alive. Where she went, nobody knows where she went." Vassiliki Psevedourou, fifty-four, of Neos Voutras, east of Athens, was calling hospitals unsuccessfully for her missing cousin's wife. Psevedourou said (Maltezou, 2018a), "We are not sure about her, we are not sure where she is."

Missing relatives was a theme in Guatemala as well. Hilda López (Perez, 2018) "cannot stop crying. He holds his face with his hands. He does not know where his mother, his sister and his brother-in-law were. Now, together with her children and her husband, she waits at a shelter to hear from her relatives." In Japan, Kosuke Kiyohara, thirty-eight, had not heard from his sister and two sons in the flooding. Kiyohara said (Japan floods: 155 killed after torrential rain and landslides, 2018): "I have asked my family to prepare for the worst."

INJURIES

Most injury examples were in Greece, including two examples in BBC stories about those from the United Kingdom—Susan Margaret Stephos, seventy-one, escaped from the fire in Mati and was hospitalized for burns and smoke inhalation (Greece wildfires: British man in hospital with burns, 2018), while Zoe Holohan was in a hospital after suffering burns to her head and hands (Irishman on honeymoon dies in Greek fire, family confirms, 2018). Another Greek fire survivor described a scary example of her cousin. Vassiliki Psevedourou said (Maltezou, 2018a): "His shoes melted from the heat, the ground was burning. He was trying to hug (his wife), to shield her from the flames, and his legs, his hands, his face were burned."

Survivors in the United States also suffered burns, including Rick Rios, who had severe burns to his hands and face. His daughter, Maria Rios, said (Arango, 2018): "Right now, it's just a recovery effort. . . . My dad is in a lot of pain—he keeps saying, 'I have no skin, no skin.'" Maurine Johnson, seventy-nine, of Paradise (California wildfires: Thanksgiving hope from ashes of Paradise, 2018), broke her nose and damaged her teeth from falling while escaping fire.

EVALUATION OF SURVIVOR STORIES

Stories about survivors offered continuity and hope by showing a positive outcome among stories filled with death and destruction. Survivors offer symbolic hope for the future by demonstrating life goes on despite tragedy, which aids healing. It could help people cope with the ongoing disaster by illustrating examples of others who have overcome tragedy. The individual trauma of survivors can influence the collective trauma of a larger audience, especially when it involves those with shared values (Ostertag & Ortiz, 2013) or common social identity (Slater, 2007). Sources directly tied to survivors— including survivors themselves and their friends or relatives—dominated survivor stories. Source usage demonstrates that the people themselves were able to help define and articulate the survivor stories.

The two wildfires put people in imminent danger, with people in Greece fleeing into the sea or through flames on land, harrowing tales of escape that offered a glimmer of hope, similar to the mine disaster survivors evaluated by Kitch and Hume (2007). People in the United States narrowly escaped by driving automobiles through flames on mountain roads and survivors dodged rocks and mudslides from the volcanic eruption in Guatemala, showing continuity and hope. Expressions of trauma, fear, and anxiety in the disasters, more prominently in the United States, revealed the humanity of those involved, giving readers relatable characteristics. Among those who lost homes and other property, some survivors took philosophical responses, offering perspective and acceptance that looks forward. These themes of survivors spread hope and aided coping to a broader audience by demonstrating a path forward into the future despite trauma.

Chapter 6

Death Stories

Victims of the natural disasters were transformed in stories from names into people with depth, sometimes by mentioning details of the victim in life, creating a written legacy. In other situations, the reaction of family or friends gave the victim depth and poignancy, triggering empathy among readers. Death stories were particularly common in the wildfires in Greece and the United States, the volcanic eruption in Guatemala, and the flooding in Nigeria.

Biographies or descriptions of people known to others were the most common among the three types of death stories. Descriptions of victims were also common, with less attention on names or numbers on victims. Witnesses, survivors, and friends or relatives of the deceased accounted for nearly nine in ten of the sources used.

BIOGRAPHIES AND DEATHS OF PEOPLE KNOWN

Biographies—which contained details and depth on victims—were particularly prominent in the wildfires of the United States, with deaths of people known to others were found in the Guatemala, Greece, and Nigeria natural disasters. Those who knew the deceased contributed all of the sourced material. The most extensive biography was in the *New York Times International* edition, which devoted nearly 1,000 words to details on several victims of the wildfires in the United States, along with photographs of the deceased. The story (Arango, 2018) was meticulously researched with background and perspective on one victim of the Camp Fire. Ernie Foss, sixty-three, was described as "a surfer and skateboarder as a young man. He grew up in San Francisco and worked at a store in the hippie heyday of Haight-Ashbury, selling candles and crystals, a job that allowed him to pursue his passion of music. And then tech money flooded the city, his neighborhood was gentrified, and like so many others he was priced out." Foss, according to his daughter, Angela Loo, settled in Paradise, but San Francisco was always in his mind. Loo said: "His San Francisco roots were very important to him. . . . It's where he got into music. And did his thing and where he raised his kids. It's his hometown and he loved it very much and he missed it all the time." Instead, Foss died in Paradise, the story explained. "His body was found outside his home, near his minivan, in what Ms. Loo believes was a desperate attempt to escape with his stepson Andrew Burt, his caretaker, as the flames engulfed the street. Mr. Foss's dog, Bernice, a little brown mutt he had rescued from a shelter, died there too." The story told about his days as a blues and rock musician in San Francisco to his last years isolated in Paradise battling lymphedema, a condition that swelled the arms and legs. Loo said: "You know, whenever something like this happens we tend to focus on all the positive attributes of a person. . . . Graciously ignoring all of their faults. My dad was not a perfect person. He struggled in life and was perfectly imperfect."

The same story also briefly told of two other victims. Jesus Fernandez, forty-eight, "died of smoke inhalation, probably trying to rescue his dog, King. Mr. Fernandez, nicknamed Zeus, had a son who lives in Las Vegas, and was described by a friend as someone 'who people counted on in rough times.'" Bill Godbout, seventy-nine, was "an influential figure in the early days of Silicon Valley who ran a popular electronics store. He was well-known in the hacker community, and remembered for his quirks, like his license to fly blimps."

One heart-wrenching example was in the Nigeria flooding, which depicted the families of Suleiman Ibrahim and Tanko Hassan (Ololade, 2018) "having lost two of their promising sons to floods. The two families were inconsolable as they received the news of the death of their sons." The article described the deceased as "hard working, tenacious, responsible and ready to take on any task." The men were graduates of the Niger State College of Education and were returning home to their families in the Lapai local government area but drowned when their canoe capsized.

Survivors of the volcanic eruption in Guatemala shared horrific tales about witnessing the demise of loved ones. BBC (Guatemala volcano: Almost 200 missing and 75 dead, 2018) told of one traumatized survivor. "Boris Rodriguez has no-one to turn to now. He lost more loved ones in a single night on Sunday than many do in a lifetime. Mr. Rodriguez's wife, both of her parents, his brother and sister-in-law and their children died when the Fuego volcano erupted. 'I saw the children's bodies. . . . They were huddled together in the bed, like they were trying to hide from what was happening.'" A story in *La Hora* told of José Manuel Sacol in El Rodeo (The survivors of the Fire

Volcano safe, 2018): "Sacol does not hide his sadness, at times his eyes fill with tears as he remembers childhood friends who died that day. 'They warned us that we should leave, but when the tragedy had passed, how could one do it? People ran everywhere, there were people crying,' he said." And the funeral of Juan Fernando Galindo was highlighted (Guatemala volcano aftermath—in pictures, 2018), including his relatives receiving a medal at the wake.

Greek wildfire survivors also told of the dead, such as Olivia Exarchakou, nineteen (Greece wildfires: 'Hundreds went into the sea', 2018): "I know two people who have died as a result of the fire. One died at home. She didn't have time to get out of her house because of the speed at which the fire spread. Another family friend lost her life at the beach. She was in the water when she was found." The same story mentioned George Vokos, who said: "Two ladies lost their lives as in my hands." And BBC ran a brief profile (Greek fires: 'Hearts empty' over death of Irishman Brian O'Callaghan-Westropp, 2018) of a newly married Irishman who died in Greece on his honeymoon. Louise Jay said that the death of Brian O'Callaghan-Westropp was "a big loss to our family. . . . Brian was such a lovely man. He would do anything for anyone, always had that happy smile and had so many friends—and they all meant something to him."

VICTIMS DESCRIBED

Sources describing victims were equally distributed among three types—businesses and nongovernmental entities, people who knew victims, and governmental representatives. Most powerful of the victim descriptions was the poignant story of twenty-six bodies found on a clifftop near Mati in the Greece fires. Although the victims were not named, the nature of their demise, as expressed by Nikos Economopoulos, head of Greece's Red Cross (Greece wildfires: Dozens dead in Attica region, 2018) was powerful: "They had tried to find an escape route but unfortunately these people and their kids didn't make it in time. Instinctively, seeing the end nearing, they embraced." Another story (Plot where 26 wildfire victims died is encroached state land, 2018) described them as "26 bodies, including those of small children, huddled together inside the plot, some of them hugging. They were only a few metres away from the sea."

Besides general descriptions of the clifftop victims, other stories told of specific people. For instance (Missing 13-year-old boy identified among wildfire victims, 2018):

> A 13-year-old boy that had gone missing in the coastal town of Mati since Monday's deadly blaze was identified among the victims . . . The news comes

a day after authorities announced they had identified the bodies of the nine-year-old twin girls and their grandparents that went missing after the wildfires. Their bodies were among a group of victims recovered by emergency crews on Tuesday lying close together near the top of a cliff overlooking a beach.

Another story showed the severe impact on one family (Firefighter's wife, baby among 93 victims of Greece blaze, 2018): "The victims also included five members of the same family—a 39-year-old chef, his wife, 38, their two children, ages 4 and 7, and the chef's 67-year-old mother. In all, 11 children died in the fire. Among them were two sets of twin girls, and the 6-month-old son of a firefighter who was called to duty that day and whose wife also was killed."

In the wildfires of the United States, survivor Robert Tuck (Arango, 2018) drove away from Paradise with his family, but his grandfather did not make it. "Mr. Tuck said through tears. 'He was listening to the radio report and thought he had a little more time.'" In Nigeria, flood victims were described (Akinrinade, 2018) as "an expectant mother" and a "visually impaired man" who "drowned while he wanted to salvage his belongings from the water."

NAMES, NUMBERS

As death tolls rose, stories included lists of the deceased and totals of the identified victims. Such mentions were most common in the Greece, Guatemala, Nigeria, and U.S. disasters. In Greece, *Kathimerini* (As fire victims named, their stories emerge, 2018) included a numbered list of ninety fire victims by name, including their year of birth and parents' names. In Guatemala, *La Hora* (These are the names of some people who sadly lost their lives, 2018) published a numbered list of sixty-six victims by name and age.

In Greece, victim names were a prominent part of stories. Examples also included "twin 9-year-old girls Sofia and Vassiliki Philippopoulou, whose pictures have featured internationally" (Greece to start burying wildfire victims, government facing criticism, 2018); Father Spyridon Papapostolous, who drowned while trying to escape flames (Burials of Greece's wildfire victims begin, 2018); teacher Vassilis Katsargyris, seventy, who was trapped in a garage (Greek fire victims sue authorities over deaths in Mati, 2018); and two Polish nationals, Beate-Teresa Korzeniowska, forty, and her nine-year-old son, Kacper-Nikolaj, who drowned (As fire victims named, their stories emerge, 2018).

Nigeria's flood victims were also depicted by name. One story in the *Nation* (Elekwa, 2018) listed "Okechukwu Osadebe, 18, son of the late highlife crooner" and "The father of nine children, Chief Ojike Ajanwu, from Umuokpalaoma kindred." Akinrinade (2018) mentioned "No fewer than five persons, including a 60-year-old visually impaired man and an 11-year-old boy." In the United States, one story (California wildfires: 'More than 1,000 missing' in Camp Fire, 2018) listed the names of five victims and another story mentioned names of those missing but presumed dead (Arango, 2018).

EVALUATION OF DEATH STORY THEMES

A handful of stories featured biographies or highlighted the deaths of people known to others, illustrating the personality and accomplishments of the deceased to readers. By turning a victim from a number into a person, it was uplifting, gave meaning to the victim's life, and aided coping by suggesting continuity. It fits into a peace journalism approach that supports identifying victims of conflict (Tenenboim-Weinblatt et al., 2016). Not surprisingly, friends, relatives, and others who knew victims contributed all of the sourced material providing details of the deceased, allowing for portrayals that helped victims come to life.

The most extensive biography appeared in the local publication in the U.S. wildfires, transforming victim Ernie Foss from a name and age into a well-rounded person with a history and a family, somewhat like the portraits of grief after the 9/11 terrorist attack (Hume, 2003). Foss was portrayed as a full-fledged person with an interesting life full of ups and downs, triggering empathy for his life story and reactions of his daughter.

Other victims in the United States, Guatemala, Nigeria, and Greece received enough attention in the news to become people with thoughts and emotions, many sharing the loss of a loved one. A story from Nigeria about two young men who died in the flooding were described as promising, hard-working, tenacious, and responsible. Descriptions of their accomplishments cut short and potential ensured that their lives would not be forgotten. This elevation demonstrates the potential of news attention to provide a glimmer of hope in making victims into people with goals in life cut short, similar to news attention toward school shooting victims (McCluskey, 2017).

Stories that described victims without names offered glimmers of hope for humanity within the tragedy, especially the discovery of twenty-six burnt bodies in the Greek fires who were found huddled together, as poignant deaths can trigger empathy. It suggested that, even in the face of death, people turned toward others and embraced humanity, a hopeful theme. Other victim descriptions showed the depth of loss, including five people in one family and one daughter seeking her missing father.

Chapter 7

Selfless Behavior

Selfless behavior in the news demonstrated kindness of others and served as aspirational models. Selfless behavior offered a glimmer of hope for society amid the chaos of the present trauma, illustrating the best of humanity and compassion for others.

Four types of selfless behavior were found in the news content—volunteerism, assistance and donations, heroic actions, and rescues. Items of selfless behavior were found in all eight of the natural disasters, especially in Indonesia and the United States. Sources used to explain selfless behavior were distributed mostly around three types—business and nongovernmental organizations (39%), volunteers (34%), and unaffiliated people (25%).

HEROES

Explicit heroism in the news coverage arose in Indonesia's twin disasters of an earthquake and tsunami, centered on air traffic controller Anthonius Gunawan Agung, twenty-one, who died while staying in the control tower during an earthquake until an airplane was able to take off. While many depictions of heroes were unattributed, the attributed sources were mostly from businesses and NGOs. Agung was called (Indonesia tsunami: Pilot calls air traffic controller his 'guardian angel', 2018) a "national hero" and a "guardian angel." State-Owned Enterprises Minister Rini Soemarno said (Nasution, 2018b): "Agung is a hero for us all. He sincerely sacrificed his life for saving the lives of those on board a commercial aircraft, which was ready for getting airborne." The pilot of the Batik Airways plane, Ricosetta Mafella, said that Agung saved his life and those of his passengers (Indonesia tsunami: Pilot calls air traffic controller his 'guardian angel', 2018). The story explained how Agung remained in the shaking tower during the plane's takeoff and died after jumping from the crumbling tower. Nasution (2018a) was more poetic in describing the heroism. "Amid the grievances and hardship left behind, there is a heroic story that can be told from generation to generation. It is the story of the brave-heart of Anthonius Gunawan Agung. . . . Agung will also remain in the minds and hearts of his colleagues and the people at large due to his dedication, professionalism, and brave heart that saved the lives of those in the commercial aircraft by risking his own life." The story added: "Agung's sincerity toward his work needs to be an inspiration for those struggling for survival amid the shortage of food and water, military and police personnel securing the disaster zones, and humanitarian workers assisting the victims."

A nurse and firefighters were heroic in the United States. Allyn Pierce, a registered nurse, narrowly escaped flames in the Paradise area, yet he did not flee the area and was explicitly named as a hero (Del Real & Nicas, 2018). "He instead returned to the main hospital, Adventist Health Feather River, where he manages the intensive care unit. He and some colleagues began treating injured neighbors. When the hospital caught fire, they moved patients and equipment about 100 yards away, to the hospital's helipad. Eventually, everyone made it out."

In Guatemala, columnist Stu Velasco (2018), under the headline "Volcano of Fire and our Heroes of Truth!," found many heroes:

> Before the dark death and desolation stand Heroes of Truth, women and men of steel, stoic thinking, unwavering temperance, able to overcome the fear to which many mortals succumb, Guatemalan flesh and blood that are planted with example of gallantry and heroism before the huge and deadly action of the volcano that has alluded to its fearsome name -of Fuego-. Our heroes of truth possess privileged names, firefighters, policemen, soldiers, rescuers, and they must be written under the title "Heroes of Truth" with letters of gold in the history of our country, to overturn without fear to be embraced by the death where not there is return, to return the life, the hope, the joy to hundreds of families, for having arrived punctually and lifted in arms to children, women and men who were about to expire the breath of life and today they are under shelter and shelter with certainty of living.

VOLUNTEERS

Japan and Indonesia provided the most examples of volunteer behavior, with at least one example found in each of the eight natural disasters. Volunteers themselves provided most of the sourced material about their activities and their motivations.

In Japan, more than 100 volunteers showed up at the city of Seiyo in Ehime Prefecture (Osumi, 2018a). Atsuhito Inoue of Seiyo's welfare council said: "I've seen some foreigners among the volunteers. . . . They are welcome as long as they can communicate in Japanese, even if it is through smartphone (translation) applications." One volunteer was American Joy Jarman-Walsh, forty-nine, a long-term Hiroshima resident, who joined other local residents to clear debris, mud, and sand from clogged drains in her neighborhood. She said (Osumi, 2018a): "That was what was really needed to get those neighborhoods back functioning." Other foreigners helped cleanup in Hiroshima Prefecture (Osumi, 2018b) despite scorching temperatures "to show gratitude for the hospitality they have received living in Japan." Mongolian Munkhbat Manduul, twenty-seven, was among 360 volunteers setting sandbags and digging out mud from houses on Ninoshima island. Manduul said: "I was planning to spend holidays in Mongolia but I ditched that plan and called other (Mongolian community members) to join me. . . . Judging from what I've seen here, help will be needed for a while, so more people should come to help." Sri Lankan Amila Lakmal, another volunteer, said (Osumi, 2018b): "I live in Japan, I love Japan, I love Japanese people—so what I can do, I do. . . . I wanted to do something in return." Piotr Szalczynski, a 29-year-old drone designer from Poland, took a 12-hour bus ride from his home to Hiroshima's Aki Ward to volunteer. Szalczynski said: "I heard on the news that they're looking for volunteers (in disaster-hit areas), so I came. . . . I work out a lot and I'm stronger than many Japanese people, so I thought I could use my strength here and could be of help."

References to volunteers in Indonesia highlighted unnamed people who worked for the sake of others. Nasution (2018b) wrote:

> Who are they? Among them are security apparatuses and rescue workers who keep on working to secure humanitarian relief operations, as well as to search for, rescue, and evacuate trapped victims in the disaster zones. Those actively working for restoring the law and order, and helping people in need in the disaster zones, including the volunteers of the Indonesian Red Cross (PMI) and Islamic Defenders Front (FPI), are all unsung heroes. . . . those actively getting involved in humanitarian mission in the disaster zones of Central Sulawesi Province are all unsung heroes though their names are not published in media and are not publicly known.

One Indonesian volunteer was singled out (Henschke, 2018b): "Erna Wahyuni is cutting up a mountain of cabbage for soup. Her house was destroyed, but she wants to help. 'I was saved so I have to give back. It's also hard just sitting in a tent in the hot sun all day, I would rather be cooking', she laughs."

Pet rescue volunteers were featured in the Greek wildfires, as nearly 600 people opened their homes to a pet who lost its home or family. Elena Dede, the head of the Dog's Voice platform for animal protection groups, said (Fotiadi, 2018a): "We've had help from a lot of experienced volunteers at shelters, from concerned citizens and from dozens of vets offering their services for free." Loukoumaki, a white poodle mix dog, was the focus of one story after he was found "traumatized and seemingly unable to move" two days after fire swept through a home in Mati (Loukoumaki the dog recovers from Greek wildfire, 2018). Artemis Kyriakopoulou, an animal rescue volunteer, found Loukoumaki and lured him out with a tin of dog food. Diana Topali, forty-two, who offered Loukoumaki foster care, said: "Even its eyelashes are burnt, I wonder how this dog survived."

In Guatemala, volunteers handed out food and other essentials to those affected by the volcano and rescue workers (Guatemala volcano: Emergency agency 'failed to heed warnings', 2018). Volunteers came from the Catholic Church of Our Lady of Guadalupe (The survivors of the Fire Volcano safe, but with uncertainty about the future, 2018) and students at the University Paraninfo, who also set up a collection center (They ask resignation of Morales and other officials after the tragedy of Volcán de Fuego, 2018). Banrural provided volunteers, donations, and other humanitarian support, along with cosponsoring a raffle (Empresarial, 2018b).

Volunteers in the United States searched for the missing and served the homeless. Trish Moutard, a volunteer with the California Rescue Dog Association, said (California wildfires: Concern over rain in search efforts, 2018): "We have been told we're to look as hard as we can, but it's still possible we may not be able to find something left of someone." Rich Wilson, sixty-eight, a volunteer helping homeless people camped outside a Walmart in Chico, said (Levine, 2018b): "They've been through the good, the bad and the ugly here."

The other tragedies had fewer mentions of volunteerism. In Papua New Guinea, Anna Mand, principal of the Lae Christian Academy, said that helping is an everyday thing at the school and students donated clothes to earthquake victims (Students give to help earthquake victims, 2018). In Nigeria, youths and others constructed embankments around their communities to contain floods (Adeyemi et al., 2018). Youths in Pakistan embarked on a massive tree-planting exercise to mitigate future heat waves (youth begins with sowing 200 neem plants in Karachi, 2018).

ASSISTANCE, DONATIONS

Papua New Guinea and the United States received the most news attention to examples of assistance or donations, with every disaster except for Pakistan including at least one mention. Businesses, schools, or NGOs contributed three-fourths of the source material on assistance and donations, with unaffiliated people accounting for the remainder.

Donations from schools and a relief fund were detailed in *The National*, a newspaper serving Papua New Guinea. The St. Paul's Lutheran Primary School in Lae donated more than K2,000 worth of water and rice (Earthquake victims receive K20,000 worth of clothes, 2018). Students felt sorry for children in the affected provinces, according to school coordinator Sesike Sawe, who said: "Disasters of such magnitude are a challenge for us to rise up and give whatever way we can and assist." Lae Christian Academy students and faculty donated bottled water and clothing to the Lae earthquake relief appeal (Students give to help earthquake victims, 2018). Principal Anna Mand said: "Our school's motto is: Sharing is caring." The Highlands earthquake relief appeal in Lae raised more than K26,000 in cash and K1000,000 worth of food and clothes (Ukaha, 2018), an effort that appeal chairperson Sarah Haoda-Todd said was "overwhelming."

Donations and assistance came from organizations, businesses, individuals, and even celebrities. Actor James Woods enlisted his 1.85 million Twitter followers to support missing person appeals, solicit donations, and attract volunteers for the fires in the United States (Bell, 2018). In Japan, top-ranked Mongolian sumo wrestler Hakuho rented a bus to transport twenty compatriots from Chiba Prefecture to Hiroshima to aid relief efforts (Osumi, 2018b). According to the story, "The Yokozuna"—referring to the top-ranked sumo wrestler in Japan—"has used his celebrity status to help collect supplies for disaster relief, alongside efforts from the rest of the Mongolian community in Japan and the yokozuna's fans."

Nonprofit organizations provided shelter, clothes, and food, including meals for the Thanksgiving holiday in the United States (California wildfires: Thanksgiving hope from ashes of Paradise, 2018). Hundreds of Red Cross volunteers ran an emergency shelter that housed 950 people one night, provided meals, dealt with a viral outbreak, and helped people search for the missing. In Indonesia, volunteers of Jokowi-Ma'ruf Amin in Malaysia conducted a donation drive for victims of the disasters (Volunteers of Jokowi-Ma'ruf in Malaysia collect tsunami donation, 2018). Coordinator Agus Dwi Purwanto said: "These volunteers are concerned about the condition of the victims of the disaster, who need help." Volunteers from Fundación Castillo Córdova in Guatemala and students of the Castillo Cordova School set up emergency kits for victims and rescuers.

Individuals cleaned up and tended to disaster victims. In the United States, people volunteered to house ill or elderly residents. Tracey Grant and her boyfriend, Josh Fox, took in 93-year-old Lee Brundige, a World War II veteran who was left homeless by the wildfires in Paradise (California wildfires:

Survivors share stories of heroic rescues, 2018). Grant, who met Brundige while distributing hamburgers to displaced residents, said: "He can stay with us as long as he would like." Kassy Parish, nineteen, was invited to spend Thanksgiving with her twin sister at the home of a stranger in the Paradise area (California wildfires: Thanksgiving hope from ashes of Paradise, 2018). Parish said: "It's brought out so much good in a lot of people in the area. . . . A lot of people have been getting together and making sure everyone is taken care of." Mee Forbes, also in the Paradise area, said (California wildfires: 'I saw cars become metal and bones', 2018): "People have really stepped up to help us find a place to stay for a night. It is really nice to have family and friends that are able to reach out to us. We are very thankful for that."

In Guatemala, Faye Dunstan, manager of the Oxford Language Centre in Antigua, said (Guatemala volcano: Lava ash like 'black rain', 2018): "I had raised some money online through Facebook so we went to the supermarket and bought supplies. We bought toilet paper and medicine." Guatemalans in Barcelona raised funds for victims of the volcano and migrants in Madrid sent donations for mostly medical materials (Herrera & Pinto, 2018). People who provided assistance during the floods of Japan were praised. One story mentioned (Johnston, 2018b) "Neighbors were seen helping each other move muddy, broken and waterlogged furniture and household items to curb sides, in a calm and efficient manner."

In Nigeria, Good Samaritans and members of neighboring communities sheltered and sustained people displaced from Zugachi, a tiny community in the Gabasawa Local Government Area (Adeyemi et al., 2018). Malam Ishyaku Yusuf, sixty, a native of Augwa Makera in Kura Local Government Area, said (Akinrinade, 2018): "I survive by the charity and kindness of my friends and brothers who make sure that at least, I eat." In Indonesia, Haritati, a local resident, planned to carry a humanitarian package on board an air flight to aid disaster victims (Wings Air resumes Gorontalo-Palu flights, 2018).

RESCUES

The wildfires of the United States triggered ample news coverage focused on rescue efforts, as people aided others trying to escape the rapidly spreading flames. Unaffiliated people, including survivors and witnesses, provided most of the sourced material on rescues. Nurse Tamara Ferguson, surgical nurse Karen Davis, and other hospital staff moved sixty-seven patients of Adventist Health Feather River Hospital in Paradise in any vehicle they could find (Hughes, 2018). Ferguson was evacuating a critically ill patient in an ambulance when she heard over the radio that an ambulance ahead of them had caught fire (Hughes, 2018). "Looking at the only house that is not burning, they decide to shelter with patients inside its garage. Tamara and her colleagues start stripping away loose vegetation from near the house to try and stop it catching fire. Others spray the roof and start stockpiling water as the fire gets closer." Nurse Allyn Pierce drove his ambulance through the fire to rescue his patients from the Adventist Health hospital (California wildfires: Survivors share stories of heroic rescues, 2018).

A group of people fleeing fire went into Lake Concow, a reservoir in the mountains above Paradise, to escape the flames (California wildfires: Survivors share stories of heroic rescues, 2018). Neighbors in a rowboat rescued one group from an island. Cal Fire Division Chief Garrett Sjolund said (California wildfires: Survivors share stories of heroic rescues, 2018): "It was a true rescue story." Waste Management employee Dane Cummings was driving his route near Paradise when he spotted a 93-year-old woman in her front yard. Cummings said (California wildfires: Survivors share stories of heroic rescues, 2018): "I decided that we were gonna get her out of there. . . . I don't know that much about fires, but I knew if that fire came over that hill they were in trouble." Margaret Newsum, who broke her back eight months earlier in a fall, said she "was going to get out of there. . . . I didn't know how, and here I got an angel driving this great big, green monster."

In Greece, Argyro Moustaka Brettou was talking on the phone to her frightened mother and aunt, who were trapped by fire (Greece wildfires: 'Hundreds went into the sea', 2018), she said, when "Out of the blue, a young man whose house was also in flames came by in a car. They got inside and he drove them away." Another dramatic rescue in Greece occurred in the sea, when the crew of a fishing boat pulled Nikos Stavrinidis, his wife, and two friends to safety (Gatopoulos, 2018). Stavrinidis said: "They jumped into the sea with their clothes still on. . . . They made us tea and kept us warm. They were great." People stepped forward to help in Guatemala, too, as "anyone with a spare seat in their care offered a lift to those walking past" who were fleeing the volcanic eruption (Grant, 2018).

The most unusual rescue took place in Japan, where a miniature horse was trapped on a roof in the Mabicho area of Kurashiki, Okayama Prefecture (Tanaka, 2018). Named Leaf, the horse was spotted by a team from Peace Winds Japan, a nonprofit organization engaged in disaster relief activities in the affected area. While waiting for assistance, the team watched as Leaf fell 2 meters to the ground, where rescuers comforted the mare, who was not seriously injured.

EVALUATION OF SELFLESS BEHAVIOR

Acts of selfless behavior provided hope and aided recovery through uplifting stories that demonstrated the best side of people, positive messages of healing. It signals to the audience that they, too, may heroically run to the aid of others or some stranger may come to their aid. Altogether, these aspirational models restore faith in humanity, raise hope, and promote healing. People in positions to best evaluate selfless behavior, including volunteers, survivors, witnesses, and NGOs that directly contributed to such activities, dominated the sources usage.

While explicit mentions of heroism were rare, the story of an air traffic controller in Indonesia was an inspirational example of selfless behavior. Stories not only told of his willingness to put his life in danger to help others, but also talked about him in mythic terms (also see Yair et al., 2014), setting an aspirational example for others. Hero stories build on collective memory to heal society (e.g., Berkowitz, 2010). Similar to analysis of heroes in school shootings (McCluskey, 2017), the air traffic controller's actions showed morality, leadership, empathy, skill, decisiveness, and character.

Volunteers aided others in the aftermath of the natural disasters, showing additional angles of selflessness. Stories from Japan's flood cleanup highlighted foreigners who volunteered to clean mud and debris, several expressing gratitude toward the country, demonstrating healing and recovery. Other volunteers joined search efforts, handing out food and other relief materials, and even providing foster care for pets. Donations from people and businesses, including school children and celebrities, were found in most of the disasters, demonstrating the depth of selfless acts. People invited those made homeless from fire into their houses in the United States. People also stepped in to rescue others from danger, especially in the two wildfires. In all, these tales of selfless behavior were inspiring to others and aided psychological and physical healing.

Chapter 8

Recovery Efforts

Natural disasters can cause severe damage to both infrastructure and people, with the eight disasters analyzed in this book each causing severe harm. The process of healing, coping, hope, and recovery begins while the disaster is still occurring and continues for days, weeks, and even years. News coverage focused on recovery was common in the eight natural disasters, with some attention found in every disaster except for Pakistan's heat wave—the only disaster of those studied that did not have severe impact on infrastructure.

Content about recovery fits into two broad categories, some focused on physical acts and the others virtual. Physical acts included shelters and homelessness; goods and assistance; escape, rescue, and search; and construction, which signaled to people that their needs were being addressed, aiding their healing and recovery. Virtual recovery themes included normalcy, and grief and emotions, each addressing psychological needs among the traumatized, factors of coping, healing, and hope. Three types of sources were most common in the news about recovery—from unaffiliated people, including victims and survivors (48%), government (27%), and businesses or nongovernmental organizations (22%).

SHELTERS AND HOMELESSNESS

The wildfires in the United States garnered the most news attention to shelters and homelessness among the disasters. People who became homeless from a natural disaster accounted for three-fifths of the source on this theme, with another two-fifths from government sources. The plight of those burned out of homes in the United States—some of whom called themselves "burnouts" (Levine, 2018b)—struggled with their current condition while also contemplating the future. People who fled Paradise, Magalia, and other burned towns in the foothills of the Sierra Nevada range ended up in business parking lots in nearby Chico, California. Others were in emergency shelters or staying with friends or relatives.

The parking lots of a Walmart store in Chico became an unofficial campground for people left homeless from the fires (Romero, 2018). Jarrad Winter, thirty-nine, a Marine Corps veteran and software developer who had recently emerged from a stretch of homelessness, only to lose everything he owned in the devastating Camp Fire. Winter said: "I never thought I'd live in a tent city. . . . I mean, this is America; we're not supposed to live this way. But here we are, man, the new normal." Some in the tent city said they felt safer there than in shelters, others liked being near friends and neighbors. The parking lot camp became a place for fire evacuees to connect and share information. James Reed, sixty-five, a retired tow-truck driver, was sleeping in his 1968 Chevrolet El Camino after his house Magalia was destroyed. Reed said: "This is my home now . . . being here, in this parking lot, I'm reminded I'm not the only one."

Campers also looked for longer-term housing (Levine, 2018b). James Brown, fifty, who lived in Magalia, said: "These people need housing, and tents are not good enough in this weather." Local officials acknowledged the need. Tom Tenorio, chief executive of the Community Action Agency of Butte County in Chico, said (Levine, 2018b): "It's heart-wrenching, because you know the people sitting across from you really, really need to be able to be housed. . . . I've had my staff in tears; it's a tough thing on our end." Most of the 500 people who had been in and out of a shelter in Chico were older people, who faced critical decisions about their future (Levine, 2018a). Some people had few options, such as Daniel Cayer, who was sleeping in a camper outside a church shelter in Chico. Cayer said (Levine, 2018a): "I have nowhere to go, I have no family."

Evacuees from Nigeria's flooding also faced challenges finding a place to live. Villagers were forced into makeshift huts and other shelters, including schools and mosques. Many lost means of livelihood, noted resident Alhaji Attahiru Isah (Ololade, 2018). A public relations officer of the national Emergency Management Agency, Ibrahim Audu Hussaini, said (Ololade, 2018): "Their houses are totally destroyed. They lost all their crops and livestock, mostly chickens and goats, and their lives are in danger." Conditions were difficult and people concerned. A relief camp at Crowder Memorial Primary School, Onitsha (Elekwa, 2018), contained mostly women and children, who faced hunger, starvation, and a "bad environment." An elderly man in Gululu village in Miga Local Government Area, Ilu Mato, said (Adeyemi et al., 2018): "As I'm talking to you I have nothing; I've lost all my stored food and cash crops, and I am not alone. Many others lost as much as I did."

Innocent Okoye, who sought refuge at the Community Primary School, Umueze-Anam, said (Elekwa, 2018): "I lost virtually everything I possess to the floodwaters and my house in the village is submerged too; that is why I came here to seek refuge and shelter."

In Indonesia, attention was devoted to how government, organizations, and businesses were aiding displaced people. Public Works Minister Basuki Hadimuljono said (Government to build new Palu city after earthquake, 2018): "Around 1.2 thousand units of temporary shelter will be set up, and each one will accommodate 10 families. They will also be complete with kitchen, bathroom, sanitary, and other facilities." About 10,000 evacuees were housed in fifty locations and were given shelter, goods, and medicine (Quake, tsunami death toll in Central Sulawesi rises to 420, 2018). Survivors lived in tents with food served from public kitchens (Situation of emergency officially extended in Central Sulawesi, 2018) and more tents and toilets were being set up in three refugee sites (Living condition of Central Sulawesi quake victims gets improved: mily, 2018). Two state-owned lenders, Bank Mandiri and Bank BNI, agreed to build temporary houses for 400 families (Mandiri, BNI to build houses for 400 quake-hit families: government, 2018).

Temporary shelters in Japan housed thousands of displaced people in school halls, gymnasiums, and other locations. About 300 people spent the night at the Okada Elementary School in Okayama Prefecture and many slept on blue mats in the school's gym (Japan flood: At least 179 dead after worst weather in decades, 2018). The Tokyo Metropolitan Government agreed to provide 220 residences of free public housing for victims despite being several hundred kilometers away from the flooded areas (Murakami, 2018). Shunro Miyazaki, an official at the Urban Development Bureau of the Tokyo Metropolitan Government, said: "We thought it would help for the victims to have a safe place to stay near their family in Tokyo." Those sheltered found that everything wasn't terrific, such as Michiko Wakisaka, sixty-nine, who moved out of one evacuation center after finding it had only squat-style toilets she could not use due to disabilities (Western Japan struggles to restore water to flood-hit towns as temperatures soar, 2018). Others gained security in houses allowing two years of residency, with rents covered by the prefectural government (Hundreds of temporary housing units planned for rain-hit Ehime Prefecture and city of Kurashiki, 2018).

A visit to shelters highlighted anecdotes of those left homeless by the volcanic eruption in Guatemala (The survivors of the Fire Volcano safe, but with uncertainty about the future, 2018), "where children performed activities to distract themselves, while men and women tended clothes and met in groups. Each of them has a story to tell." At a shelter of the Simón Bergaño Institute, "A photo of a missing person can be seen in the entrance and a list of the people who are in the place are part of the welcome." María Nelly Segura, who ended up in the shelter after being forced to abandon her home in the village of El Rodeo, said (The survivors of the Fire Volcano safe, but with uncertainty about the future, 2018): "Here I do not complain about anything, but it worries to know what they will do with our houses, there we have our little houses, they have not said how long they will have us here. We slept on mats, they gave us clothes and some doctors came to see us."

In Greece, there were just brief mentions of accommodations for those left homeless. Argyro Moustaka Brettou (Greece wildfires: 'Hundreds went into the sea', 2018) said: "Our beautiful small town is completely destroyed. We find victims every day. Everybody lost their fortune. These were our houses. Most of us have no place to go. We don't have any money to move to another place—we have to start all over again." In Papua New Guinea (Relief operations ongoing in earthquake affected areas, 2018), K5 million had been spent on shelter, food, water, and nonfood items (medicines, tents, mosquito nets, tanks, pumps).

GOODS AND ASSISTANCE

Recovery involving goods and/or assistance was mentioned in seven of the eight disasters, with many examples in news about the disasters in Indonesia. Goods and assistance appeared in two primary contexts—one focused on how authorities and other provided help, the other on the unaddressed needs of the victims. Source distribution was nearly equally divided among unaffiliated people, government, and businesses or NGOs.

Proving goods and assistance to aid people coping with the twin disasters that hit Indonesia were a focus of news attention. A spokesman of 132/ Tadulako Military Resort Command, Colonel Agus Sasmita, ensured the availability of food for quake and tsunami victims in Donggala District (Living condition of Central Sulawesi quake victims gets improved: mily, 2018). Sasmita said that security officials flew six sorties of aid to villages via helicopter and distributed goods by four trucks. Additionally, the military set up emergency kitchens in several villages. People queued up at roadside stalls, buying petrol in bottles to take into the affected area (Indonesia earthquake: Huge surge in death toll, 2018).

Assistance in the United States included finding physicians and medication. Doctors, nurses, and volunteers tracked down physicians and pharmacy records to replace medication for those burned out of homes (Levine, 2018a). Joy Reich, a Paradise resident staying at a shelter, needed immediate attention for respiratory problems when she arrived (Levine, 2018a). She said: "I have asthma . . . and that smoke and asthma did not mix well. It's been awful." A makeshift camp in the parking lot of a store in Chico included portable toilets and donated food and clothing (Romero, 2018). Kassy Parish and her family, who were burned out of their home, set up a crowdfunding page to seek help (California wildfires: Thanksgiving hope from ashes of Paradise, 2018).

In Guatemala, organizations, businesses, and government aided those affected by the volcano's eruption by installing a mobile kitchen and administering donations. The National Coordination for Disaster Reduction of Guatemala installed mobile kitchens in the Alotenango hostel, allowing volunteers of Fundación Castillo Córdova to provide three hot meals per day (Empresarial, 2018a). Through the program "Guatemalans to the rescue!," Cervecería Centro Americana, SA and the Castillo Cordova Foundation assisted vulnerable populations. In Japan, more than 70,000 troops, police, and firefighters tackled the aftermath of the floods (Western Japan struggles to restore water to flood-hit towns as temperatures soar, 2018) and Mongolian volunteers were digging out walls of sand around homes in Hiroshima (Osumi, 2018b). In Okayama, workers scraped mud and water was distributed to residents who had walked from their damaged homes, sometimes hundreds of meters away (Johnston, 2018b).

In Papua New Guinea, the Lae mayor's office presented secondhand clothes to earthquake victims in the Highlands area and the Morobe government allocated K200,000 for supplies and transport (Earthquake victims receive K20,000 worth of clothes, 2018). Community affairs manager Paul Sapake of Oil Search announced the company would prepare recovery kits for affected communities (Nalu, 2018c). Sapake said: "The kit will include gardening tools, building materials, water tanks and whatnot. This is the next phase of the programme after we've given them food rations that can last them for some time."

Stories also reflected the unsatisfied needs of victims. Indonesian president Joko Widodo asked the Central Sulawesi governor to urge the public to resume their economic activities and shop owners to open their shops (Logistic distribution for earthquake victims needs to be improved: president, 2018). The president said: "We invite them to open their shops with security guarantee by police and military officers in economic areas so that the economy will be back to normal." Wasliha, who trekked with her family 10 hours from her devastated village of Lolu Sigi Biromaru to Palu airport, said (Henschke, 2018b): "We had no clean water or food and all we have is the clothes we are wearing." Her children, who hadn't drunk anything since the previous day, gulped down the water given them.

The lack of an evacuation plan in Japan irked Mototaka Inaba, a doctor with the NPO Peace Winds Japan (Johnston, 2018b). Inaba said: "Ambulances and rescue vehicles could not initially get through as the roads were out. So we ended up evacuating people by boat and by helicopter." Among the sad tales of victims was Ya'u Ibrahim of the Galadima Fulani settlement in Auyo

Local Government Area of Nigeria, who said (Adeyemi et al., 2018): "We migrated from our original community because the flood submerged our huts and farm produce." Asadu Bossi, whose family rice farm was submerged, said (Akinrinade, 2018): "Never in my imagination did I think of this. The rice farm is gone; our houses are gone, and there is nothing left."

ESCAPE, RESCUE, AND SEARCH

Sources in stories about escape, rescue, and search came primarily from survivors and other unaffiliated people, allowing for poignant anecdotes. One sad tale of searching in Greece involved a father trying to locate his missing nine-year-old twin daughters. Yiannis Philippopoulos had not heard from the girls, Sophia and Vasiliki, or from their grandparents, who they were with on the day they went missing (Greece wildfires: Search for missing family members after eighty people die, 2018). Philippopoulos said: "We went to the hospitals and police and then the fire brigade said the last resort would be to look for them in the mortuary." After giving DNA to the mortuary, Philippopoulos and his wife saw a TV report showing two girls who resembled their daughters being rescued. Later, the parents hired a private investigator, who discovered that the girls and their grandparents died on a cliff overlooking a beach (Woman dies in hospital, raising number of wildfire fatalities to eighty-eight, 2018).

Others in Greece used social media to search for the missing, posting photographs online (Greece wildfires: British man in hospital with burns, 2018) and a website was set up to help relatives find family (Greece wildfires: At least seventy-four dead as blaze 'struck like flamethrower', 2018). People wandered the streets, some searching for burned-out cars, others for their pets (Triandafllou & Konstantinidis, 2018). Desperate relatives appeared on television to plead for information on those missing (Maltezou & Konstantinidis, 2018).

Two recovery-oriented examples of rescue involved pets. In Greece, many rescued pets at a clinic near the coastal resorts of Rafina and Mati had been reclaimed by their owners (Pemble & Hadjicostis, 2018). Another rescued pet was a miniature horse who survived three days stranded on a roof in Japan before being rescued by aid workers, who fed her carrots and cabbage to calm her (Japan flood: At least 179 dead after worst weather in decades, 2018).

The escape examples in the news all came from Indonesia. Wasliha walked through the mountains for more than 10 hours with her young family to seek help after days of waiting for aid (Indonesia tsunami: Frustration in remote areas waiting for aid, 2018). Wasliha had heard the military was flying out and joined hundreds of people at the Palu airport hoping to get a seat. Another waiting for a flight out of Palu was Wiwid, a forty-four-year-old food vendor (Head, 2018), who said: "I'd get a plane anywhere. I've been waiting for two days." Hartati, who was trying to reach Palu, said (Wings Air resumes Gorontalo-Palu flights, 2018): "I have been contemplating for three days on whether I should go to Palu by land or sea, as there is no flight to Palu. Today, I get notified that a commercial flight for Palu has resumed. I will book a ticket."

CONSTRUCTION

Japan and Guatemala were the most frequently mentioned as engaging in construction to aid recovery, with government officials providing most of the sources. Providing housing, especially temporary shelter, was a common type of construction, with infrastructure a secondary focus. In Japan, Prime Minister Shinzo Abe mentioned a plan to build temporary housing for people left homeless by floods and landslides in the city of Kurashiki (Water outages continue in flood-hit areas across western Japan, as death toll tops 170, 2018). Work had already started on 158 temporary housing units in Ehime Prefecture, while the government of Okayama planned 200 temporary housing units in the city of Kurashiki (Hundreds of temporary housing units planned for rain-hit Ehime Prefecture and city of Kurashiki, 2018). The Okayama Prefectural Government earmarked funds for 1,000 temporary housing units. Kurashiki mayor Kaori Ito said: "We've picked spacious sites for the temporary housing so that people who will move into the housing can maintain their communities to a certain extent."

Housing for victims of the volcanic eruption was one sign of recovery in Guatemala. Funds from El Mundo del Millón Banrural promotion were targeted for the TECHO Guatemala Foundation to pay for building emergency housing (Empresarial, 2018b). Edgar Guzmán, general manager of Banrural, said: "Moved by this tragedy, we decided to channel together with the TECHO foundation the destination of the funds of the promotion so that the proceeds are channeled exclusively for the construction of housing for the affected families because of the eruption of the Volcano of Fire. We know that as Guatemalans, we will move forward and that we will come together to support those who today need our helping hand." Authorities in Guatemala determined that 1,000 homes would be built (The survivors of the Fire Volcano safe, but with uncertainty about the future, 2018). The Inter-American Development Bank agreed to support Guatemala with loans for rehabilitation and reconstruction (Mata, 2018). Construction companies anticipated years of work to clean up and rebuild after the volcanic disaster (Reyes Lopez, 2018).

In Indonesia, the government announced a master plan for the rehabilitation and reconstruction of Palu, including resettlement of residents (Residents in Palu to be relocated to safer regions, 2018). Minister of Agrarian and Spatial Planning/Head of the National Land Agency Sofyan Djalil said: "If the area can no longer be inhabited, its residents will be moved." The National Disaster Mitigation Agency announced that rehabilitation and reconstruction programs would begin soon in Central Sulawesi (Foreign NGOs should have local partners: BNPB, 2018). In the United States, federal and state funds were targeted for Paradise to rebuild streets, public utilities, and buildings (California wildfires: Thanksgiving hope from ashes of Paradise, 2018). Paradise Mayor Jody Jones believed that the town will be reborn. Jones said: "We're committed to rebuilding. It's not an 'if', it's 'How long is it going to take? I know it's going to take a couple of years until Paradise is rebuilt but I have lived here all my life.'"

NORMALCY

A sense of normalcy was more likely in news coverage from the disasters in Indonesia and Japan. Contexts of normalcy included infrastructure, transportation, businesses and services, homes and social conditions, and planning for future needs. Government officials accounted for most of the sources used, followed by businesses or NGOs and unaffiliated people.

Infrastructure normalcy involved restoration of electric power and water, along with communication systems, roads, and bridges. In Indonesia, electrical power was restored to Palu, Donggala, and Sigi, all areas affected by the natural disasters (Minister Soemarno revisits Palu to review economic recovery efforts, 2018). State Enterprises Minister Rini Soemarno said: "Alhamdulillah (Thank God), electricity supply in Palu has reached nearly 90 percent, thanks to the hard work of PLN technicians and pioneers. Thanks to the hard work of the technicians, all economic activities resume quickly." In Japan, water was restored to Kurashiki, where about 200,000 residences had been without water (Western Japan struggles to restore water to flood-hit towns as temperatures soar, 2018). Roads connecting the center of Hiroshima with the Yano district reopened (Osumi, 2018c), along with the Togetsukyo bridge in Kyoto, a popular tourist site that crosses the Katsura River and offers great views of the surrounding mountains (Johnston, 2018a). In Papua New Guinea, Digicel offered free telephone service to affected areas while work continued to restore transmission towers in the Highland region (Digicel to provide free calls to earthquake-affected areas, 2018). Digicel chief executive Valde Ferradaz said: "We are working to have our network back to full capacity by this weekend to support the requirements of emergency services and government support teams. As we return services to each of the areas, we are providing free calls for a period of 24 hours to allow people to speak with loved ones. Our six teams plus transmission and tower specialists are working around the clock to re-establish the network to allow the emergency services and rescue efforts to co-ordinate effectively to save lives."

Transportation improvements included air and train travel. Indonesia's Wings Air resumed flights from Gorontalo to the Central Sulawesi city of Palu, perceived as good news for several Gorontalo residents who planned to meet their relatives in Palu (Wings Air resumes Gorontalo-Palu flights, 2018). Hartati, a local resident, said she felt relief after knowing that a flight for Palu has been operated. Bullet trains between Shin-Osaka and Hiroshima stations in Japan resumed operations (Johnston, 2018c).

Business and services were restored and manufacturing facilities reopened. Trading resumed at Indonesia's Masomba traditional market (Minister Soemarno revisits Palu to review economic recovery efforts, 2018) and conditions improved for people in Palu as several markets and hospitals resumed operation (Living condition of Central Sulawesi quake victims gets improved: mily, 2018). Colonel Agus Sasmita praised disaster mitigation and restoration processes for the resumption of daily activities. In Japan, several manufacturing plants resumed operations, including Daihatsu Motor Co. and farm equipment manufacturer Kubota Corp. (Rescuers race against time as death toll in western Japan floods rises to at least 176, 2018), along with Mazda Motor Corp. and Mitsubishi Motors Corp. (Kyodo, 2018a). Employees of a home improvement center in Mabicho, a district in the city of Kurashiki, assessed damage in preparation for reopening (Johnston, 2018b).

In Greece, signs of normalcy included camps reopening. For instance (Seaside town remembers lives lost to fire, children's camp reopens, 2018), "there were also signs of a return to normality as a children's camp, which closed due to the blaze, was reopened on Sunday. The mayor of Athens invited youngsters affected by the fire to come along." Athens mayor Giorgos Kaminis announced that the camp would host children whose families lost their homes in the wildfires (Municipal camps evacuated during wildfires to reopen on Sunday, 2018).

In the United States, a special sporting event helped restore normalcy for one teen. After Paradise High School track runner Gabe Price missed a state qualifying event due to the fire, athletes in nearby Chico hosted another event (California wildfires: Survivors share stories of heroic rescues, 2018). Price said: "The fire took just about everything we had, but at the same time, it didn't take our family." Students from Chico High School cheered as Price successfully qualified for the state meet. Chico student Charlie Giannini said: "We've been racing against Gabe for all of our years. . . . And to see him not go to state, that would just be another tragedy on top of what's going on."

Planning for future needs was a focus in Indonesia and Papua New Guinea. The Indonesian central government set a target of two years to finish the rehabilitation and recovery efforts (Nasution, 2018b). The government announced plans to build a new city to replace Palu (Government to build new Palu city after earthquake, 2018). Public Works Minister Basuki Hadimuljono said: "Palu has changed entirely, and so we plan to build a new Palu city. We have to make a new master plan that will adopt all (elements of the old city)." Hadimuljono said that temporary school buildings, hospitals, and universities would be finished within two years. In Papua New Guinea, a budget for emergency restoration was announced at K100 million to support and restore essential public services including roads and bridges, health, education, power supply, communication, government office repairs, transportation, logistics, and disaster management (Relief operations ongoing in earthquake affected areas, 2018).

GRIEF AND EMOTIONS

Recovery through grief and emotions was found most frequently in news about the wildfires in Greece, with a handful of examples in the United States and Indonesia. People providing mental health assistance accounted for most of the sources. Fotiadi (2018b) focused on steps that parents in Greece should take to help children overcome grief and other emotions. "Experts say parents should also focus on the positive aspects, such as the brave victims who were able to battle their fear and save themselves, the rescue crews who fought hard against the odds, but also the many teams of volunteers who tried to help in the wake of the disaster. . . . Managing this situation, experts say, can be a great challenge if the child has suffered the loss of a loved one in the wildfires." The story mentioned psychologist Chryssa Karakana saying that "grieving is important so as to alleviate the emotional pain. Following the initial stages of grievance, parents or guardians can proceed with helping the child cope with the loss. It is very important for the child to be able to move on." Additionally, "Shock and trauma are not exclusive to children. The Association of Greek Psychologists encourages all people affected by the recent disaster to seek professional help if they are suffering symptoms such as sadness, hyperactivity, sleep disturbance, focus problems, short-term memory loss or suicidal thoughts." Law enforcement officers were also affected by the disaster (struggle for survivors of fire trying to return to normalcy, 2018), with police officers attending sessions with a specialized psychologist.

Dealing with the emotion plight of the elderly who lost their homes was a focus in the United States, with Levine (2018a) noting how difficult it can be for those in their seventies and eighties. Mari Stewart, the nursing supervisor for the clinic at the East Avenue Church in Chico, said: "Half of them don't have it in them to start all over again." Dr. David Eisenman, the director of the UCLA Center for Public Health and Disasters, said: "For them to not be allowed to rebuild and live in their community again might produce a kind of harm that's much greater than if you or I or younger people had to rebuild and move away." Ron Zimmer, the pastor of the East Avenue Church, said that younger families "tend to have larger social circles" but "our seniors tend to have closing social circles, so they don't have anywhere else to go."

Two women in their thirties suffering depression were receiving treatment in an Indonesian hospital (Depression cases surface at hospitals following earthquake, tsunami, 2018). The director of Madani Hospital, Palu, Nirwansyah Parampasi, said: "We provided both of them assistance through psychologists with psychiatric approach programs, with the hope that both of them would recover quickly."

EVALUATION OF RECOVERY

An initial step toward recovery was to deal with the existing natural disaster through steps like providing housing, restoring infrastructure, and addressing emotional needs. This combination of physical and psychological acts helped restore normalcy and aided coping by providing a path forward after a devastating natural disaster. These influences existed on more than one level. Recovery efforts were a pragmatic response to the natural disaster by assistance to those directly affected by the events, a type of healing. Additionally, recovery acts brought a virtual sense of help by demonstrating that others are aiding present and future needs, affecting even those indirectly affected by the disaster. Further, recovery efforts signaled that individuals in the area are not alone, that that need for healing is being acknowledged and addressed.

Source usage showed that people in a position to provide insights or authoritative information were used the most often. For instance, survivors and unaffiliated people accounted for most of the sources on escape, rescue, and search, along with shelters and homelessness, giving them a chance to tell their own dramatic and tragic tales. Government officials were in position to provide authoritative information about reconstruction. Mental health practitioners explained grief and emotions.

Shelters addressed the immediate needs of those displaced, organized by government, organizations, volunteers, and sometimes the people themselves, such as the fire victims in the United States who set up camp in a commercial parking lot. Shelters provided both physical and psychological recovery by addressing immediate needs and suggesting that there is a path forward.

Normalcy was established through the restoration of electricity, roads, businesses, and services, plus improving conditions and planning for future needs. This tapped most directly into immediate and physical needs that aided healing, but also moving people forward. The grief and emotions of disaster survivors led to intervention by mental health professionals much like what was found in analysis of school shootings (McCluskey, 2017) and advice from experts to parents having to deal with distressed children. This directed effort assisted both healing the immediate crises and coping to show a positive path to the future.

Chapter 9

Community, Cohesion, and Intimacy

Elements of community, cohesion, and intimacy were found within seven of the eight natural disasters (absent only in Japan) and were particularly prominent in the Greece and Guatemala disasters. Community, cohesion, and intimacy fell into four distinct types—mourning and sorrow, collectivity and solidarity, emotions, and honors/thanks. These physical and virtual examples of people coming together displayed continuity, solidarity, and intimacy among mourners and survivors, raising hope and helping people cope.

Government officials accounted for nearly half of the sources on community, cohesion, and intimacy, with about one-fourth each drawn from businesses or NGOs and unaffiliated people, including survivors.

MOURNING AND SORROW

One common theme was stories featuring the nation's leader mourning for the country, explicitly mentioned in Greece, Guatemala, and the United States. Two-thirds of sources about mourning and sorrow came from government officials. Both Greek prime minister Alexis Tsipras (Triandafllou & Georgiopoulos, 2018) and Guatemalan president Jimmy Morales declared three days of national mourning (Guatemala volcano: Dozens die as Fuego volcano erupts, 2018). Tsipras said (Triandafllou & Georgiopoulos, 2018): "It is a difficult night for Greece" and (Triandafllou & Konstantinidis, 2018): "Greece is going through an unspeakable tragedy." In the United States, President Donald Trump said (California fires: Firefighters hold containment lines in north, 2018): "We mourn the lives of those lost and we pray for the victims and there were more victims than anybody would ever think possible."

Other government officials expressed mourning or sorrow as well. In Nigeria's Anambra State, Governor Willie Obiano said (Elekwa, 2018) that he is "profoundly touched by the powerful sense of solidarity which Nigerians from different sections of the country and from all walks of life have been demonstrating with the people of Anambra State since the flood disaster." Indonesian vice president M Jusuf Kalla offered condolences and sympathy for victims of the earthquake and tsunami (Iskandar, 2018). Kalla said: "We are very surprised, (and) will soon help (regarding) the sorrow and sympathy of the entire nation, the government will prepare what the victims need." The government-run Bank of Greece, in a press release, stated (Greek central bank pledges financial assistance to fire victims, 2018): "The General Council expressed its deep sorrow for the loss of life and for the economic and environmental devastation caused by the recent wildfires."

Religious-based examples of mourning and sorrow were all found in Greece. During a memorial service in a Mati church, the senior local Greek Orthodox Church official, Bishop Kyrillos, said the Mati community was grieving the simultaneous loss of family, neighbors, and friends (Death toll from Greek wildfire reaches ninety-one as village grieves, 2018). Hundreds attended the memorial service (Seaside town remembers lives lost to fire, children's camp reopens, 2018) "where they wept and lit candles in memory of those killed." Additionally, hundreds attended a funeral for Father Spyridon Papapostolous in his parish of Halandri, a northern suburb of the Greek capital (Burials of Greece's wildfire victims begin, 2018).

People came together to recognize victims during other public memorial events in Greece. Hundreds of people gathered on Syntagma square in Athens to commemorate the victims, placing candles, flowers, and messages on the square in front of the Greek Parliament (Vigil held in Athens for wildfire victims, 2018). Pitas and Maltezou (2018) quoted people who participated in the mourning event. A woman named Vasso, weeping as she lit a candle, said: "We are mourning those lost souls, those people who left (us) clasped in embrace." George Karakostas, sixty-five, said: "This candle shows our respect to the dead. May God forgive the living."

Businesses, organizations, and celebrities expressed feelings of mourning and sorrow as well. In Guatemala, Andrés Porras, general manager of the Castillo Córdova Foundation, the charitable branch of the Cerveceria Centro Americana, S.A. brewery, said (Empresarial, 2018a): "We are deeply dismayed and join the national pain for all the victims of this tragedy and the thousands of families affected and affected. Cervecería Centro Americana and the Castillo Córdova Foundation are present to help our Guatemalan brothers." Flags at all Piraeus Port Authority facilities in Greece's biggest harbor flew at half-mast as the Chinese-controlled company participated in the national mourning (Piraeus Port Authority expresses solidarity with wildfire victims, 2018).

Writers delivered sentiments of sorrow and mourning as well in Guatemala. Columnist Alfredo Saavedra (2018) wrote: "Our condolences to the relatives of our compatriots who died . . . and our exhortation of solidarity and help for the survivors." Journalist Sonia Perez (2018) wrote: "Guatemala woke up today in the midst of the pain of the death of dozens of people." Columnist Stu Velasco (2018) wrote: "We are in national mourning, our Guatemala will flourish because it has Heroes of Truth!". In Indonesia, journalist Otniel Tamindael (2018) wrote: "Now Indonesia is grieving again with the occurrence of tsunami and earthquake disaster in Central Sulawesi. This unexpected natural disaster was very heartbreaking and caused deep sorrow and trauma for Indonesians." In Papua New Guinea, one article (Earthquake suffering, 2018) stated: "We mourn the dead of loved ones and wait for ceremonial formalities to be concluded before we deal with the accused and suspects. . . . Please let us all express remorse and sympathy to those who have suffered."

COLLECTIVITY AND SOLIDARITY

Guatemala featured the most story emphasis on collectivity and solidarity, with businesses or NGOs and government officials providing most of the sources. A common focus in Guatemala was people coming together, both virtually and physically. Faye Dunstan, manager of the Oxford Language Centre in Antigua, said (Guatemala volcano: Lava ash like 'black rain', 2018): "Everyone is coming together. There are endless supplies of water, food and clothes. It's a big community effort." Juan Pablo Duhalde, director of Social Areas of TECHO International, said (Empresarial, 2018b): "Solidarity is the key tool to face the emergency at this moment. This sense of solidary urgency that today moves us as a society must remain until the survivors can inhabit a safe and dignified space." The Roman Catholic Diocese of Escuintla wrote (Diocese of Escuintla sympathizes with those affected by eruption of Fuego volcano and offers alternative aid, 2018): "We present to families and people affected our sense of closeness and solidarity." People outside the country pledged solidarity with Guatemala as well, including several international artists (Perez, 2018). Spanish actor Antonio Banderas wrote on Twitter: "My heart with Guatemala. #FuerzaGuatemala # volcanofuego." Venezuelan singer Carlos Baute wrote: "My people in Guatemala are very strong! I love you all. All vibrates from here." Spanish singer-songwriter Pablo Alborán said: "All my thoughts are in Guatemala." Guatemalans living in Spain showed solidarity as they gathered in Barcelona to inform the public about the humanitarian needs and sold typical Guatemalan food and crafts, with proceeds going to the Adentro Foundation of Ricardo Arjona to aid reconstruction (Herrera & Pinto, 2018). Additionally, Guatemalan singer-songwriter Ricardo Arjona wrote (Perez, 2018): "Brothers of Guatemala. My solidarity with the victims of this disaster of nature and my condolences to the families of the deceased."

Columnist Stu Velasco (2018) pushed for solidarity in Guatemala, too:

> Let us turn to provide support to our Guatemalan brothers, and to the State so that together as a Guatemalan we show that we know how to put aside our ideologies, differences, and even our political and social confrontations when it comes to reaching out and doing that in the face of desolation and death our country is reborn and the hope of a better country continues. To those who have already spoken and started their support, thank you very much.

Political leaders expressed solidarity in Greece, including New Democracy leader Kyriakos Mitsotakis saying (Search continues as wildfires death toll climbs to 80, 2018) priorities were "unity and solidarity." Alternate minister of Public Order and Citizen Protection Minister Nikos Toskas lauded the solidarity of other countries aiding Greece (Italy, Romania sending more aircraft, minister says, 2018). Additionally, the Stavros Niarchos Foundation, while announcing a 25 million euro grant to the Greek fire department, stated (SNF to support Greek fire department with 25 mln grant, 2018): "This national tragedy, which has cost the lives of so many and destroyed the households of thousands, requires that all of us, as a society, find ways to provide a collective remedial response. Through this grant initiative, the SNF hopes it can contribute towards the response to a grave national matter—one that transcends politics—in a manner that unites the country's leading forces against current and widespread polarization."

In the United States, the upcoming Thanksgiving holiday was the focus of solidarity. A BBC article stated (California wildfires: Thanksgiving hope from ashes of Paradise, 2018): "As the rest of America sits down to celebrate Thanksgiving on Thursday, those left homeless by the raging Camp Fire are contemplating their futures." The story mentioned 15,000 meals being donated by nonprofit organizations and celebrity chefs joining Paradise-area restaurant owners to prepare Thanksgiving Together event meals. A post on the World Central Kitchen website read: "We have seen the power of food to bring communities together, especially in times of great need." Another theme of solidarity from the California wildfires came from Governor Jerry Brown, who tweeted (California wildfires: Trump visits state's deadliest blaze, 2018): "Now is a time to pull together for the people of California."

In Papua New Guinea, a business official and a diplomat raised similar themes of unity and solidarity. Lae Biscuit Company chairman and chief executive Ian Chow said of the company-sponsored rugby team, which was aiding the relief efforts (Andrew, 2018): "Off the field, we are one family and we are all united." In Indonesia, an official from the campaign team of Indonesia's president, Hasto Kristiyanto, said (News Focus—Indonesian government moves swiftly in handling Gonggala quake victims, 2018): "Let us boost solidarity and work together with the president to help the victims of the earthquake disaster in Donggala and Palu." In a written statement, DPR Commission VI member Bowo Sidik Pangarso said it was necessary to work together to ease the burden of the victims of the disaster (Minyak, 2018). The memory of the heroic AirNav Indonesia air traffic controller who died (Nasution, 2018a) "will remain alive in the minds of his families, his colleagues, the pilot and those on board the plane, as well as the next Indonesian generation." A physical example of solidarity occurred in Pakistan, where "hundreds of believers gathered at the metropolitan's prominent mosque to offer Salat Al-Istisqa (Prayer for Rain) to plead relief in the form of rainfall" during the heat wave (Karachiites gather to offer special prayer for rain, 2018).

EMOTIONS

News mentioned anger, fear, joy, and anxiety, mostly expressed by unaffiliated people. Anger toward public officials was expressed in Greece, such as Chryssa, a survivor in Mati, who said (Koputantou, 2018): "They left us alone to burn like mice. No one came here to apologize, to submit his resignation, no one." Greece pole vaulter Ekaterini Stefanidi, interviewed after winning the pole vault at the European Championships, connected her victory to the people at home (Katsounaki, 2018). "We can only hope to offer some joy to the people [affected]," she said. Survivor Tamara Ferguson expressed a mix of emotions after escaping the wildfire in the United States. Ferguson said (Hughes, 2018): "I will forever be changed, as so many thousands of others were. . . . Not by what was physically lost, but by the reminder that life changes quickly." In Nigeria, stories mentioned "a pall of grief" in the Ahoada West Local Government, Rivers State (Akinrinade, 2018) and fears of "an imminent outbreak of diseases" (Adeyemi et al., 2018).

HONORS, THANKS

Sentiments of community and cohesion through honors or thanks were part of news coverage about the natural disasters in Greece and Indonesia, coming primarily from government and business officials. In Greece, the foreign ministry offered a collective message of appreciation to "the countries, institutions and ordinary people who offered assistance" to firefighting efforts (Greece thanks 'friends and partners' for support with deadly wildfires, 2018). The foreign ministry statement read:

> We once again express our warmest thanks to Greece's friends and partners for their immediate response and their offer of firefighting aircraft and vehicles, as well as personnel, to assist in extinguishing the wildfires in Attica. . . . We also thank the members the Greek community abroad and the foreign friends of Greece who, from the very outset, expressed their support and solidarity, stating their willingness to provide essential supplies and financial assistance to bring relief to the victims and to repair damages caused by the wildfires.

The collective thanks in Indonesia targeted Anthonius Gunawan Agung, an air traffic controller who died after guiding the safe takeoff of a commercial airplane during an earthquake (ICAO honors Anthonius Agung for saving air passengers during earthquake, 2018). The International Civil Aviation Organization presented a plaque to commemorate the air traffic controller's sacrifice.

EVALUATION OF COMMUNITY, COHESION, AND INTIMACY

Stories about people pulling together, both physically and virtually, signaled hope and recovery. Public acts of commemoration help restore collective psychological health (Alexander, 2004), while mourning through news help communities return to normal (Berkowitz, 2010) and serve as a forum for memorialization (Kitch, 2000). Government officials, especially leaders expressing mourning or sorrow, accounted for most of the sources used.

Memorial events were mentioned—much like those found in previous traumas (Kitch, 2003; Laderman, 2002; Walsh, 2001). Mourning and sorrow demonstrated the depth of feeling and sensitivity to others, especially coming from the country's leader, part of news from three of the natural disasters. The national leaders declared days of national mourning and spoke of the disaster as affecting the entire country, raising the sense of togetherness and a common experience. The national leader became a consoler-in-chief to lead mourning after several of the disasters. Religious services and memorials drew hundreds of mourners in collective action, including several examples in Greece, representing spiritual strength like those after the 9/11 terror attack (Walsh, 2001) and religious coping like mourners after school shootings (McCluskey, 2017).

Collectivity and solidarity included perceptions of people coming together in action and in spirit, especially in Guatemala. Columnists from *La Hora* (e.g., Saavedra, 2018; Velasco, 2018) were especially likely to bring a sense of solidarity into their writing about the aftermath of the volcanic eruption. Ideas attributed to a source came mostly from businesses, NGOs, and government officials. Expressions of emotions like anger, fear, joy, and anxiety demonstrated people sharing feelings that matched that of others, a sense of intimacy that aided healing. Honors or thanks were expressed as a collective experience, signaling how people came together to cope with the disaster.

Chapter 10

Faith, Belief, and Salvation

Of the eight natural disasters, all except Nigeria included mentions of faith, belief, and salvation. The most common were themes of fate or destiny, use of prayer or religion to cope with the disaster, and expressions of God's will. Faith themes were most common in Papua New Guinea, which featured the most examples of fate or destiny and nearly all of those classified as representing the word of God. Faith, belief, and salvation themes were also prevalent in Indonesia and Greece. Such themes aided healing, coping, hope, and recovery by giving survivors and victims a solid foundation for their spiritual needs. More than half of the source usage came from religious officials, with another one-third from unaffiliated people.

FATE, DESTINY

Themes of fate or destiny tied to religion became a source of blame for the disaster or a step toward recovery in Greece, Papua New Guinea, and Guatemala, with two-thirds of sentiments coming from unaffiliated people and the other third from religious leaders. In Greece, religion was the focus of a dispute between religious leaders. Bishop Amvrosios wrote that Greece's "atheist prime minister" was to blame for the wildfires ('Atheist PM' to blame for deadly fires, says Greek bishop, 2018), claiming that "Their (atheism) draws the wrath of God!". Archbishop Ieronymos responded (Archbishop slams 'wrath of God' comments, 2018): "This is a sad phenomenon. God is love. God does not take revenge but urges all to love one another."

A Pentecostal church pastor in Papua New Guinea urged people to turn to God in the aftermath of the earthquake. Pastor Monica Ano, from Upa village in Mt. Hagen, Western Highlands, said (Pastor calling on people to focus on

God as PNG counts cost of earthquake, 2018): "Many forgot that the earthquake and everything was created by God and they have to find protection in him.... God is the only hope we have to find protection and not anything else." Additionally, Ano said the earthquake caused people to lose faith in God and were therefore missing out on his protection and grace. Several reader letters in the newspaper from Papua New Guinea debated God's role in the earthquake. "Alphonse Roy (Servant), Bible Study Teacher" wrote (Still on earthquake, 2018): "Never forget: God the Creator is observing everything that is going on here in our country and around the world as well.... Therefore, we must honestly repent from evil in our land and obey and please Him always." Perhaps in response, Kiluwe Solo of Port Moresby wrote (Earthquake is not punishment, 2018): "GOD is not angry with Papua New Guinea simply because the Papua New Guinea team at the United Nations voted against Israel. God doesn't think like me nor does he act like us as his ways are higher than our ways. That's exactly what most Papua New Guineans are thinking now that God destroyed Southern Highlands and Hela because of Papua New Guinea's vote against Israel. God did not destroy PNG."

A columnist in Guatemala turned to his faith to understand the volcanic eruption. Juan Francisco Reyes Lopez (2018) wrote: "God created the world and undoubtedly allowed the eruptions of volcanoes, earthquakes and tsunamis to evolve and take place. Man has contributed to these disasters by changing the ecology.... In any case, may God protect us."

Fatalism was part of comments from Indonesia and Guatemala. Indonesians used religion to cope with personal issues, such as Ermi Liana, who did not know the fate of her parents, saying (Indonesia earthquake: Huge surge in death toll, 2018): "I can only pray they are alive."

A story about the death of the heroic air traffic controller in Indonesia expressed fatalism in religious terms (Nasution, 2018a): "he attempted to escape the ATC tower that began shaking and collapsing but God had decided his destiny." One survivor of the volcanic eruption in Guatemala turned to his faith to provide hope of finding his family. Boris Rodriguez (Grant, 2018) said: "God willing, I'll find them.... This has been an act of God and if he has taken them, then there's nothing we can do. But I would like to bury them properly, so that we don't have to suffer any more." In the United States, wildfire survivor Jed St. Henry tied his good fortune to faith (Nicas et al., 2018): "I didn't expect my house to be here.... The grace of God."

PRAYERS, SERVICES

Religious leaders accounted for most of the attributed material about prayers and services. The heat wave in Pakistan prompted a special prayer for rain, in which (Karachiites gather to offer special prayer for rain, 2018) "Hundreds of believers gathered at the metropolitan's prominent mosque to offer Salat Al-Istisqa (Prayer for Rain) to plead relief in the form of rainfall." The Greek tragedies led to calls from the church for priests around the country to hold special prayers (Holy Synod calls for prayers after deadly wildfires, 2018). Two stories talked about Pope Francis, who prayed for victims (Pope prays for victims of Greek fires, 2018) and expressed solidarity with all those affected by the tragedy (Pope Francis sends message of support to Greek president, 2018).

Government leaders called for prayer. Indonesian president Joko Widodo called on his countrymen to pray for victims (Tamindael, 2018). The article explained that "the President certainly believes that prayer is the answer to all problems of life. For the prayer is the breath of the soul, the organ by which one can receive peace and comfort into his or her parched and withered heart." Indonesia's head of state attended a mass prayer event with other government officials (Waskita, 2018). In Japan, Prime Minister Shinzo Abe (Western Japan struggles to restore water to flood-hit towns as temperatures soar, 2018) visited an area hit by flooding and "offered silent prayers at the site and met residents affected by the disaster."

Additionally, people and business leaders turned to prayer. In the United States, reality TV star Kim Kardashian on Instagram urged people to "pray for Calabasas," where her home was located (California wildfires: Nine dead and more than 150,000 evacuated, 2018). Greece resident Angeliki Galiatsatou said (Death toll from Greek wildfire reaches ninety-one as village grieves, 2018): "I came to pray for the people who were lost and I pray that God blesses us all." In Guatemala, Andrés Porras, general manager of the Castillo Córdova Foundation, said (Empresarial, 2018a): "We put our hearts and prayers with all the people affected." In Papua New Guinea, Digicel chief executive Valde Ferradaz said (Digicel to provide free calls to earthquake-affected areas, 2018): "Our thoughts and prayers are with everyone effected by this tragedy."

WORD OF GOD

Letter writers in Papua New Guinea were the most likely to communicate the word of God. Kiluwe Solo of Port Moresby (Earthquake is not punishment, 2018) cited Christian biblical verse declaring that Jesus Christ "came not to destroy men but to save them" and advised:

> "We must not make our conclusions outside the Bible. We must only act and talk within the written word of God." Letter writer Paul Waugla Wii of Wandi

wrote (What else can trigger an earthquake, 2018): "Humans grope for answers as soon as they step into the unknown. That is where God is and he wants us to know our bounds and limitations." In addition, Pastor Monica Ano (Pastor calling on people to focus on God, 2018) "said that when such disasters took place, people must not fear death but focus on the Word of God so that they could remain strong. She said God's word protected people and helped them stand firm and overcome fear and doubt."

The only other example of word of God came from Indonesia, in which Tamindael (2018) asserted: "No matter in what distress one may be, distress of body or of soul, he or she needs but look unto Him who is always near with that healing power which can immediately overcome the death-dealing poison and its terrible consequences both to body and soul."

EVALUATION OF FAITH, BELIEF, AND SALVATION

Religious institutions aided healing, hope, and recovery by attending to the needs of survivors through faith and belief. Individuals turned to their faith as well to find comfort in the aftermath of the disaster, including lost family, friends, and goods. Themes of faith, belief, and salvation suggest a larger purpose in the aftermath of a natural disaster, helping people cope and provide a sense of hope. Religious leaders set the foundation for expressions of faith, with unaffiliated people providing supporting ideas.

Fate and destiny were tied to religion, such as in establishing blame for the disaster or a step toward recovery through faith and belief. Some survivors took fatalistic perspectives tied to faith in reflecting upon those missing or killed, helping them heal by providing comfort for the fate of others. Prayers were explicitly mentioned to address the current problems—such as the ongoing heat wave in Pakistan—and calls from religious leaders and national leaders for people to pray for victims and others dealing with tragedy. This gave people a direct way to use faith to deal with the ongoing crisis. Parallel themes were found in evaluation of religion in school shootings (McCluskey, 2017). The word of God was invoked by survivors who quoted biblical verse or otherwise suggested faith-based sentiments.

Chapter 11

Reassurance, Purpose, or Meaning

Explicit mentions of reassurance, purpose, or meaning were rare, most frequently found in Indonesia and the United States, while no examples were found in Japan, Nigeria, and Pakistan. The three subthemes found were calmness, safety, and assurance; remembrance and sacrifice; and sorrow and sadness. Coming from columnists, disaster survivors, and others, these expressions put the disaster into meaningful perspective, signaling that the disaster is just one tragic event and not a whole life. With perspective comes coping, increased hope, and a path toward recovery. Just a handful of passages were attributed to a source, led by unaffiliated people.

CALMNESS, SAFETY, AND ASSURANCE

Examples of calmness, safety, and assurance were found in five of the natural disasters—Greece, Guatemala, Indonesia, the United States, and Papua New Guinea. Columnists raised themes of calmness and assurance. Alfredo Saavedra (2018) expressed a philosophical tone following the Guatemala volcanic eruption:

> Nature, which gives life and death, is presented to us in its kind aspect as the source for sustaining the existence of the human being with its consequent fauna and flora and the vitality of water with its generosity for the life in all its forms, but also with a nature transformed into the worst of the enemies of the forms of life described, in effect now demonstrated in Guatemala with the calamity of the Volcano of Fire that has unleashed its fury with the outbreak of an eruption that has devastated an entire population in a phenomenon that apparently has no historical antecedent.

Perspective and meaning came from survivors of the wildfires in the United States. Fire survivor Joseph Metcalfe woke his children around midnight to evacuate. Metcalfe said (California wildfires: 'I saw cars become metal and bones', 2018): "It has really put into perspective the value of life and the things we own, as the wealthy and the struggling alike have to face new challenges of rebuilding their lives." The approaching Thanksgiving holiday brought special appreciation from those displaced by the Camp Fire. Meals donated by nonprofit organizations brought comfort to Kassy Parish, nineteen (California wildfires: Thanksgiving hope from ashes of Paradise, 2018). Survivor Liza Johnson, who escaped the fire around Paradise, said (California wildfires: Rain brings threat of mudslides, 2018): "It's probably the best Thanksgiving of my life. . . . Being alive—and my family being alive—it makes you realise."

The performance of an athlete triggered a broader meaning tied to the wildfires in Greece. "A glimmer of hope" by columnist Maria Katsounaki (2018) mentioned Greek women's pole vaulter Ekaterini Stefanidi winning a gold medal in the European Championships and quoted the athlete: "This is the only thing that we can do. This is the only thing we are good at." The author added (Katsounaki, 2018): "Sports, globalized sports, represent a pocket of excellence amid the country's breakdown. And one question that emerges is: Can this country provide a context in which an individual can dedicate him or herself to what they are good at doing and become really good at it?"

Superstitious readers in Papua New Guinea were assured in one article that the fatal earthquake was not caused by humans. A professor of geology at the University of Papua New Guinea, Hugh Davies, said (Wani, 2018a): "Right now we need to be out there talking to the people, explaining what has happened, reassuring them, attending to their immediate needs." In Indonesia, calm and assurance came from President Joko Widodo (President orders government agencies to prepare for quake effects, 2018): "I hope people remain calm and are all safe."

REMEMBRANCE AND SACRIFICE

A Guatemalan columnist (Saavedra, 2018) put sacrifice and remembrance into a broader meaning: "The Volcano of Fire has been in permanent activity and those who lived (each in his time) in places of the capital, from where you could admire the majesty of these giants, we could observe the permanent presence of fire in the dome of that now monster that has brought death and pain to thousands of compatriots who have lost their lives and their property for that calamity, the first according to the corresponding records."

In Indonesia, special attention went to Anthonius Gunawan Agung, an air traffic controller who died heroically assuring the safety of air travelers. Nasution (2018b) wrote that "Agung will also remain in the minds and hearts of his colleagues and the people at large. . . . Agung has prioritized service and safety beyond his personal interests." Further, the hero "set a fine example for the entire nation." Remembrance and sacrifice were found in the two wildfires as well. A Greek father of two missing girls expressed hope that they were alive after viewing television footage (desperate Greeks search for missing after fires, 2018). In the United States, President Donald Trump (California fires: Firefighters hold containment lines in north, 2018) paid tribute to emergency crews' "incredible courage in the face of danger."

SORROW AND SADNESS

Just the Indonesian disaster had evidence of sorrow and sadness attached to meaning. In a story on Anthonius Gunawan Agung, the heroic air traffic controller, Nasution (2018b) wrote: "His death saddened so many people who love him." A story about the World Bank contributing a large grant for reconstruction mentioned World Bank CEO Kristalina Georgieva (World Bank offers 5 million dollars of grant for C Sulawesi earthquake reconstruction, 2018) "expressed deep sorrow for the events that occurred. 'But we know from experience that the best memories that can be built from disaster victims are to rebuild better.'"

EVALUATION OF REASSURANCE, PURPOSE, OR MEANING

People responded to the natural disaster by finding a broad sense of reassurance or purpose, especially by reacting with calmness and assistance, such as the value of life and comfort. Such sentiments helped people cope with the disaster and gave them hope. Themes of reassurance, purpose, or meaning both summarize a sentiment immediately after a natural disaster and suggest perspective for the future.

A writer in Guatemala (Saavedra, 2018) assumed a pastoral role (e.g., Berkowitz, 2010) in urging calmness and assurance to people traumatized by the natural disaster. This gave readers and others a suggested path to deal effectively with the ongoing disaster. The same columnist expressed remembrance and sacrifice to bring a broader meaning to the destructive volcano's eruption, similar to sentiments of reassurance expressed by Kitch and Hume

(2007). These sentiments aided coping and healing. Calmness, safety, and assurance came from disaster survivors, a national leader, and others, reassuring people through words of perspective and encouragement. This reassurance served as a coping mechanism and purpose (McCluskey, 2017). A heroic air traffic controller in Indonesia brought themes of remembrance and sacrifice, along with sorrow and sadness, giving his death a broader purpose.

Chapter 12

Actions

The natural disasters brought efforts by authorities to help those in need. A heavy volume of news attention went to actions, the most of any theme analyzed in this book. Actions demonstrated that others, including government, recognized the suffering and were taking steps to deal with the immediate problem and plan for the future, helping people cope and recover. Recognition of the problems aided others through both concrete and virtual acts. Action-oriented themes fell into two broad categories—physical and verbal.

Source use was dominated by government officials (76%), with 16% coming from the national leader and the remainder from others in government. Businesses and nongovernmental organizations accounted for 11% of the sources, followed by unaffiliated people (7%) and unattributed passages (6%).

PHYSICAL ACTIONS

Types of physical actions were rescues and evacuation; rebuilding, cleanup, and planning; goods, supplies, and relief aid; and medical activities. Government officials represented 61% of the sources used, with 17% unattributed and 13% from businesses or NGOs.

Rescues, Evacuation

The most common of the physical types of actions were found in seven of the eight disasters (excluding Pakistan) and most common in the Greece, Indonesia, Japan, and U.S. events. Several subthemes emerged in the news content, with stories about rescues and searches the most common.

Rescue, Search

Rescue efforts in Greece took place in towns, forests, and even water. Some people walked into the Aegean Sea to escape the flames, which led to the coast guard rescuing 700 people from the coastline, along with nineteen survivors and four bodies pulled from the water (Greece wildfires: Dozens dead in Attica region, 2018). Private vessels picked up hundreds of people. The coast guard and volunteer divers searched the water and a deserted island (Greek officials see 'serious indications' arson led to fire, 2018). A research vessel equipped with specialized sonar and a remotely operated underwater vehicle also was deployed (Becatoros & Gatopoulos, 2018). On land, rescuers mounted a house-by-house search of the burnt areas (Kantouris & Becatoros, 2018) and examined burnt cars and the scorched shoreline (Greek wildfires death toll rises to 79, 2018). Dionysis Tsiroglou and his team of volunteers searched a scorched and blackened pine forest (Tagaris & Konstantinidis, 2018). Tsiroglou said: "We're going from house to house, anywhere we believe there may be someone trapped, someone who burned inside, someone missing." Some people turned to social media and Greek television stations with appeals for information on their loved ones (Greek wildfires death toll rises to 79, 2018). Rescuers also saved pets, which were turned over to a clinic, where veterinarians treated seventy injured animals (Pemble & Hadjicostis, 2018).

The wildfires in the United States had a similar mix of rescue and search actions. In Paradise, rescuers used a bulldozer to move abandoned cars to reach a hospital and evacuate patients as the fire engulfed the building (California wildfires: Nine dead and more than 150,000 evacuated, 2018). Forensics teams searched for human remains (California fires: Firefighters hold containment lines in north, 2018), police dogs were used to pick up the scent of bodies buried in piles of ash (Hughes, 2018), and more than 400 volunteers joined the search (California wildfires: Concern over rain in search efforts, 2018).

In Indonesia, more than 8,500 military and police personnel, assisted by thousands of rescue workers, led search efforts (Living condition of Central Sulawesi quake victims gets improved: mily, 2018). President Joko Widodo said (Henschke, 2018b): "There are some main priorities that we must tackle and the first is to evacuate, find and save victims who've not yet been found." Rescue teams dug by hand to free twenty-four people trapped in the rubble of the Roa-Roa hotel in the city of Palu (Indonesia earthquake: Huge surge in death toll, 2018). Aftershocks, however, made it unsafe for rescuers to enter buildings in Palu (Indonesia earthquake and tsunami: Desperate search for survivors, 2018).

In Japan, more than 70,000 people were involved in search and rescue efforts (Japan flood: At least 179 dead after worst weather in decades, 2018).

An unnamed official said: "We are checking every single house to see if there are people still trapped inside them. We know it's a race against time, we are trying as hard as we can." An unnamed official with the Hiroshima Municipal Government said (Osumi, 2018c): "Some people are still missing, so we're prioritizing rescue operations to have firefighters, the police and the Self-Defense Forces continue searching for survivors." Rescue workers made slow progress through roads caked with mud around Mabicho (Johnston, 2018a), while boats searched for locals trapped in Kurashiki, Okayama Prefecture (Scenes of chaos after floods and landslides wreak havoc in western Japan, 2018). In Guatemala, firefighters, police, and soldiers led the search and rescue efforts, although the danger of landslides or new volcanic eruptions interrupted actions. In Escuintla, rescue teams reentered the scene just after the major eruption (Aguilar, 2018a). In Papua New Guinea, teachers were mobilized to help the rescue efforts, with some dropped by helicopter in the middle of the jungle (Papua New Guinea quake: An invisible disaster which could change life forever, 2018). In Nigeria, Delta State governor Ifeanyi Okowa directed speedboats to rescue stranded residents along the Niger River (Akinrinade, 2018).

Evacuation

The floods in Nigeria and Japan featured many examples of evacuation, perhaps because floods were an ongoing event. In Nigeria, Vincent Owen, a director of National Emergency Management Agency, said (Deaths, destruction as floods ravage states, 2018): "The Anambra government should as a matter of urgency begin immediate evacuation of people living in the flood prone areas to the emergency shelter centres in the state." Anambra's executive director of the State Emergency Management Agency, Cprian Agupugo, said (Deaths, destruction as floods ravage states, 2018): "Now that it is evident that the flood is rising, the displaced persons will be evacuated and taken to centers closest to them in no distant time."

Evacuation was also a major issue in Indonesia, where the earthquake and tsunami led to ongoing emergencies across a wide area. Military, police, and national search-and-rescue personnel evacuated victims (Tsunami waves hit several parts of central Sulawesi: BNPB, 2018). Minister/State Secretariat Pratikno said, referring to President Jokowi (President Jokowi visits quake, tsunami-stricken areas, 2018): "He would give directives regarding priorities that must be taken and make decisions needed in dealing with the impact of the disaster on the field. The main focus now is evacuating victims." A state-owned shipping company was utilized to move thousands of displaced people from Palu, Indonesian Military Chief Marshal Hadi Tjahjanto said (Residents to depart from earthquake-hit area aboard Pelni ship, 2018): "Some three to five thousand people will be transported aboard a Pelni ship."

In Japan, evacuation was under way in the flooded town of Saka, Hiroshima Prefecture, and from a mudslide in Iwakuni, Yamaguchi Prefecture (Scenes of chaos after floods and landslides wreak havoc in western Japan, 2018) and government prepared for the potential large-scale evacuation of millions of people in preparation for the possibility of major flooding in Tokyo (Suk, 2018). The two wildfires included brief mentions of evacuation. In the United States, Kathleen Schori, information officer for the California Department of Forestry and Fire Protection, emphasized the need for people to obey evacuation orders (California wildfires: Is smoke toxic to the East Coast?, 2018). In Greece, staff at a Ramada hotel evacuated hundreds of tourists (Lee, 2018), while authorities in Attica evacuated children's summer camps (Attica regional governor declares state of emergency, 2018).

Disaster Response

Actions to directly deal with the ongoing disaster were almost exclusively from the two wildfires. In Greece, firefighters battled more than thirty-three forest fires fed by dry winds and hot weather in the Peloponnese and on the Ionian islands of Zakynthos and Kefalonia (Konstantinidis & Fronista, 2018). Flames around Kineta drew more than 200 firefighters, 60 fire engines (Triandafyllou & Maltetezou, 2018), and five water-dropping helicopters, aided by homeowners with their own hoses (residents flee wildfire raging west of Athens, 2018). One story (Athens wildfires: Death toll rises to twenty-four as huge fire sweeps through holiday resorts, 2018) mentioned the challenge and logistics: "Winds reached 80 kph (50 mph) as authorities deployed the country's entire fleet of water-dropping planes and helicopters to give vacationers time to escape. Military drones remained in the air in the high winds to help officials direct more than 600 firefighters on the ground."

In the United States, stories mentioned firefighters holding containment lines (California fires: Firefighters hold containment lines in north, 2018). The director of California's fire service, Chief Ken Pimlott, said (California wildfires: Town of Paradise will need 'total rebuild', 2018): "We continue to engage in the fire fight. We continue to keep our eye on the ball."

Rebuilding, Cleanup, Planning

One significant element of actions that showed both recovery and hope were mentions of efforts to rebuild, clean up damage, and/or plans to prevent or mitigate future natural disasters. The floods of Nigeria led to the most rebuilding, cleanup, and planning, with significant attention also in Greece and Indonesia. Five separate subcategories were identified—relief, planning, rebuilding, cleanup, and logistics.

Relief

Actions to directly provide relief to victims and survivors were especially common in the news content about Nigeria, along with Greece and Indonesia. Governmental action was mentioned often, including the head of state in Indonesia, Greece, and Japan. Relief in Nigeria involved government action at the federal, state, and local levels. Some were messages of cooperation, such as an Edu state official who announced that state government was collaborating with sixteen local governments areas to reduce the flood disaster (twelve states may experience flooding 2018—NIHSA, 2018). Government officials defended or highlighted their relief efforts, such as declaring that adequate measures were taken and specific actions that were under way (Adeyemi et al., 2018). Vice President Yemi Osinbajo commended the government of Anambra for proactive steps to check the effects of the flood (Elekwa, 2018).

Nigerian governmental officials also were reassuring victims. Jigawa state deputy governor Hassan Hadejia said the state would take care of every victim (Adeyemi et al., 2018). Kano state governor Abdullahi Umar Ganduje visited affected areas, where he consoled victims and promised to alleviate their pains (Adeyemi et al., 2018).

Another theme in Nigeria was requesting help or speculating on what needed to be done. The Minister of Agriculture and Rural Development, Chief Audu Ogbeh, said (Flood: Ogbeh predicts rice shortage in 2019, 2018): "We have to find out a way to assist farmers, who were affected by the flood.... We are also hoping that as soon as the rain seized, we are encouraging farmers to replant." A resident of Gadumo, Ajaokuta Local Government Area, Asadu Bossi, said (Akinrinade, 2018): "The Vice President was here, and he gave us assurance that something will be done. We await help from above please, because our suffering is heavy on us."

Relief actions by the government were prominent in Indonesia as well. President Joko Widodo ordered government agencies to prepare for mitigation efforts (president orders government agencies to prepare for quake effects, 2018): "I am monitoring the situation and have ordered all the government agencies concerned to be ready to meet any eventualities after the quake." Other officials carried out relief efforts, such as State Enterprises Minister Rini Soemarno, who visited Palu, Central Sulawesi, to review economic recovery operations (Minister Soemarno revisits Palu to review economic recovery efforts, 2018). Soemarno said: "Since the earthquake struck, the daily activities of the public were disrupted.... I come back again to personally see the progress and ensure that public activities have returned to normal."

Governments in Greece announced a long list of relief measures, including payments to families of victims and the offer of public sector jobs for victims' spouses (Koputantou, 2018), exemptions from property tax payments and loan obligations for fire victims (Search continues as wildfires death toll climbs to 80, 2018), and compensation for damaged homes and permanent physical injuries (Souliotis, 2018c). Efforts were under way to demolish haphazard buildings that were presumed to have fueled the fires (Greece to start burying wildfire victims, government facing criticism, 2018) and Prime Minister Alexis Tsipras vowed (Greece to demolish 'illegal buildings' after wildfire, 2018) to check the "chaos of unruly construction." Another governmental measure was to reforest areas destroyed by fires to reduce flooding (Reforestation to begin without delay, says minister, 2018). In Japan, Prime Minister Shinzo Abe pledged to provide emergency relief, saying (Rescuers race against time as death toll in western Japan floods rises to at least 176, 2018): "We will assess the needs of victims and push for quick reconstruction."

In Papua New Guinea, a local professor and businesses were tied to relief actions. Hugh Davies, professor of Geology at the University of PNG, said (Wani, 2018a): "Right now we need to be out there talking to the people, explaining what has happened, reassuring them, attending to their immediate needs—food, shelter and safe drinking water—recovering bodies, and reconstructing damaged roads, bridges and buildings. . . . I hope we in PNG and donor countries will give the disaster the attention it deserves, not only now but in the months ahead." A team from a Barrick Ltd. mine went to one damaged area to assess the damage (Barrick's power facility damaged by earthquake, 2018), teams from Mineral Resources Development Company went to the communities of Moro, Hides, and Kutubu (Nalu, 2018b); and Oil Search, operator of Papua New Guinea's producing oil fields, visited seventy-eight villages in the aftermath of the earthquake (Nalu, 2018c).

Planning, Prevention

The aftermath of natural disasters led to proposals from governments and other entities to prevent or mitigate future traumatic events, which was most common in Nigeria, Greece, and Indonesia. The flooding in Nigeria prompted actions to strengthen emergency responses and help residents deal with future floods. Edo state worked with the Economic Community of West Africa States to strengthen emergency management teams (Flooding: Edo distributes relief materials to victims, 2018). Dr. Femi Oke-Osanyintolu, head of ECOWAS—Early Warning Mechanism for Nigeria, said: "We . . . agreed that emergency management is everyone's business, as such all should work together as a team in tackling the challenges of flooding in the state." The partnership between Edo and ECOWAS included sensitizing people to adopt practices to safeguard the environment (Flooding: Edo, ECOWAS re-strategize on disaster management, 2018). People in Kwara state were targeted in a campaign to stop dumping refuse on drainage and building along water channels (twelve states may experience flooding 2018—NIHSA, 2018).

In Greece, planning or prevention actions included a major grant from a nongovernmental organization and advice from journalists. Authorities collected aerial photos of the burned areas and information to designate areas for tree planting (Reforestation to begin without delay, says minister, 2018). The Stavros Niarchos Foundation supported the Greek fire department with a 25 million euro grant for maintenance and equipment. A commentary in *Kathimerini* (Ellis, 2018) pushed government to carry through with promises to plant new trees in burned areas: "Everybody agrees on that but 'something' always happens and after a while homes spring up on burned land—sometimes even villas with pools. . . . What else has to happen, how many more people have to lose their lives, before we sit down and draw up long-term plans together and, above all, agree to implement them consistently and continuously?"

A commentary by Andrew Tzembelicos (2018) offered direction for the future. "Going forward, cooperation can and should involve governments, communities and citizens. It can and should include identifying and implementing low-cost measures that can be quickly implemented, as well as solutions requiring larger investments over the longer term. . . . Though cooperation and preparedness may not prevent loss of life or disasters from happening in the future—be they wildfires, floods, earthquakes or other events—moving forward together is the best way to honor the lives lost and plan for the future. Ultimately, this will help better prepare Greece and its resilient citizens for when future disasters strike."

Government was the focus of planning or prevention efforts in Indonesia. A member of the National Awakening Party (PKB) proposed to make "new spatial arrangements in disaster-affected areas" for structuring cities and areas (Government urged to propose new spatial arrangements for Palu, 2018). PKB member Abdul Kadir Karding proposed including knowledge and anticipation over natural disasters to be included in school curriculum. Karding said: "If the Indonesian people have knowledge about natural disasters and their anticipation from a young age, then in the event of a disaster, they can be more prepared."

In Pakistan, the focus was on agriculture. Green Team members began planting 200 neem herbs across Karachi, designed to provide shade and reduce temperatures (Youth begins with sowing 200 neem plants in Karachi,

2018). Other reforms to deal with worsening heat included creation of urban green spaces and subsidies for families to retrofit their homes with energy-efficient air conditioners (Matthews-Trigg, 2018). The other angle on agriculture was to protect fields and fruit farms to create a "green shield" ('Revival of agriculture fields in rural Karachi can minimise heatwave effects', 2018). Town planner and architect Arif Hassan said: "By making rural Karachi economically viable we can make Karachi city cooler."

In Japan, a commission was formed to develop evacuation plans and emergency shelters (Suk, 2018). A Tokyo Metropolitan Government official said: "We will have to determine the ability (of areas outside flooded zones) to accept evacuees and how many people they can take, also considering situations such as whether they themselves are located near minor rivers or whether they are likely to be vulnerable to landslides." The government planned to widen the Oda River and lower the water level (Risk of deadly flood in badly hit area of Okayama Prefecture known in advance, 2018). In Guatemala, the government identified fifty-four communities in the path of lahars that would factor into planning and mitigation efforts (Figueroa, 2018).

Rebuild, Repair

Papua New Guinea government officials focused on rebuilding and repairing roads and bridges. Works and Implementation Secretary David Wereh said (Wereh points out roads badly affected by earthquake, 2018): "Roads at this time are critical in terms of moving fuel and other goods up to the affected sites." Repairing tsunami detection buoys was a prime effort in Indonesia (President issues orders to repair tsunami detection buoys, 2018). President Joko Widodo said: "This is the importance of securing instruments that are useful to detect tsunami and earthquake. We also need public awareness on this." Intermittent power outages during the heat wave in Pakistan led to ongoing repairs (Bhatti, 2018c). Officials set up portable generators to restore telecommunications services in Indonesia (Azly, 2018).

Cleanup

Nearly all examples took place in the Greece wildfires, especially brief mentions of ongoing cleanup. Precautions were noted as well (Struggle for survivors of fire trying to return to normalcy, 2018). Nikos Michalopoulos, the head of the Athens Observatory's Institute for Environmental Research and Sustainable Development, said "Residents, workers and volunteers must be careful in the burnt areas as toxic compounds have entered the soil." Cleanup in Greece also included demolishing illegal construction. An estimated 1,046 buildings needed to be demolished (Pitas & Maltezou, 2018). In Japan, resident Teruo Sasai, whose house, along with nearly a dozen others in one part of Mabicho, had been flooded, said (Johnston, 2018a): "We're still cleaning up. But I'd guess that, in order to recover, it's going to take at least a year, and cost hundreds of millions of yen or more."

Goods, Supplies, Relief Aid

Six types of goods and supplies were provided to survivors of the natural disasters and were most commonly mentioned in the Indonesia and Nigerian disasters.

Food and Water

Supplying food, water, and related items was especially common in the Indonesian and Nigerian disaster responses. Edible items provided in Indonesia included side dishes and boxes of ready-to-eat foods, along with public kitchens (Social ministry sends logistic assistance for donggala earthquake response, 2018). In Nigeria, Gombe state government provided 1,200 bags of maize (deaths, destruction as floods ravage states, 2018) and in Kogi, the state provided foodstuffs to flood victims (Akinrinade, 2018). Flooding contaminated water supplies, so safe water was another need in Nigeria. Yakubu Suleiman of the National Emergency Management Agency, said (Akinrinade, 2018): "We have brought water treated plants to be installed in the camp, so, that the people will have access to portable water."

Dry Goods

Distribution of aid was a focus following the Indonesian disaster. Social Minister Agus Gumiwang Kartasasmita (Azly, 2018) "coordinated with the Armed Forces (TNI) commander in order to mobilize relief goods and evacuation equipment prepared from the Ministry of Social Central Warehouse in Bekasi." The story mentioned other governmental entities that provided and transported goods. Stories also detailed the range of items being provided—2,000 beds, 3,000 tents, two packages of public kitchen equipment, 1,500 mattresses, 3,000 blankets, 200 family kits, 200 kids items, and 100 clothing packages.

Another theme from Indonesia was identifying the need, with governmental officials again at the center. President Joko Widodo said (Government to deliver food aid in large quantities: president, 2018): "I think these problems must be handled soon before we tackle the second phase of disaster response." Coordinating Minister for Political, Legal, and Security Affairs Wiranto said (Indonesia needs more tents, fogging for earthquake-hit area,

2018): "We need a lot of tents. Clean water is limited. We need electricity for the well pump. Therefore, we will ask for gensets from these donor countries."

Similarly, governmental efforts were at the center of goods being distributed to people in Nigeria. Anambra state government opened centers for distribution of relief materials (Elekwa, 2018). Edo state government made similar efforts to distribute goods to flood victims (Flooding: Edo distributes relief materials to victims, 2018). The National Emergency Maintenance Agency supplied mattresses, blankets, and mats (Akinrinade, 2018). In Greece, a collective effort of municipalities, the Hellenic Red Cross and other nongovernmental organizations, and volunteers gathered supplies for those left homeless and they appealed for donations (search continues as wildfires death toll climbs to 80, 2018). Skai TV's Oloi Mazi Boroume (Together We Can) campaign and the workers' union at the Center for Disease Prevention and Control collected donations (Karamanoli, 2018).

Transportation and Logistics

Logistical assistance and transportation goods were a prominent focus in Indonesia, where aircraft of the Indonesian Air Force were deployed to transport aid to Palu (Air Force aircraft evacuate quake, tsunami victims, 2018) and the federal government provided thirty satellite telephones to coordinate disaster management (Azly, 2018). Trucks under police escort from the state-owned oil and gas company Pertamina provided fuel to petrol stations around Palu so people could resume normal activities (Nasution, 2018a). In Nigeria, Delta state deployed speedboats to rescue stranded residents (Akinrinade, 2018) and about 100 canoes were procured for transporting victims (Adeyemi et al., 2018).

Monetary Aid

In Greece, eighteen wildfire victims in Attica received a lump sum of 5,000 euros from the Ministry of Finance (First eighteen Attica fire victims receive aid, 2018) and more than 1,700 applications for compensation were received in three days (Applications for wildfire aid reach 1,761 in three days, 2018). The Hellenic Red Cross drew contributions of 100,000 U.S. dollars through Facebook (Karamanoli, 2018) and the Bank of Greece promised to donate 5 million euros to help wildfire survivors and support reconstruction (Greek central bank pledges financial assistance to fire victims, 2018). The Indonesian government pledged financial support of 10,000 Rupiah per person for three months to survivors of the natural disaster (Purnamawati, 2018) and 15 million Rupiah for each heir (Social ministry sends logistic assistance for donggala earthquake response, 2018). Adhy Karyono, spokesman of the ministry's Central Sulawesi Disaster Command Center, said (Purnamawati, 2018): "The residents, who have joined an exodus of disaster zones, will not lose their rights for receiving the social aid fund because it depends on their home addresses." Stories also mentioned the overall financial commitment from government. Nigeria pledged 6.2 million euros for relief efforts (Why does Nigeria keep flooding?, 2018), Indonesia prepared 560 billion Rupiah (Fatir, 2018) and Japan agreed to disburse 2.1 billion yen (Kyodo, 2018b). Japan also agreed to help victims receive special administrative benefits, including extension of licenses and permits (Kyodo, 2018b).

Shelter

In Nigeria, the Edo state government opened resettlement camps for residents who lost home and provided mattresses (Flooding: Edo distributes relief materials to victims, 2018) and Anambra state set up twenty-eight emergency shelters (Deaths, destruction as floods ravage states, 2018). The federal government mounted 110 tents and worked to ensure every affected home was assisted (Akinrinade, 2018). Indonesia president Joko Widodo promised tents and other goods (President receives aid offers from various countries, 2018).

Medical Supplies

Nigeria's National Emergency Management Agency checked victims for diseases. Yakubu Suleiman, NEMA coordinator, said (Akinrinade, 2018): "The medical teams are on ground from the Federal and State Ministries of Health, to be assisted by members of the Red Cross Society, to avoid the spread of diseases as a result of polluted water." The Indonesian military sent paramedics, medical supplies, and a hospital ship (Quake, tsunami death toll in Central Sulawesi rises to 420, 2018), while the Health Ministry was ordered by the president to provide field hospitals (President Jokowi outlines four priorities in Central Sulawesi disaster handling, 2018).

Medical Care

Two types of actions focused on medical care were dealing with physical trauma and handling psychological concerns. Just a handful of stories mentioned actions related to death, including postmortem inspection and burials.

Physical treatment

Indonesia, the United States, and Greece featured the most examples of treating physical trauma; in each disaster, medical personnel provided treatment outside of normal settings. Trauma from Indonesia's earthquake and tsunami required fast and flexible action to treat the injured. That included patients "being treated in the open outside city hospitals" and setting up a military field hospital (Indonesia earthquake: Huge surge in death toll, 2018). With people facing difficulty getting clean water, the Health Affairs Ministry sent water purification tablets to Palu (Three battalions of army troops dispatched to Palu: mily commander, 2018) and the Indonesian Islamic Da'wah Institute sent medicine and other basic necessities to disaster victims (Prihantoro, 2018). In the United States, emergency crews around Paradise carried out triage on patients, with nurse Tamara Ferguson (Hughes, 2018) treating "two women who have just undergone caesarean sections." Staff moved patients to the hospital's helipad and drove other patients to nearby hospitals (Hughes, 2018). In Greece (Athens wildfires: Death toll rises to 24 as huge fire sweeps through holiday resorts, 2018), "The dock area became a makeshift hospital as paramedics checked survivors when they came off coast guard vessels and private boats. The operation continued through the night."

Psychological Treatment

The most detailed psychological support was advice from psychologist Chryssa Karakana helping parents guide children through the trauma (Fotiadi, 2018b). Karakana said:

> My advice to parents is to minimize their children's exposure to sounds and images that originate from the area of disaster, and, overall, keep them away from receiving excessive information on the matter. . . . We should all discuss the events with our children so as to give them a solid idea of what happened, without however exposing them to graphic images that feature explicit content. We must educate our children so that they understand what can start a dangerous fire, how to eliminate or avoid bad habits that can spark a fire, and how we can protect ourselves in the event of a fire.

VERBAL ACTIONS

While physical actions were visible to many in the affected areas, other types of actions were less public. Verbal actions included responses by government agencies and leaders; advice and suggestions, including comments from journalists in their stories; donations and volunteerism; and police investigations and other activities from authorities. The national leader provided 22% of the sourced passages and others in government another 59%. Unaffiliated people appeared in 22% of the sourced material and businesses or NGOs another 10%.

Government

Actions involving government were a significant element in the news coverage, especially in Greece, Indonesia, and Guatemala. Government actions fit into four categories—policies, visits by governmental officials, articulating existing and future needs, and political activities.

Policies

Emergency declarations targeted the ongoing disaster or governmental reorganization to deal with future disasters. Policy actions by Greek governments included declarations of a state of emergency at both the federal and local levels, along with financial help from international bodies, including the European Union (Athens wildfires: Death toll rises to twenty-four as huge fire sweeps through holiday resorts, 2018). Prime Minister Alexis Tsipras heralded the creation of the National Emergency Management Service to integrate all services, research institutes, and volunteer teams (Antoniou, 2018b). The Greek government announced subsidies and tax breaks for fire-stricken residents of Attica (Iordanidis, 2018).

In Japan, most governmental policy news was found in one article that articulated the need for a new disaster prevention ministry to coordinate rescue and relief efforts (Johnston, 2018b). Much of the justification came from a book by Shigeru Ishiba, a former LDP secretary general from Tottori Prefecture, who wrote: "Japan is a country with a lot of different kinds of natural disasters, and we're very experienced in dealing with them. Isn't it necessary to scale things up by centralizing this knowledge in one location, including knowledge gained from infrastructure issues and evacuations?". In another section of the book, Ishiba wrote: "The development of scientific technologies for disaster prevention would receive a lot of support. As a national policy, putting efforts into making this sector would lead to new industries and make Japan a world leader in innovation with regards to disaster prevention techniques."

Indonesia president Joko Widodo outlined four priorities in handling efforts to rescue and assist victims of the earthquake and tsunami: search, rescue, and evacuation efforts; medical assistance; helping refugees in shelters and emergency tents; and infrastructure reconstruction efforts (President Jokowi outlines four priorities in Central Sulawesi disaster handling, 2018). One agency's task was to fight hoaxes on social media, Indonesia's Ministry of Information and Communication produced a point-by-point rebuttal of fake news (Indonesia tsunami: Authorities fight hoaxes, 2018). In Guatemala, Congress authorized emergency funds to provide housing and other aid (Ortiz, 2018). In Nigeria, Cross River State Emergency Management Agency appealed to the national agency for relief materials (twelve states may experience flooding 2018—NIHSA, 2018). In the United States, President Donald Trump declared a major disaster in California, making federal aid possible (California fires: Winds propel fires as death toll rises, 2018).

Visits

In five of the disasters, visits by the country's leader were highlighted. Trips by Indonesia president Joko Widodo to affected areas included the ruins of the collapsed Hotel Roa Roa in Palu (Indonesia tsunami: Frustration in remote areas waiting for aid, 2018); Undata Hospital, where hundreds of victims were being treated (Tamindael, 2018); and Talise Beach, a tourist area hit by the tsunami (Indonesia earthquake: Huge surge in death toll, 2018). Widodo also reviewed the handling of rescue efforts and visited several refugee camps (President Jokowi again visits quake-hit C Sulawesi, 2018).

Appearances of Prime Minister Alexis Tsipras were prominent in news from Greece. As the fire broke, Tsipras cut short a visit to Bosnia to coordinate the disaster response (Maltezou, 2018d). Later, Tsipras visited Mati, the worst-affected area, tweeting that he spoke with "citizens, engineers, soldiers, firefighters and volunteers." In the United States, President Donald Trump surveyed damage from the fires in California and visited those affected (California wildfires: Number of missing leaps to 631, 2018). In Paradise, Trump praised the efforts of local law enforcement, politicians, and the teams searching for survivors (California wildfires: Trump visits state's deadliest blaze, 2018).

In Guatemala, President Jimmy Morales, along with his wife Patricia Marroquin, visited an emergency center and a shelter (Lopez, 2018a). Morales said: "In this type of situation we are only going to leave, uniting all our efforts and transferring the aid to those who need it." In Japan, Prime Minister Shinzo Abe inspected damage in Okayama (Japan flood: At least 179 dead after worst weather in decades, 2018). At a school in Kurashiki, Abe shook hands and spoke with evacuees (water outages continue in flood-hit areas across western Japan, as death toll tops 170, 2018). In Nigeria, Niger state governor Alhaji Abubakar Sani-Bello visited affected communities via a police helicopter (Ololade, 2018).

Needs

News content that addressed needs to government was most common in Guatemala, with detailed advice from writers. The most thorough critique came from one columnist for *La Hora*, who pushed Guatemala's government to learn from the volcanic eruption and make changes. Edgar Villanueva (2018) wrote: "The lesson learned, in my opinion, is that we must invest in strengthening the disaster prevention system. In addition to being the first line to save lives, it is also the first line to save state funds that have to be invested after disasters. It is proven that it is cheaper to prevent than having to spend large amounts of resources to alleviate the consequences of a natural disaster, without accounting for the loss of human lives." Additionally, Villanueva stated:

> We must prevent entire communities from being built on the slopes of active volcanoes, just as we cannot continue to have entire communities in the ravines of the capital city. It is important not only to create awareness and be prepared for a disaster, but also to have planning laws that help us all, regardless of socioeconomic status, to live in safe places." Finally, he wrote: "We cannot stop the force of nature, but we can learn today at least three lessons that tragedy leaves us. We must strengthen our disaster prevention system and the institutions under its responsibility. Likewise, we must streamline the mechanisms they use and the way we locate and plan the villages, hamlets and cities of the future.

Another columnist for *La Hora* offered advice to Guatemalan government as well. Stu Velasco (2018) wrote:

> In the face of the tragedy that occurred and the genuine example of our Heroes of Truth, it is up to us not to disappoint them; . . . work without delay, without excuses, to activate any relief mechanism that the law establishes to meet the urgent need for help that thousands of families urgently need. . . . Bear in mind that what the victims of this tragedy want to hear, like all Guatemalans, are messages that denote security and capacity in the face of the calamity that has occurred, that public-financial funds flow for its attention and that they be executed with agility, transparency and quality of expenditure.

A member of Pakistan's National Assembly delivered advice to his government. Dr Ramesh Kumar Vankwani wrote (2018):

> The government must focus on preparing a proper action plan to prevent and handle a heatwave with the coordination of various departments, individuals, the media and the civil society. There is a dire need to run public awareness campaigns and issue heatwave alerts. We must recognise this phenomenon as a major health risk and identify vulnerable communities. We must devise a strategy to protect shopkeepers, auto mechanics, taxi and rickshaw drivers,

labourers, police officials and security guards, who are extremely vulnerable to heatwaves and its adverse impacts, such as dehydration and sun strokes.

Vankwani also advised: "The government must initiate massive plantation drives in the city on a priority basis, whereas citizens must also plant trees in their homes and gardens for the sake of protecting the environment. . . . Those who live in apartments should consider the environmental benefits of having green roofs. According to my knowledge, a green roof can help keep the temperature down in a home by as much as six to eight degree Celsius."

Nigerian author Banji Ojewale wrote (2018): "The federal government, in collaboration with relevant state agencies, especially states along the coastal regions, should as a matter of urgency evacuate residents of flood-prone areas and other danger zones to avert any flood devastation." In Greece, an editorial (Our good side, 2018) called for government attention to "a more active civil society that will be able to provide solutions to big problems. The Greek state has reached its limits. . . . The country needs to develop a culture of volunteerism and social contribution, together with steps to better organize local communities."

Expressions of government need also came from experts, celebrities, and victims. In Guatemala, Ricardo Barrientos, an economist at the Central American Institute for Fiscal Studies, raised concerns about the effectiveness of government (Lopez, 2018b). Barrientos said: "There is concern about the use and quality of spending of resources because the Government has been characterized by corruption." The Pakistan Meteorological Department urged (Karachi hit by sweltering heatwave, 2018): "Considering the ongoing observance of Ramadan and people fasting, authorities have to ensure adequate supply of power and water."

In the United States, celebrities suggested government actions, some criticizing President Donald Trump (California wildfires: Death toll rises to 25, 2018). Singer Katy Perry called it an "absolutely heartless response" and singer-songwriter John Legend said Trump "can't bring himself to show some empathy to Californians dealing with a horrific disaster." A victim of Nigeria's flooding, Innocent Okoye, pushed for governmental support (Elekwa, 2018): "I am also using this medium to appeal to government to assist our people who have virtually lost everything they have to the floodwaters."

Politics

All of the political actions were in Greece, where several government officials faced pressure to leave office. The leader of the opposition New Democracy Party, Kyriakos Mitsotakis, accused the government of shirking responsibility (Greek PM to unveil new plan for civil protection, 2018). Calls to resign came from the municipal council of Marathon, which voted unanimously for the resignation of city Mayor Ilias Psinakis (Marathon municipal council votes to oust mayor over wildfire tragedy, 2018). Dimitra Lambarou, the deputy mayor of Marathonas, which has administrational jurisdiction over much of the devastated coastal town on Mati, resigned (Woman dies in hospital, raising number of wildfire fatalities to 88, 2018). Lambarou said: "Since no-one else did it, I will." Prime Minister Alexis Tsipras replaced the heads of the police force and fire brigade (Police, fire chiefs replaced in wake of deadly Attica blazes, 2018). Alternate Citizens' Protection Minister Nikos Toskas submitted his resignation (Nedos & Georgiopoulou, 2018).

Advice

Three subcategories of advice attached to actions were expressions of caution, suggestions for people to flee, and offers of assistance. Caution was most likely in Pakistan, and advice to flee and assistance were especially prominent in Greece.

Caution

The ongoing heat wave in Pakistan prompted calls from experts, governmental officials, and article writers for the affected population to help themselves. Some advice was specific, such as to avoid exposure to the sun and wetting heads (Blistering heatwave continues to grip country, 2018). Karachi Met Office chief Abdur Rashid (Bhatti, 2018a) said: "For the next four to five days, people, especially those who are fasting, the elderly and children, are advised not to venture out in the sun, while labourers should also refrain from hard labour under the sun." Other cautionary advice was general, such as from Dr Ghulam Rasool, director general of the Pakistan Meteorological Department (Yet another heatwave to hit city in a week, 2018): "In this scenario, I would request people and the state organisations to remain on high alert in the coming months. Keep warning people to adopt precautionary measures to protect themselves from heat stroke."

Caution also targeted local governments in Pakistan, as when the Ministry of Climate Change (Climate Change minister says provinces warned of heatwave, 2018) "took a proactive approach" and sent letters the previous month to provinces and federating units to prepare for heat waves, demanding "comprehensive steps at all level to deal with issue." Climate change ministry spokesperson Mohammad Saleem proposed an early warning system so (Pakistan's heatwave woes to worsen further as summer temperatures spike steadily, 2018) "authorities can boost their ability to prevent a lot of suffering, illness, and death from heat waves through timely response and preparedness." Further, Saleem suggested health awareness campaigns and improvements such as expanding cool roofs, solar reflective paint on buildings, encouraging gardens on rooftops, increasing access to drinking water, and training medical personnel.

In Greece and the United States, caution was targeted at the effects of pollution from the wildfires. Experts advised people in Greece to wear surgical masks and rubber gloves when cleaning their homes and keep their stays there brief (Elafros, 2018). Health officials in the United States warned people to stay indoors (California wildfires: Air quality rated 'world's worst', 2018); the Sacramento County Public Health Office said: "Wearing a mask may encourage outdoor activity when staying indoors is the best way to minimize exposure to smoke." Hygiene was a theme of cautionary advice in Japan as well, where governmental agencies (Western Japan struggles to restore water to flood-hit towns, 2018) promoted video tutorials on measures such as "making a diaper from a towel and plastic shopping bag."

Fleeing

Continued danger from fires in Greece raised messages to flee. Achilleas Tzouvaras went on state TV to appeal to people to leave the Megara area (Residents told 'just leave' as wildfire rages near Athens, 2018): "People should leave, close up their homes and just leave. People cannot tolerate so much smoke for so many hours." Stories (e.g., Triandafllou & Maltezou, 2018) urged people in coastal areas threatened by fire to abandon their homes. More pointed advice from Greek Fire Service officials (Athens wildfires: Death toll rises to twenty-four as huge fire sweeps through holiday resorts, 2018) "to comply with evacuation orders and not stay on in an effort trying to save their homes." People in the United States were told to flee in vehicles from the fast-moving Camp Fire (California wildfires: Is smoke toxic to the East Coast?, 2018).

In Nigeria, the focus of caution was the risk of further flooding, to ensure preparedness among residents in flood-prone areas and advising some residents to vacate the area (Flooding: Avoiding the fury of nature, 2018). The Kwara state government advised people along the Niger River to "immediately relocate to safe areas" to avoid loss of lives and property (Akinrinade, 2018). Further, government officials also urged people to comply with evacuation orders and move upland during tidal changes and ocean surges (Akinrinade, 2018).

Assistance

Most of the advice for assistance was targeted at friends and family of those missing in the Greek wildfires. They were urged to report missing relatives and friends and (Souliotis, 2018a) to "provide DNA samples so that forensic investigators can complete the process of identifying dozens of victims." Another request in Greece was for volunteers to help tackle fires (Triandafllou & Konstantinidis, 2018). One example from Indonesia was an appeal from the government for people "to be its eyes and ears on social media" to battle against hoaxes and fake news (Indonesia tsunami: Authorities fight hoaxes, 2018).

Donations, Volunteerism

News content mentioned donations most frequently in the Guatemala and Greece disasters. Nearly all details about donations appeared in the local publications.

Donate

In Guatemala, churches in the Diocese of Escuintla set up a special collection day during masses (Diocese of Escuintla sympathizes with those affected by eruption of Fuego volcano and offers alternative aid, 2018). The Greek Orthodox Holy Synod called on parish priests to encourage donations from their congregations (Holy Synod calls for prayers after deadly wildfires, 2018). Names and account numbers for donations were found in Guatemala (Empresarial, 2018b) and in Greece, where the Hellenic Red Cross and the Municipality of Rafina opened bank accounts for donations (Karamanoli, 2018). In Guatemala, *La Hora* (Empresarial, 2018a) announced that all Super 24 convenience stores were available as collection centers. Guatemalans were invited to purchase tickets for a raffle, with proceeds going to those affected by the volcanic eruption (Empresarial, 2018b). The inter-American Development Bank approved $200,000 to the Guatemalan Red Cross to cover immediate humanitarian needs of families affected by the disaster, along with a 20 million dollar rehabilitation loan (Mata, 2018).

In Greece, the American Hellenic Institute, a Greek-American charitable organization, set up a relief fund and noted immediate needs for food, water, clothing, and shelter (AHI calls for donations to help Greece's wildfire victims, 2018). The organization stated: "Together, we can help the people of Greece in their darkest hour." The National Blood Donation Center organized a major donation drive and the country's associations of pharmacists and doctors called on members to provide supplies and services (Karamanoli, 2018). Health authorities appealed for donations of blood and blood components (Search continues as wildfires death toll climbs to 80, 2018). The board of the Athens and Epidaurus Festival offered 20,000 euros in proceeds from an upcoming concert (Athens Festival to donate proceeds to fire victims, 2018). The Stavros Niarchos Foundation contributed a 25 million euro grant (SNF to support Greek fire department with 25 mln grant, 2018) to the Greek fire department.

In Papua New Guinea, private businesses donated to aid earthquake victims. Mineral Resources Development Company offered to fly in relief supplies to earthquake-ravaged areas (Nalu, 2018b). Bart Yacop, the company's petroleum coordinator, said: "Starting (today) we'll be getting medical and food supplies into those areas." ExxonMobil humanitarian aid manager Aaron Grogan said (Nalu, 2018c): "Our team in Port Moresby is working closely with the national coordination committee and controller, so that information flow is shared among the group. . . . It's been a phenomenal effort from our team who have worked very, very hard."

Volunteerism

Examples of volunteer efforts were rare. In Greece, the American Hellenic Educational Progressive Association mobilized members to offer assistance and coordinated volunteer physicians to go to Greece (AHEPA announces post-fire aid program, 2018). The Greece foreign ministry offered to coordinate potential volunteers and others offering help (Greece thanks 'friends and partners' for support with deadly wildfires, 2018). In Indonesia, the Islamic Da'wah Institute deployed its members to help the earthquake- and tsunami-affected victims in Central Sulawesi (Prihantoro, 2018). Volunteers were acknowledged as helpful in Japan (Osumi, 2018a).

Investigations, Police Activities

Natural disasters triggered actions to understand what happened and how to deal with existing problems. Investigations and planning were found in news coverage of three of the natural disasters, with just two disasters including news about police activities and security.

Investigation, Planning

Stories about investigation into causes or emergency responses were found in the Greece, Nigeria, and U.S. disasters. The wildfires in Greece led to multidimensional approaches to determine the cause and evaluate the response. Prime Minister Alexis Tsipras said (Firefighter's wife, baby among 93 victims of Greece blaze, 2018): "We have a duty to take a deep and careful look at everything that happened, to learn and to correct possible lapses." Tsipras promised an inquiry as to why hundreds of people found themselves trapped by flames with no means of escape (Identified wildfire victims reach 76, eight remain missing, 2018). Stories from Greece mentioned investigations by police, the fire service's arson section, and selection by the Supreme Court of an appeals court prosecutor to expedite an investigation.

In Nigeria, one story (Deaths, destruction as floods ravage states, 2018) emphasized planning and education. Two states announced campaigns to educate residents to stop dumping refuse on drainage and building along water channels. The director of Legal Services for the National Emergency Management Agency, Umar Mohammed, said (Deaths, destruction as floods ravage states, 2018): "The essence is to articulate some proactive measures, identify flash-points as well as inspect equipment that could be deployed to tackle flood within the shortest possible time." Deputy Governor John Jonah said: "Every flood-prone area should have a high ground identified and a big hall built to accommodate displaced persons whenever there is flood." In the United States, a team of ten investigators interviewed as many witnesses as possible (Johnson, 2018). Many people fleeing the fires recorded video on their phones and posted it to social media, giving investigators an additional tool to see how the fire spread.

Police Activities, Security

In Indonesia, three battalions of army troops were dispatched to Palu (Three battalions of army troops dispatched to Palu: mily commander, 2018). Indonesian Military Commander Marshal Hadi Tjahjanto said: "They will secure important places, including airport, seaport, patrol stations, shops, and automatic teller machines." Troops guarded trucks transporting humanitarian aid (Three battalions of army troops dispatched to Palu: mily commander, 2018). Tjahjanto said: "All aid packages should be able to reach the disaster survivors in need." Another 2,000 police safeguarded business centers and shops from being looted (Nasution, 2018a). In Greece, worries about arson drew police attention, including requests for drones to detect any suspicious activity (Greece wildfires: Dozens dead in Attica region, 2018). Four people were arrested for suspected looting in an area hit by fire (Search continues as wildfires death toll climbs to eighty, 2018).

EVALUATION OF ACTIONS

News content focused on actions, while mostly validating efforts by government to address the problem, also included elements that offered relief and hope for the affected. Both the physical and verbal actions sent a message that government and others recognized the problems and were taking steps to address those problems, aiding hope and recovery. Not only do actions provide for physical needs, but the efforts also serve as a strong psychological signal that authorities are looking out for people and their future. Stories reflected the magnitude of efforts, details of acts, and determination to aid those in need and plans to move forward.

Government dominated the source usage, suggesting that actions were primarily tied to authorities. The national leader was prominently tied to examples of verbal actions—primarily promising something—while others in government were frequently mentioned in both physical and verbal actions. Businesses or NGOs accounted for one in nine sources, showing that rebuilding or suggestions outside of government were somewhat common but of secondary importance. Unaffiliated passages were somewhat common in describing physical actions.

Physical actions evaluated were rescues and evacuations; rebuilding, cleanup, and planning; good, supplies, and relief aid; and medical care. In each case, the examples in the news demonstrated actions to deal with the immediate and ongoing needs of disaster survivors, directly aiding those affected. Those actions, in turn, indirectly aided those who identified with the survivors and victims. Many of these actions were led by government officials, providing a sense of psychological comfort that authorities were looking out for people, which can aid healing.

Rescues and evacuations were common across the disasters, with search and rescue most common in the two wildfires, evacuation in the two floods, and disaster responses nearly all in the wildfires. Examples of rebuilding, cleanup, and planning included relief actions aiding victims and survivors (especially in Nigeria); planning and prevention efforts from governments to prevent future disasters (most common in Nigeria, Greece, and Indonesia); rebuild and repair actions, such as fixing roads and bridges in Papua New Guinea; and cleanup efforts (near all in Greece). Themes of goods, supplies, and relief aid were especially common in the disasters of Indonesia and Nigeria. This included food and water, dry goods, transportation and logistics, monetary aid, shelter, and medical supplies. Medical care, including physical and psychological treatment, was most found in Greece, Indonesia, and the United States.

Verbal actions included governmental actions, advice, donations and volunteerism, and investigations and police activities. Verbal actions centered on government and its policies showed compassion for victims. Many of the verbal actions offered hope by showing that authorities had recognized the needs of disaster survivors and promised efforts to help them. The benefit was mostly psychological in providing assurance to aid coping and healing, fitting within a peace journalism perspective to explain courses of action needed by society (Tenenboim-Weinblatt et al., 2016).

Government actions included policies (especially in Greece, Japan, and Indonesia), visits by governmental leaders and officials (in five disasters), needs being addressed to government (most common in Guatemala), and politics (all in Greece). Advice took several forms, including caution over the ongoing heat wave in Pakistan, fleeing from continued fire danger in Greece, and assistance aimed at friends and family of the missing in Greece. Donations and volunteerism included stories about how and where to submit donations in Guatemala and a handful of volunteer activities. Investigations and police activities included investigations into the causes or emergency responses to the disasters in Greece, Nigeria, and the United States, plus law enforcement and security actions in Indonesia.

Chapter 13

Blame, Responsibility

Government was the most common target of blame or responsibility—especially in Greece, Guatemala, and Papua New Guinea—mostly for failing to prevent the disaster or poor response to the disaster. Other common targets were nature, such as weather patterns (Pakistan) or climate change (Greece, the United States), and infrastructure (Greece, Nigeria).

Blame or responsibility primarily came from unattributed sources (26%, especially in the Greece and Papua New Guinea local newspapers), government (23%), and unaffiliated people (16% mostly in Nigeria, Greece, and Guatemala). Those in government blaming others in government, especially local officials blaming federal government, was a rare combination. More common were political foes placing responsibility upon the existing government (especially in Greece) and unaffiliated people blaming government. Attribution of blame or responsibility helped the audience see that their concerns were being aired, a type of control that could aid coping, healing, and recovery.

GOVERNMENT

More than half of the blame toward government appeared in the Greek wildfires and some blame appeared in each of the eight disasters. Article writers were the leading source of affixing blame (28%), with unaffiliated people (19%), governmental officials (14%), and opposing political officials (12%) providing blame as well. Themes of blaming government are organized around the party expressing the blame or attributing responsibility.

Writer

Criticism toward government came from opinion articles and other writers, especially in the Greece and Papua New Guinea disasters. Writers in Greece (published in *Kathimerini*) attacked an inadequate initial response to the wildfires, poor preparation, overall governmental incompetence, and inadequate explanations. Costas Synolakis (2018) argued that an accelerated response was needed and "the fire should not be allowed to reach people's yards before they are ordered to abandon their homes. Authorities need to have evacuation plans that factor in available resources and traffic flow on the national and secondary road network." A further critique: "As we saw from yesterday's events, though, neither the Civil Protection Agency's command center nor the municipal authorities in the area had knowledge of the possibilities offered by modern technology for planning the evacuation of densely populated woodland areas. There would have been fewer victims if a few simulations had been carried out in the area, because the authorities would have had a clearer picture of the challenges of an evacuation and would possibly have informed residents as well."

Another negative evaluation came from Notis Papadopoulos (2018):

> The Mati tragedy could have been avoided if the fire service had done its job, ... Someone has to take the blame for this operational failure, for the state's inability to prevent the disaster and guide people to safety. Greece must finally get to the point where it is able to work out a plan and procedures when necessary and not have to depend on the self-sacrifice of firemen, the coast guard and volunteers. We must finally stop losing people to such tragedies. Our politicians must stop resorting to overnight meetings broadcast live on TV just for the sake of appearances.

Governmental incompetence was a focus of Alexis Papachelas (2018): "The mess that starts at the top of the country's power structure spreads all the way down to the smallest local authority. ... The long and short of it is that Greece needs to rebuild its state apparatus from the ground up. The funds, willingness and know-how to achieve this are there. We need to come to an understanding and get our act together because with a state machine like this one, we are extremely unlikely to make progress." A similar critique from an editorial (No remorse, no accountability, 2018):

> The state apparatus is dangerously lax and nothing works as it should, yet the government cares only about the public handling of the tragedy, dividing people instead of uniting them. First it hid, then tried to convince the public that everything had been done properly. Following a public outcry, the prime minister assumed political responsibility. However, no apology was made and

no resignation offered. . . . People expect honest answers and a sincere apology. Their anger is fully justified, because they have got neither.

Another criticism from writers castigated the Greek government's responses to the public reaction (Nedos, 2018) "particularly in the days immediately after the inferno, was all but insulting. Officials switched to a damage control campaign before being swallowed by the inefficiency of the Greek state apparatus, which is, almost by definition, unable to fulfill tasks far less complicated than civil protection."

The primary critique of government in Papua New Guinea appeared in one article that focused on an insufficient disaster response. According to "Let's get earthquake relief aid moving" (2018): "On the ground, those affected are already frustrated with the no-show of essential support. That bewilderment, tinged with anger towards officials at local and national level, was shared at the scene of the disaster as witnessed by *The National*. The scenario is an indication that any form of disaster response is plagued by bureaucratic and at times political obstacles. It is incredible, that there is no evacuation or emergency operation plan." The article detailed the lack of relief supplies and the writer stated: "The questions which remain are how the current system came to be, what our expectations of the system should be and how we ought to shock the political bureaucracy into action to repair the obviously ailing system."

In Pakistan, writers criticized the Sindh government for failure to deal with people affected by the heat wave. "Karachi heatwave" (2018) suggested that the government minimized the impact: "Denial seems to have become a hallmark of the Sindh government. Instead of doing their job, they think their job is just to claim that there is no crisis. . . . It is clear that very little emergency measures were taken to combat this. Pakistan has continued to be reminded of the dangers global warming poses to the country. Experts warn that even more heatwaves should be expected in the coming years." Additionally, "Heatwave in Karachi" (2018) argued that the Sindh government didn't take action to address a heat wave in 2015 that killed 1,000 people. The article suggested: "The provincial government should start a campaign to plant trees to create a natural environment to reduce the effect of heat. Heatstroke units with facilities of basic life support should be made available at every hospital to offer emergency treatments. Cold water dispensers should be kept in public places. Although no authority can directly influence climate, it can at least take some efforts to minimise the losses as much as possible."

In Japan, writers critiqued ineffective advance notice of flooding dangers. For instance (Find and fix the weak points in disaster defenses, 2018): "To learn lessons for future disasters, the review of the response to the heavy rains should scrutinize whether the evacuation orders were given early enough to allow residents—particularly the elderly—sufficient time to safely evacuate before the floods or landslides took place; whether sufficient efforts had been made in advance to share the disaster-risk information—by the local authorities, at the community level and by the residents themselves—and whether evacuation advisories and other emergency information were properly communicated to all residents."

In Nigeria, criticism dealt with the impact of an expanding population and a lack of proper planning (Why does Nigeria keep flooding?, 2018): "If the impact of flooding is to be reduced in the future, the consequences of rapid urbanisation and poor urban planning need to be addressed. . . . And greater co-operation with Nigeria's neighbours in the control of river levels will need to be achieved in order to avoid dangerous surges in water levels during the periods of heavy rain."

Unaffiliated People

Survivors and other people not affiliated with an entity like government or business delivered sharp criticism of government on six of the eight natural disasters, with most news attention in Greece, Guatemala, and Nigeria. Survivors of the wildfires in Greece called for resignations and vented anger toward government officials over failures in the evacuation and slow response to fight the fires. A woman in tears shouted at Defense Minister Panos Kamenos, who visited Mati (Maltezou, 2018b): "This shouldn't have happened, people perished for no reason. . . . You left us at God's mercy!". An unidentified survivor, in response to watching the prime minister on television, said (Maltezou, 2018d): "Words are nice . . . but I want him to tell me and the people who perished, our friends . . . whose fault it is, if not his. I've reached my limits." Failures in the Greek evacuation riled survivors such as Phoebe Angelopoulos, who said (Maltezou, 2018c): "The church bells didn't ring, the sirens didn't go off, no one alerted us." The same story quoted an elderly survivor, who said: "No alert, there was nothing, nothing, nothing." A woman who lost her family claimed a "total lack of communication and confusion" caused the tragedy (Fire survivor sues officials, 2018).

Survivors of the disaster in Guatemala had similar complaints as those in Greece—that the emergency response was "woefully disjointed and disorganized" (Grant, 2018). Conred, the national emergency agency, drew sharp criticism from Arnulfo Santos, who said (The survivors of the Fire Volcano safe, but with uncertainty about the future, 2018): "They never told us to be alert, did not arrive or warn." Guillermo Castillo, an immigrant from the United States, said (Gamez, 2018): "It is unacceptable that in the midst of pain and suffering, we have authorities so incompetent, mediocre and arrogant that instead of helping, they get in the way." Demonstrators, carrying torches and signs, claimed that (They ask resignation of Morales and other officials after the tragedy of Volcán de Fuego, 2018) "the disaster and the humanitarian crisis" were the product of an inept government. Some complained of poor response from Guatemalan leaders to accept international assistance. Journalist Nacho Lozano traveled from Mexico to cover the disaster and told of rescuers from Mexico who were delayed entry to the country for three days (Gamez, 2018). Former foreign minister Fernando Carrera said (Lopez, 2018b): "The impression I got was that the government was more concerned with showing that it could be alone and that is what made the request for aid late."

People in Nigeria expressed disappointment with their representatives in the state and national assemblies for their aloofness (Adeyemi et al., 2018). Displaced people appealed for government intervention, warning that there might be outbreak of epidemic in the camp if urgent steps were not taken (Elekwa, 2018). Mallam Ndamitso Umar in Niger State said (Ololade, 2018): "Even if I say anything now, would it make the government to forget the loan? . . . Will they have pity on us because we have lost our farms?" Survivors in Indonesia complained about the lack of help, especially outside of the hard-hit Palu area. Dede Diman said that rescuers had not even begun to search the area where he believed his sister was (Indonesia tsunami: Search for victims to end, though hundreds still missing, 2018): "We don't agree with giving up. Even if they give up, we won't. We want to find our sister." Yahdi Basma, from an area south of Palu, said (Indonesia tsunami: Frustration in remote areas waiting for aid, 2018): "There are hundreds of people still buried under the mud in my village. I lost many members of my family and neighbours. There is no aid whatsoever which is why we're leaving."

Public concerns in Japan focused on rebuilding homes and providing necessities. Prime Minister Shinzo Abe, in response to concerns from a displaced 88-year-old woman, mentioned a plan to build temporary housing (Water outages continue in flood-hit areas across western Japan, as death toll tops 170, 2018). Shigenobu Ikeda, seventy-four, said (Osumi, 2018c): "I'd like (the government) to help us restore our house, which I worked hard for and feel attached to—I raised my daughter there." Hiroshi Oka, forty, an Okayama resident, said (Western Japan struggles to restore water to flood-hit towns as temperatures soar, 2018): "We need the water supply back. . . . What we are getting is a thin stream of water, and we can't flush toilets or wash our hands."

Government

Most of the news content featuring governmental officials blaming government for the disaster or response came from Greece, which has a vibrant and contentious political environment. Guatemala featured several examples, with less attention in Nigeria, Pakistan, Papua New Guinea, and Indonesia (and none in Japan and the United States).

In Greece, much of the blame targeted mayors and other local officials for poor response to the fire and lax oversight of construction that may have contributed to the fires.

Criticism of the immediate response came from federal, regional, and local officials. Eleni Tsoupra, the regional governor of civil protection, pointed at insufficient response from local mayors to evacuate from the approaching wildfire (Maltezou, 2018c). Tsoupra said: "Evacuation plans are with the municipal authorities, who are also responsible for drafting them." The mayor of the Marathon region, Elias Psinakis, said that evacuating Mati was not his responsibility. Later, the municipal council of Marathon voted unanimously for the resignation of Psinakis, whom they accuse of negligence (Marathon municipal council votes to oust mayor over wildfire tragedy, 2018). Dimitra Lambarou, the deputy mayor of Marathonas, said (Woman dies in hospital, raising number of wildfire fatalities to 88, 2018): "I'm really ashamed for all those people who are in positions of responsibility." She accused Psinakis of "not rising to the occasion." The mayor of the northern Athens suburb of Maroussi, Giorgos Patoulis, accused Attica Regional Governor Rena Dourou of "lies and inaccuracy" after she accused the municipality of not taking the necessary preventive measures before floods that hit areas burned by wildfires (Maroussi municipality accused of indifference after floods, 2018). In turn, the Attica Regional Authority criticized Maroussi of failing to prevent illegal construction. Greece's union of forest rangers attributed responsibility to those who failed to stop a wildfire (Forest rangers see operational failures in tackling deadly blaze, 2018). Another form of blaming government in Greece looked ahead. Interior minister Panos Skourletis announced (Government says it will knock down illegal properties, 2018) the government would unveil "a plan for the radical overhaul and replanning of civil protection," to limit future tragedies. A government source pushed for the demolition of illegal structures (Government issues decree for demolition of illegal construction, 2018).

Criticism toward government from others in government over the evacuation was a key issue in Guatemala. Eddy Sanchez, director of the National Institute of Seismology, Volcanology, Meteorology and Hydrology, said he warned disaster officials about the threat of an eruption but evacuation did not proceed (Castanon, 2018). Deputies asserted that Sergio Cabañas, executive secretary of the Coordinator for Disaster Reduction (Conred), must resign due to negligence for his handling of the emergency (Figueroa, 2018). Later, deputies of the Parliamentary Front for Transparency denounced Cabañas and filed a complaint for culpable homicide. Deputy Enrique Álvarez said

(They denounce Secretary of the Conrad, Sergio Cabañas, for the tragedy of the Volcán de Fuego, 2018): "We are confident that the complaint will move forward because we are providing evidence, where it is detailed that despite the alert, people were not evacuated."

In Nigeria, the primary context of criticism dealt with the government's role in aiding farmers. Government officials pushed for better coordination between government and rice farmers (Okereocha, 2018) and more support from the state governors to improve the quality of seeds (Flood: Ogbeh predicts rice shortage in 2019, 2018). In Pakistan, Met Office Karachi chief Abdur Rashid suggested a major shift in urban planning to mitigate the effects of climate change (Bhatti, 2018c). In Papua New Guinea, Western Governor Taboi Awi Yoto said the provincial government lacked the capacity to respond to the disaster and called upon help from the National Disaster Office (Wani, 2018b). In Indonesia, the agency that manages the country's tsunami buoy warning system acknowledged that minimal attention had been paid to predisaster anticipation (Indonesia earthquake and tsunami: How warning system failed the victims, 2018).

Opposition Political Entities

The aftermath of the Greece wildfires generated most of the critical comments toward government from opposition parties. Criticism came primarily from the conservative New Democracy Party, but also from the Panhellenic Socialist Movement (PASOK Party) and the centrist and social-liberal To Potami Party. New Democracy leader Kyriakos Mitsotakis received prominent attention in *Kathimerini* to criticize the ruling party. Under the headline "Mitsotakis blasts 'deplorable' government reaction to deadly wildfire" (2018), the lead sentence was "conservative opposition leader Kyriakos Mitsotakis slammed the government's 'deplorable' reaction to the deadly wildfire that ripped through the east coast of Attica, killing more than 90 people and injuring scores, saying his party will ensure that responsibility is attributed to those who failed to prevent the disaster." Mitsotakis called for the resignation of five officials. Mitsotakis accused the government of attempting to blame others (Mitsotakis: Government wanted to shift blame for deadly blaze, 2018): "Instead of bowing their heads . . . all they cared about was raising their finger, blaming others—those who own illegal buildings, citizens, even the dead." New Democracy spokeswoman Maria Spyraki said (Koputantou, 2018): "This government has just added unbridled cheek to its abject failure in protecting lives and people's property." In response to an official's resignation, New Democracy stated (PM accepts resignation of Citizens' Protection Minister Toskas over Attica fires, 2018): "Responsibility has a name: Alexis Tsipras. He and his government do not have the courage to assume it, eleven days after the tragedy." Another statement (Kammenos defends government's response to blaze, 2018): "The people, however, are no longer convinced by publicity stunts. They want to know the whole truth as to how so many lives were lost for no reason."

PASOK party leader Fofi Gennimata also criticized the ruling party (Koputantou, 2018): "Why didn't they protect the people by implementing on time the available plan for an organized and coordinated evacuation in the areas that were threatened? They have confessed they let people burn helplessly." To Potami leader Stavros Theodorakis said Greeks "paid dearly" for Toskas' tenure (PM accepts resignation of Citizens' Protection Minister Toskas over Attica fires, 2018).

In Guatemala, opposition politicians attacked the head of the emergency response agency Conred for failure to heed advance warnings about the volcano. Senior opposition figure Mario Taracena said the government should investigate whether there was criminal negligence (Guatemala volcano: Emergency agency 'failed to heed warnings', 2018), arguing that orders to evacuate were not clearly or sufficiently communicated. In Indonesia, a federal emergency agency was challenged by Head of the House Commission V Fary Djemi Francis for lifting a tsunami warning (BMKG should clarify lifting of tsunami early warning, 2018). He said, "We demand the reason why the tsunami early warning was lifted. They must clarify it."

Country's Leader

The national leaders in the United States and Greece criticized government for its role in the destructive wildfires. U.S. president Donald Trump blamed state forest officials for their management of timber in California. In a tweet, Trump accused state authorities of "gross mismanagement" (California wildfires: Fears of further damage as winds strengthen, 2018). Trump said (Kingsley, 2018): "You look at other countries where they do it differently . . . (in Finland) they spent a lot of time on raking and cleaning and doing things. And they don't have any problem." While surveying fire damage in Paradise, Trump said (California wildfires: Finland bemused by Trump raking comment, 2018): "We've got to take care of the floors. The floors of the forest." Greek prime minister Alexis Tsipras blamed previous government policies, weak response to the disaster and pledged changes. Tsipras vowed to crack down on unlicensed construction (Identified wildfire victims reach seventy-six, eight remain missing, 2018), a responsibility of local governments. Tsipras replaced four top officials in response to criticism over the emergency response (Greek PM to unveil new plan for civil protection, 2018) and contemplated an overhaul of his cabinet to appease public discontent (Papadiochos, 2018b). Finally, the prime minister pledged a new national plan to correct decades-old building violations (PM finally takes blame for deadly conflagration after outcry, 2018).

Experts

Criticism and blame from experts were most common in the disasters of Guatemala, the United States, and Greece. Experts typically critiqued the performance of government in planning prior to the disaster or noted deficiencies in response. In Guatemala, two stories from *La Hora* brought critical perspectives from experts to blame government for response to the volcanic eruption. Ricardo Barrientos, an economist at the Central American Institute for Fiscal Studies, pointed out deficiencies in the government's process to receive help from other countries (Lopez, 2018b). The same story cited Luis Linares, an analyst at the Association for Research and Social Studies, who criticized the establishment of shelters: "Definitely, the actions of the authorities in general are not satisfactory, there are many complaints about the lack of attention to many of the affected communities and people." Deputy Enrique Álvarez of the Parliamentary Front for Transparency asserted that government officials were minimizing data on those missing. He said (They denounce secretary of the Conrad, Sergio Cabañas, for the tragedy of the Volcán de Fuego, 2018): "The attempt to manipulate the figures is evident, they want us to believe that there are a little over a hundred people disappeared, but there are data that detail that in those communities lived more than 5 thousand people."

Forest management practices were the main target of experts in the aftermath of wildfires in the United States. Scott Stephens, an authority on wildfires at the University of California, had for years questioned forest management priorities and he argued for (California wildfires: Is Trump right when he blames forest managers?, 2018) emphasis on more sensible management of the environment and better land use to avoid "catastrophic burning." In the same story, Prof. Stefan Doerr of Swansea University suggested that the modern policy of putting out all fires in wild areas may have been misguided, creating "a tinderbox of vegetation." Chad Hanson, a fire ecologist at the John Muir Project, an environmental group, also criticized land management policies. Hanson said (Johnson, 2018): "When it got to the logged area, it spread very rapidly and people just didn't have much time to evacuate in Paradise, so this whole notion that logging—so-called hazardous fuels reduction—was going to save the town is a dangerous falsehood."

In Greece, experts targeted mistakes in managing the wildfires and prevention. A preliminary inquiry into the fires by the University of Athens blamed authorities' failure to issue a timely warning and left (Lack of early warning, town planning led to high death toll, study finds, 2018) "almost zero time between realizing the danger and reacting to it." Costas Synolakis, professor of natural hazards at the Technical University of Crete's School of Environmental Engineering, wrote that the outcome of a fire always depends on the initial intervention and highlighted the need for preventive planning (Ellis, 2018). In Japan, Susumu Nakano, the head of the Research Center for Management of Disaster and Environment at Tokushima University, said (Water outages continue in flood-hit areas across western Japan, as death toll tops 170, 2018): "Compared to earthquakes, there are not enough measures. It is necessary to make efforts on the assumption that there will be flooding." In Nigeria, World Meteorological Organization Secretary General Petteri Taalas attributed flooding to poor meteorological data (Yahaya, 2018). Taalas said: "This is demonstrating that there is need for a stronger national meteorological services and stronger WMO and that is why we have the feeling that there is more demand for WMO expertise and demand for national expertise of meteorological services."

Businesses, Organizations

The disasters in Greece, Guatemala, and Japan brought the most themes of businesses or organizations blaming government. Environmental organizations targeted Greece's government in a statement (Pitas & Maltezou, 2018): "This tragic event shows the full inadequacy and ineffectiveness of the current forest protection system." The World Wildlife Fund Greece director Dimitris Karavellas said, of people trapped by flames (Maltezou & Konstantinidis, 2018): "These people should have been ordered out of this area." News media blamed government as well, pointing to an absence of coordination and planning that delayed the arrival of fire trucks to western Attica (Synolakis, 2018). In Guatemala, Jorge Santos of the Unit for the Protection of Defenders of Human Rights argued that the government had failed to act adequately in previous emergencies. Santos said (Gamez, 2018):

> They have blatantly lied to us, they have told us half-truths, the inability to approach the communities and ask for their immediate evacuation, the ability to order the humanitarian aid process, the reception of help from friendly countries, is in question. that is, if outside and this is really the sensation, if not for the strength of the population itself, of the rescue workers, of the firefighters of the capacity to organize themselves in front of an event of these dimensions, the drama would be even greater.

In Japan, a doctor with NPO Peace Winds Japan, Mototaka Inaba, said that there had been no evacuation plans prior to the flood (Johnston, 2018b). Another complaint was people reluctant to use outdoor toilet facilities. Atsushi Kato, who heads Japan Toilet Labo, a Tokyo-based nonprofit group conducting lavatory research, said (Western Japan struggles to restore water to flood-hit towns as temperatures soar, 2018): "It is a problem that is directly linked to people's health." In Papua New Guinea, Scott Waide, deputy editor at local news organization EMTV, said (Papua New Guinea quake: An invisible disaster which could change life forever, 2018): "People are organising themselves because it's been difficult for the government to get in. When people get a mobile phone signal they are sending texts to the authorities saying 'we have 2,000 people here and no food or water—can you send help?'" Waide also argued that the political process of freeing up and delivering aid has been slow and the national disaster agency has been unprepared to cope with a disaster of this size.

Judicial

Most of the criticisms from judicial authorities were found in the Greece wildfires. Supreme Court prosecutor Xeni Dimitriou ordered a probe amid indications that the state response to the emergency had been slow and that no evacuation plan had been in place (Search continues as wildfires death toll climbs to eighty, 2018). Prosecutor Varvara Gnesouli received testimonies from the chiefs who were responsible for the prevention and containment of the fire (Lack of early warning, town planning led to high death toll, study finds, 2018). The investigation focused on apparent shortcomings by the fire service and regional authorities (Souliotis & Elafros, 2018). One apparent finding was that high-ranking fire service officers did not heed the warnings of firefighters who called them from the scene (Souliotis & Mandrou, 2018). In Guatemala, a complaint with the Public Prosecutor's Office targeted Sergio Cabañas, executive secretary of the Coordinator for Disaster Reduction, for the crimes of culpable homicide, breach of duties, serious injuries, very serious injuries, and mistreatment against minors (They denounce Secretary of the Conrad, Sergio Cabañas, for the tragedy of the Volcán de Fuego, 2018).

NATION'S LEADER

Blaming the country's leader for the natural disaster was much more common in the Greece wildfires than in the other events. Representatives of other political parties or entities issued more blame of the leader than other sources, followed by unaffiliated people. All of the political opposition parties blaming the leader occurred in Greece, targeting Prime Minister Alexis Tsipras. Many of the stories mentioned the opposition without being any more specific, such as (Maltezou, 2018d) "Tsipras was accused by the opposition of burying his head in the sand. He rejected the accusations during the cabinet meeting" and (Pitas & Maltezou, 2018) "Tsipras has been attacked by opposition parties for the government's handling of the disaster, which also left dozens injured." Another article (ND slams Tsipras's early Monday visit to Mati as PR stunt, 2018) cited the opposition New Democracy Party downplaying Tsipras' visit to a burned seaside resort "as a 'publicity stunt' aimed at deflecting public attention from the government's failings during the tragedy" and wrote in a statement "Mr. Tsipras must realize that [people] must be held accountable for the mistakes and omissions made on July 23."

Less common were criticisms from named officials. New Democracy leader Kyriakos Mitsotakis called out Tsipras (Mitsotakis insists heads must roll, 2018) "over the fact that no one has resigned over last week's deadly wildfires. When someone undertakes political responsibility it should be accompanied by an act, and resignation is an act of personal responsibility." Even sharper comments came from New Democracy spokeswoman Maria Spyraki (Antoniou, 2018a): "A wretched prime minister, who refuses to assume responsibility for the criminal lack of preparation, the nonexistent coordination and the tragic management of the crisis at Mati, today announced the demolition of illegal structures which should have been done three years ago." Socialist Pasok party spokesman Pavlos Christides criticized the prime minister as (Maltezou, 2018d) "more focused on the 'communications aspect' of the crisis than 'what really matters.'"

Greece's prime minister criticized himself as well, taking responsibility for the tragedy (Seaside town remembers lives lost to fire, 2018) "and pledged a series of changes, including on illegal and haphazard construction which is thought to have worsened the blaze." One editorial (Too little, too late, 2018) harshly criticized the prime minister: "Given that all previous efforts to spin the tragedy failed and seeing that the political cost was bearing down heavily on the shoulders of the government, Prime Minister Alexis Tsipras at long last was forced on Friday to take political responsibility." A much different criticism of the prime minister was based on spiritual grounds. Bishop Amvrosios of Kalavryta in the Peloponnese wrote on his blog ('Atheist PM' to blame for deadly fires, says Greek bishop, 2018): "Atheist Prime Minister Alexis Tsipras draws the wrath of God. . . . The atheists of SYRIZA are the causes of the general disaster! Their atheis, draws the wrath of God!" Writers pounded Tsipras as well. An opinion commentary stated (Damage control without accountability, 2018): "Nor of course was there any attempt to assume a degree of political responsibility . . . Tragedy is bound to happen when you have a state apparatus that is at best incompetent and at worst nonexistent—and apparently only getting worse under this administration." Another editorial (Everything is wrong, 2018): "The question is whether Prime Minister Alexis Tsipras will finally comprehend just how badly he manages issues of public safety. SYRIZA's policy, people and laxity are all wrong."

In Guatemala's volcanic disaster, people of the country delivered most criticism of President Jimmy Morales. People demonstrated against the inefficiency of the Morales government's handling of the tragedy (They ask resignation of Morales and other officials, 2018) and asked for Morales and other leaders to resign. Survivor Mardoqueo González (The survivors of the Fire Volcano safe, 2018) "sent a message to President Jimmy Morales, to make him present, 'we want him to come and tell us what they are going to do with us, we need support, here where we are we have water, but it is not enough.'" Japan's prime minister was criticized for appearing insensitive when photos on Twitter showed Shinzo Abe (Japan flood: At least 179 dead after worst weather in decades, 2018) "at a party with lawmakers just as rains intensified. Many social media users have criticised their actions. 'Has he read the news and heard about the rains and landslides?' one user asked on Twitter. 'Is the word refrain in his dictionary?' 'They're inside safe and drinking, when others are outside struggling. Senators, I thought you'd care more for your people,' another added."

Leaders of Indonesia and the United States came in for less criticism. President Joko Widodo of Indonesia was criticized by villagers (Indonesia tsunami: Frustration in remote areas waiting for aid, 2018). Yahdi Basma, from an area south of Palu, said: "The president is not hearing about the remote areas, only about the tsunami and about Palu." President Donald Trump of the United States, who had blamed forest management policy for the severity of wildfires, was criticized by the California Professional Firefighters (California wildfires: Is Trump right when he blames forest managers?, 2018).

INFRASTRUCTURE

Blaming infrastructure for shortcomings in prevention or response to the natural disaster was an element of coverage in seven of the eight disasters and was especially common in the wildfires of Greece. Most of the blame was from governmental officials and article authors. The infrastructure blaming fell into two interlapping themes, one based upon causes of the disaster and the other responses to the disaster, including problems during escape from danger.

Causes

In Greece, infrastructure causes included land use and road-building practices. For instance (Lack of early warning, town planning led to high death toll, 2018), "Researchers found that the narrow streets and numerous dead-ends that blocked off escape routes to the sea, as well as the absence of large public spaces in Mati, an area built up with no town planning, also contributed to the high death toll." Similarly, Prime Minister Alexis Tsipras (Mitsotakis insists heads must roll, 2018) "has promised that the state will conduct an inquiry as to why hundreds of people found themselves trapped in the flames with no way of escape. He has also vowed to crack down on unlicensed construction, which the investigation has revealed blocked off escape routes toward the sea." The other main target of infrastructure overlapped with response—illegal construction (Greek government sent out spin guidelines after lethal wildfires, 2018). "Officials were also instructed to make the case that illegal construction was the main reason behind the high death toll at the seaside settlement." In addition (Government issues decree for demolition of illegal construction, 2018), "Rampant illegal construction in eastern Attica, where dozens of people died in wildfires last month, has been widely blamed for the magnitude of the tragedy."

In Nigeria, drainage was the primary infrastructure cause. For instance (Ojewale, 2018), "The causes are clear. Sewage system blockages and rise in ground water level have been cited by some environmental experts as the main causes of flooding in Nigeria." Dam management was another cause, including eighty-nine communities that were flooded when water was released from Jebba Dam (Ololade, 2018), with a public relations officer of NSEMA stating that people should have been resettled before the construction of the dam. A Nigerian government engineer, Mustapha Maihaja, mentioned drainage and offered a more complex cause (Flooding: Avoiding the fury of nature, 2018): "The felling of trees without replacement leaves more carbon dioxide in the atmosphere which causes ozone depletion. This simply means that the iceberg separating the sun from having direct impact on the earth causes rapid melting of the ice from above, while excess carbon dioxide from the earth also enhances rapid melting of the ice from under. Thus, there is need for tree planting by everyone to checkmate the continuous heavy rainfall."

In Pakistan, infrastructure was blamed for the heat wave through construction and development, pollution, and the lack of trees. Environmentalist Nasar Usmani said (As sea breeze resumes, Karachi gets some respite, 2018): "There is an urgent need to stop constructions in Karachi and to bring an end to the city's vertical and horizontal expansion. . . . Now this city needs more trees, not more buildings and concrete structures." As explained by "Yet another heatwave to hit city in a week" (2018), "The urban heat island effect is another cause of concern in Karachi. In the absence of sea breeze for several days, the city's temperature remains hot even in the night as the trillions of tons of concrete which traps heat during the day, starts radiating the heat in the night and there is no respite for the people during the day and night for several consecutive days, experts said." Dr Noman Ahmed, dean of Architecture and Management Sciences, listed several causes for hot weather in Karachi, including development and environmental pollution, fed by a luxurious lifestyle ('Revival of agriculture fields in rural Karachi can minimise heatwave effects', 2018).

In Papua New Guinea, letter writer Kelly Matoli argued that oil and gas extraction activities contributed to the earthquake (Matoli, 2018):

> I therefore negate the "Rim of Fire" explanation and hold the assumption the extraction operations could have had a contributing factor, especially if franking was used. This earthquake is now a lesson that as custodians of our natural resources, we must be informed and be made aware of during the initial negotiating stages of any development proposals, of the likely positive and negative impacts of the extraction techniques proposed so that we can be better prepared.

The wildfires in the United States were blamed on problems with electric transmission lines (California wildfires: Town of Paradise will need 'total rebuild', 2018), along with people living in houses built of combustible materials (California wildfires: Is Trump right when he blames forest managers?, 2018). In addition, the hills and forests around Paradise made evacuation difficult (Nicas et al., 2018). In Indonesia, an advanced tsunami warning system was in place, but was not working and a replacement system had been delayed (Indonesia earthquake and tsunami: How warning system failed the victims?, 2018). In Japan, Shiro Maeno, an Okayama University professor of river engineering, said the flood disaster might have been reduced if a project to widen the Oda River had been completed (Risk of deadly flood in badly hit area of Okayama Prefecture known in advance, 2018).

Responses

Responses that reflect blame were especially common in the wildfires of Greece, with the head of state and other governmental officials the most frequent sources. These responses to the disaster suggested that the officials recognized the problem, accepted blame, and were taking steps to prevent future disasters. An issue in Greece was demolishing illegal buildings that may have caused or worsened the wildfires and preventing such construction in the future. According to investigators (As fire victims named, their stories emerge, 2018), "most of the properties in Mati, the settlement in eastern Attica that was hardest hit in the fires, had been illegally built." Addressing future hazards was also tied to the prime minister. For instance (Kambas & Papadimas, 2018), "Tsipras, whose government has been accused of a slow response, said Greece must no longer allow illegal construction that has been common for decades in a country dogged by bureaucracy and corruption. 'The chaos of unruly construction, which threatens human lives, can no longer be tolerated,' Tsipras said." Greek government spokesman Dimitris Tzanakopoulos announced (More than 3,100 illegal buildings slated for demolition, 2018) "the government will begin work to crack down on illegal construction, which experts said made the fire even worse."

In the U.S. wildfires, responses explored the ongoing threat of people living in risky areas. One article (California wildfires: Is Trump right when he blames forest managers?, 2018) cited a 2010 federal report estimating nearly one-third of California residents lived in fire-prone areas. Nicas, Fuller and Arango (2018) stated: "Many California towns, especially those near wildlands, are vulnerable. 'It could happen anywhere,' [said Paradise mayor Jody Jones]. 'It seems like we have more natural disasters now that come at us quicker and affect large numbers of people at the same time. There's no easy solution for it.'"

In the other natural disasters, just a handful of passages dealt with infrastructure as a response. In Nigeria, governmental officials planned to manage future flooding. One article (Flooding: Avoiding the fury of nature, 2018) suggested "government may consider building more water channels like canals, dikes and levees. Our preparedness for the peak of rainy season, effective natural disaster management and emergency response can, to a large extent, reduce the risk of flood disaster. We may not be able to prevent rains from unleashing floods, but we can mitigate adverse humanitarian effects."

In Japan, infrastructure blame revolved around emergency crew access to flood victims. Mototaka Inaba, a doctor with the NPO Peace Winds Japan, said (Johnston, 2018b): "Ambulances and rescue vehicles could not initially get through as the roads were out." In Indonesia, said Sutopo Purwo Nugroho, spokesman for the National Disaster Mitigation Agency (Indonesia earthquake and tsunami: How warning system failed the victims, 2018), "Communication is limited, heavy machinery is limited." Similarly, a communication breakdown affected the response in Papua New Guinea, with mobile phones and landlines not operating (Let's get earthquake relief aid moving, 2018).

NATURE

Weather and climate change were blamed in several natural disasters, especially in the two wildfires, flooding in Japan and the heat wave in Pakistan. Source of blame came mostly from the writer of the article, governmental sources, and experts.

Climate Change or Global Warming

Organizations, governmental sources, experts, miscellaneous sources, and writers of articles were among those directly tying or speculating that climate change or global warming was at least partially responsible for the natural disasters. This was particularly common in the wildfires. Environmental organizations (Pitas & Maltezou, 2018) and a European Union expert (Becatoros & Gatopoulos, 2018) blamed climate change as a factor in Greece's forest fires. In the latter story, Christos Stylianides, the EU commissioner for humanitarian aid and crisis management, said: "Climate change is real. It's not fake news." Greek leaders also attributed the fire severity to climate change. Prime Minister Alexis Tsipras linked the fires to challenges posed by climate change (Nedos et al., 2018). Greece's alternate minister of Public Order and Citizen Protection, Nikos Toskas, blamed climate change for the gale force winds that fanned the fires in Greece, adding that the country had never before experienced such strong winds (Italy, Romania sending more aircraft, 2018). Alternate Minister for Agriculture Yiannis Tsironis linked the fires to global warming and said (Souliotis & Antoniou, 2018) he felt responsible "because we cannot explain to our people what climate change will bring." Writers made mostly indirect connections between the Greek fires and climate change. One story read (Greece wildfires: Search for missing family members after 80 people die, 2018): "While no individual weather event can be linked to climate change, a general correlation does exist between warmer global temperatures and the dry conditions that can spark several dangerous fires at once."

Climate change, along with weather and population shifts, was mentioned as causes of wildfires in the United States (California wildfires: Trump visits state's deadliest blaze, 2018), perhaps tied to drought as well (Johnson, 2018). The National Climate Assessment report, issued by the federal government before the wildfires, listed global warming as reasons for fire becoming bigger and more dangerous (Krugman, 2018). California governor Jerry Brown said (California wildfires: Death toll reaches grim milestone, 2018): "This is not the new normal, this is the new abnormal. . . . We are vulnerable because of climate change; the extreme weather events and our extended drought is part of it." Some stories made indirect mention of climate change and wildfires, for instance (California wildfires: Death toll reaches grim milestone, 2018) "Historically, California's 'wildfire season' started in summer and ran into early autumn. But experts have warned that the risk is now year-round."

Global warming or climate change was also listed as a cause for disasters in Nigeria, Pakistan, and Japan. Professor Junaid Asimiyu Mohammed attributed flooding in Nigeria to climate change mixed with human activities (Adeyemi et al., 2018). Increasing rainfall in Nigeria was attributed by some to climate change (Why does Nigeria keep flooding?, 2018). Pakistan climate change ministry spokesperson Mohammad Saleem linked extreme heat waves to global warming (Heatwave woes to worsen further as temperature spikes steadily, 2018). A community activist in Pakistan held heat waves responsible for ocean warming, killing crabs. Gulab Shah said (Khaskheli, 2018): "Marine heat waves may become more common in coming years." In Japan, scientists argued that flooding and heavy rains in recent years was due to climate change, causing warmer air and rainfall (Feeling the heat of climate change, 2018).

Story writers asserted that climate change was a cause of flooding in Japan (Feeling the heat of climate change, 2018): "This is not a one-off experience: This is the new normal. . . . Governments and societies must do more to stop climate change—reduce greenhouse gas emissions—as well as work to mitigate the impact of this grim reality." An editorial argued (Protect the socially weak from heat waves, 2018):

> What we seem to be witnessing is that extreme weather events are happening so frequently—due at least partly to the effects of climate change—that they can no longer be dismissed as 'unusual.' Long-term forecasts on weather patterns worldwide indicate that the extreme weather conditions that we're experiencing with increasing frequency may not be so uncommon in the future. . . . The concentration of heat-related health problems among elderly people, coupled with the growing risk of extreme temperatures caused by climate change, means that Japan must take additional measures to protect its rapidly growing population of elderly people—particularly as an increasing number of them live alone and some may be isolated from the rest of the local community. . . . As weather patterns continue to change, it is society's weakest members whose health will be impacted the most. Society as a whole must think of what can be done to protect them.

Weather

Weather was a source of blame in stories about natural disasters, especially in suggesting the reasons why the latest incident was so severe. This was common in the Pakistan heat wave, as stories warned people that weather patterns, including low pressure in the sea and upper Sindh, would lead to continued hot weather (Mercury soars to 42 degrees again, 2018). Pakistan Meteorological Department chief Dr. Ghulam Rasool said (As sea breeze resumes, Karachi gets some respite, 2018): "These low pressure areas cut off sea breeze towards the coast, especially towards Karachi, and under the influence of warm and dry winds the city's temperature starts shooting." According to Karachi Met Office Director Abdur Rashid, the rise occurred after sea breeze stopped and wind from northwesterly direction started blowing in the city (Mercury soars to 42 degrees again, 2018).

In the United States, President Donald Trump rejected climate change and blamed the scale of the fires on a lack of rain (California wildfires: Trump visits state's deadliest blaze, 2018). Scott Stephens, a leading authority on wildfires at the University of California, pointed to the larger number of dead trees due to drought and disease (California wildfires: Is Trump right when he blames forest managers?, 2018). Weather exacerbated the response to the wildfires in Greece, as high-speed winds that abruptly changed directions interfered with evacuation (Maltezou, 2018b). In Japan, one editorial speculated that (Find and fix the weak points in disaster defenses, 2018) "Extreme weather of unprecedented scale, like the heavy rains that caused the extensive damage in western Japan, is expected to occur with increasing frequency. We need to scrutinize our defenses against such disasters, identify the weak points and fix them." Another editorial opined (protect the socially weak from heat waves, 2018): "Given the greater frequency of such extreme weather, society must make more concerted and continuous efforts to better protect its weakest members from the hazards of extreme temperatures, including heatstroke, which claims hundreds of lives each year."

CRIMINALITY

Establishing criminal behavior as responsible for the natural disaster was nearly all tied to the wildfires in Greece, especially speculation from government officials that the fires were deliberately set. One suggestion was that arsonists were looking to loot abandoned homes (Greece wildfires: Dozens dead in Attica region, 2018); government spokesman Dimitris Tzanakopoulos said, "Fifteen fires had started simultaneously on three different fronts in Athens." Alternate Citizens' Protection Minister Nikos Toskas (Minister says 'serious indications' of arson behind deadly wildfire, 2018) said: "We have serious indications of criminal acts . . . lots of fires appeared in a very short period of time." Authorities blamed illegal construction for blocking escape routes (Greece wildfires: Emergency chiefs replaced, 2018) and the Hellenic Fire Service's arson department suggested the main fire that reached Mati was due to negligence (Man arrested for arson in Marathonas, 2018), leading to the arrest of one man for multiple acts of arson. However, other government officials disputed arson as a cause. For instance (Greek gov't shrugs off blame in handling of deadly fire, 2018) "a report from the fire service's arson department (DAEE), which suggested the cause was negligence." Article writers attributed some fires to (Georgiopoulos & Kambas, 2018) "a crude attempt to clear forest land for building."

The only other natural disaster in which criminal behavior was blamed was in the aftermath of the earthquake and tsunami in Indonesia. According to Nasution (2018), "Certain individuals who rob, steal, and loot the properties of other people, who are also suffering from this devastating disaster, particularly goods which are not basic necessities, should be treated as criminals."

BUSINESSES, ORGANIZATIONS

Nearly all of the blame targeting businesses or organizations was from government or people blaming an electrical utility for the wildfires in the United States, as (California fires: Winds propel fires as death toll rises, 2018) the "electrical companies may have suffered malfunctions near the sources shortly before the fires began." Most of the blame went to Pacific Gas & Electric, a privately owned utility. According to Penn and Eavis (2018), "State officials have determined that electrical equipment owned by PG&E, including power lines and poles, was responsible for at least 17 of 21 major fires in Northern California last fall. . . . PG&E's 'safety culture' has been the subject of a three-year investigation by the state's Public Utilities Commission." Several people filed a lawsuit against Pacific Gas & Electric, causing a stock market plunge that equaled a market value of $16 billion (California wildfires: Town of Paradise will need 'total rebuild', 2018). Critics said that poor maintenance of power poles and failure to trim vegetation around power lines was a cause of fires (Penn & Eavis, 2018).

PEOPLE, CULTURE, SOCIETY

Government officials, experts, and article writers were most likely to blame people, culture, or society for the disaster and/or its aftermath, with blame scattered across five disasters. Blame from government was registered in the Guatemala, Nigeria, and U.S. disasters. In Guatemala, the government asserted that alerts were issued, but were ignored by people (Guatemala volcano: Emergency agency 'failed to heed warnings', 2018). In Nigeria, a government official pointed his finger at deforestation as responsible for serious flooding (Why does Nigeria keep flooding?, 2018). In the United States, a story (California wildfires: Is Trump right when he blames forest managers?, 2018) noted that California law requires homeowner to clear or reduce vegetation near their properties, which may have contributed to the wildfires.

Experts blamed people and culture for the two wildfires. In Greece, European Commissioner for Humanitarian Aid and Crisis Management

Christos Stylianides said (Peloni, 2018): "We urgently need to cultivate a culture that responds to the effects of climate change." In the United States (California wildfires: Is Trump right when he blames forest managers?, 2018), "research by the Hoover Institute earlier this year raised concerns over public awareness, enforcement and the availability of up-to-date information about the areas at most risk." An expert suggested "other types of landscape such grass and shrub land" to clear out vegetation (California wildfires: Is Trump right when he blames forest managers?, 2018).

Other blame toward people, culture, or society came from an article writer in Nigeria, who wrote (Why does Nigeria keep flooding?, 2018): "The dumping of waste in the streets can also prevent the steady flow of water and put pressure on the few urban drainage systems." Another example came from the Greek Orthodox Church during a memorial service, stating that (Tears, grief at memorial service for Greek wildfire victims, 2018) "the burden of responsibility weighs upon everyone to avoid actions that hinder the protection of the environment."

EVALUATION OF BLAME, RESPONSIBILITY

Attributing blame or responsibility potentially served a cathartic role in allowing people upset by the natural disaster to vent their concerns. In turn, this could remove anxiety from readers, allowing them to cope by giving them a sense of control. A natural disaster appears overwhelming, so having a focal point to target blame restores some control and suggests it could be prevented. Peace journalism (Tenenboim-Weinblatt et al., 2016) suggests attributing responsibility as a means to address conflict.

Government was the most common target of blame or responsibility, with common themes of an inadequate response to the disaster (evacuation plans, support and relief supplies, addressing the ongoing disaster), failure to prevent or mitigate the disaster (lack of warning, inadequate planning, poor management), general governmental incompetence, and poor response to the public. Blame or responsibility came from a wide range of sources, including article writers, government, unaffiliated people, and the country's leader, suggesting a wide-open opportunity for the airing of grievances.

The nation's leader was targeted for similar reasons, with more emphasis on political responsibility and calls to resign, along with poor response to the crisis and lack of sensitivity toward those affected. Infrastructure blame arose primarily from government officials and writers, with causes (including poor planning, construction, insufficient roads, or drainage) more common than responses. Nature was blamed through climate change or weather, with climate change depicted as the new normal, hinting the possibility of more disasters in the future. Lesser blame or responsibility went to criminality (especially arson in Greek wildfires); businesses and organizations (primarily one private electrical utility in the United States); and people, culture, society (such as ignoring warnings, contributing to the disaster and a lack of awareness).

Chapter 14

External Validation

Examples of external validation contained messages that inferred the affected area was not alone, that others outside the community and nation were offering support. Tangible support aided healing and recovery, while intangible sentiments promoted hope. Outside validation was especially common in the Indonesia and Greece disasters. The most common sources were other governments, with businesses and nongovernmental organizations also providing some support. The most common subthemes were sympathy and solidarity.

Help to Indonesia, ranging from material assistance to condolences, came primarily from countries in Asia and Europe, along with international sources. A partial list of countries providing external validation includes regional powers like Japan, South Korea, China, Singapore, and India; the European Union and members such as Germany and the United Kingdom; plus Russia, the United States, and Saudi Arabia. Additional support came from the International Monetary Fund, the World Bank, an affiliation of fourteen UK charities, and other relief organizations. In the Greece wildfires, external validation came from governments of Europe, especially the European Union, Cyprus, Germany, and Italy. Turkey, Australia, and the United States also offered support, along with Prince Charles and Pope Francis. Among the other countries, most of the external validation in Guatemala came from the United States, Mexico, the United Nations, the Central American Bank for Economic Integration, Bolivia, and Spain. In Japan, external validation came primarily from the United States and France.

Chapter 14

SYMPATHY

In Indonesia, world leaders sent messages of condolences to the president. Philippine foreign secretary Alan Peter Cayetano said (Assegaf, 2018): "We grieve with our Indonesian brothers and sisters and stand hand in hand with them in praying for all of those who lost their lives in this tragedy." The German ambassador designate to Indonesia, Peter Schoof, led a moment of silence for victims and those affected by earthquake and tsunami (Fitriyanti, 2018). UN secretary-general António Guterres said (Assegaf, 2018): "Our hearts go out to all affected by the earthquake and tsunami. My deepest condolences to all who have lost family and friends."

In Greece, sympathy was a major part of external validation, mostly coming from fellow Europeans. Prince Charles offered condolences in a letter to the Greek president (Condolences pour in over Greek fires, 2018) "Our hearts go out to all the families who have been so cruelly bereaved, and our deepest sympathy to those who have been injured or whose property has been destroyed." French president Emmanuel Macron wrote (Triandafllou & Konstantinidis, 2018): "Our thoughts go to Greece and the victims of the terrible fires." Norway's Ambassador to Greece, Jørn Gjelstad, wrote (Norwegian envoy 'shocked' by wildfire deaths in east Attica, 2018) "My deepest compassion & condolences to the victims and their families." Italy's president Sergio Mattarella expressed his "sincere and deep support" for the families of the victims, the injured, and the rescue workers (Condolences pour in over Greek fires, 2018). European Commission President Jean-Claude Juncker wrote to Greek prime minister Alexis Tsipras (Commission chief writes to Greek PM to express condolences over deadly fires, 2018): "It is with a heavy heart that I have learnt that many people have tragically lost their lives in devastating fires in Athens, Greece."

In Guatemala, sympathy arrived in a statement saying that South Korea (Aguilar, 2018b) "hopes that Guatemala will overcome as soon as possible the immeasurable pain caused by this painful event." Japan prime minister Shinzo Abe used Twitter to thank U.S. president Donald Trump and French leader Emmanuel Macron for offering their condolences (Johnson, 2018). Abe tweeted: "Sincerely appreciate Donald's warm words of condolences and solidarity, and precious support from the U.S. including volunteers from the U.S. Forces in Iwakuni." Trump wrote: "Our prayers are with those affected by the flooding in Japan. We commend the rescue efforts and offer condolences to all who were injured or lost loved ones."

SOLIDARITY

Stories highlighted friendship between Indonesia and other countries around the world. United States Department spokesperson Heather Nauert said

(Assegaf, 2018): "The United States and Indonesia are strategic partners and friends, and we stand ready to assist in the relief effort." Indonesia president Joko Widodo saw aid as recognition; for instance, he said (Economic activities begin to recover in tsunami devastated Donggala, 2018): "We are not alone in facing this difficult time." And, in a story listing support from eleven world leaders, Widodo wrote on his Facebook account (Assegaf, 2018), "It sends across a strong message that we are not alone in these difficult times." Other themes of external validation were recognition of the country's solidarity and expressions of sympathy. World Bank CEO Kristalina Georgieva said (World Bank offers five million dollars of grant for C Sulawesi earthquake reconstruction, 2018): "On behalf of the international community, I say your solidarity is very strong, so we really appreciate and respect the government and the community."

In Greece, support from Turkey was particularly noteworthy due to their long and complicated history, including a war in the early twentieth century. Residents of the Turkish town of Izmir displayed banners of support (one read "hold strong neighbor"), lit candles, and laid flowers at a makeshift shrine to the victims (Turks express solidarity for Greeks outside consulate in Izmir, 2018). The United Nations and NATO offered support, along with Australia, China, and the United States. Pope Francis expressed solidarity with the Greek people (Pope Francis sends message of support to Greek president after wildfires, 2018).

Another theme was others vowing to support Greece or express solidarity. European Council President Donald Tusk said (Tusk: 'Europe will stand by our Greek friends', 2018): "Europe will stand by our Greek friends in these difficult times. Help is on its way from several EU countries." German chancellor Angela Merkel said (Germany offers help to combat Greece fires, 2018) that "in these difficult hours Germany stands firmly by the side of our Greek friends." NATO secretary-general Jens Stoltenberg said that the transatlantic alliance "stands in solidarity with the Greek people" (NATO 'in solidarity with the Greek people,' alliance chief says, 2018). Australia's Prime Minister Malcolm Turnbull wrote (Australia PM: 'A tragedy that affects Greece also affects Australia', 2018): "Australia and Greece share a special relationship nurtured by strong family and community ties," adding that, "A tragedy that affects Greece also affects Australia." Additional support came from nongovernmental entities. Media outlets in Cyprus organized a charity concert and collection drive in support of wildfire victims in Greece ('Tsunami' of support for Greek fire victims in Cyprus, 2018). Airbnb opened homes to displaced residents for no charge (Suliman, 2018).

In Guatemala, solidarity was a key attribute of support from Spain, in which Guatemalans in Barcelona (Herrera & Pinto, 2018) "joined the solidarity and contributed their grain of sand." The executive president of the Central

American Bank for Economic Integration, Dr. Nick Rischbieth (Aguilar, 2018b) "expressed his solidarity with the people of Guatemala and expressed his condolences to the relatives of the deceased." Solidarity was also used to describe support from the United Nations and friendly countries (Perez, 2018). U.S. vice president Mike Pence said (Pence will visit Guatemala and meet with victims of the Volcán de Fuego, 2018): "Today I promise you that we will continue to support the people of Guatemala while recovering and rebuilding because that is what good neighbors do."

In Papua New Guinea, the United States Agency for International Development offered aid as well; U.S. ambassador Catherine Ebert-Gray thanked USAid and said (Wahune, 2018): "As Americans, we have been waking up every day thinking of our colleagues up in the earthquake-affected areas.... Americans have a long history of working in the Highlands, mostly as missionaries, anthropologists, health workers, and all sorts of different aspects of service."

OTHER EXTERNAL VALIDATION THEMES

One prominent feature in Indonesia's *Antara News* was to link external validation to Indonesia's president or government. Stories explicitly mentioned respect for the president; for instance, China's president Jinping (Assegaf, 2018) "believes that under the strong leadership of President Jokowi and the Indonesian government, Indonesians will certainly overcome this disaster." Even within the country, aid was attached to the president (Indonesia needs more tents, fogging for earthquake-hit area, 2018). Coordinating minister for Political, Legal, and Security Affairs Wiranto attributed the international aid to "President Joko Widodo's visits to foreign countries were aimed at enhancing bilateral, as well as multilateral ties. We appreciate all this help." International Monetary Fund executive director Christine Lagarde said she appreciated the Indonesian government's handling of the disaster (IMF managing director visits victims of Lombok earthquake, 2018): "We are amazed at the way the government has handled the situation, allowing the children to go back to school to pursue their studies." Similarly, a written statement from the U.S. Embassy in Jakarta was cited (Trump calls Jokowi, offers US aid for earthquake victims, 2018): "Trump appreciated the leadership of the Indonesian government in responding to the crisis." In turn, Indonesia's president was portrayed as appreciating the support, such as a Facebook post that thanked King Salman Al Saud and to the Saudi people (Saudi King expresses condolences over Central Sulawesi earthquake, 2018).

In Papua New Guinea, most of the external validation came from businesses within the country, including Ela Motors (Ela Motors gives K50,000 to earthquake victims, 2018) and the Lae Snax Tigers rugby team (Andrew, 2018). In Nigeria, the nongovernmental organization and the Economic Community of West African States provided the bulk of external validation, primarily through offering improved prevention for future flooding (Flooding: Edo distributes relief materials to victims, 2018). The European Commission allocated funds for climate service development (Yahaya, 2018), including Africa.

EVALUATION OF EXTERNAL VALIDATION

Sympathy and solidarity from countries outside the affected area brought a sense of compassion from others, leading to perceptions that others care about their plight. Monetary support gave those affected tangible and material support that can aid physical recovery. External validation also aided healing, hope, and recovery by raising a large psychological sense of concern by showing that others cared about the damaged. The nature of external validation, primarily involving the affected nation, other governments, and nongovernmental organizations, meant that sources were exclusively drawn from top-level officials.

Sympathy came from world leaders and was directed at the people of the affected countries, often addressed to the country's leader. Compassionate words from the international community and celebrities can make others feel comfortable. Solidarity themes stressed how foreign countries and other entities sent messages of a shared relationship with the afflicted country and promised support. External validation was also represented by themes such as stories from Indonesia that explicitly mentioned respect for the president from leaders of other countries and how that respect led to aid. This could reassure Indonesians that their president was benefitting their lives.

Chapter 15

Analysis By Country

Analysis of news coverage about the eight natural disasters covered in previous chapters was focused around themes related to healing, coping, hope, and recovery. This chapter reviews the patterns of emphasis related to each disaster, taking into account the context and journalistic conditions present in each disaster.

GREECE'S WILDFIRES

Nearly two in five of the stories analyzed in this book were about the Greek disaster, far more than any other event, with 94% of those appearing in the local news source, *Kathimerini*. The nature of the wildfires—which often have clear and confined boundaries—may have made reporting easier by establishing safe zones where people escaping the fires could gather and be interviewed by journalists. The most devastating fire took place in Mati, a densely populated resort town on the Aegean Sea, further limiting where people could find safety. Since Mati is just 32 kilometers by road from Athens, it was a short trip for journalists from the country's largest city. Greece's status as having a partly free press and high levels of political freedom meant few governmental limits on reporting.

By theme, stories about the Greek wildfires drew relatively high levels of blame or responsibility, death stories, actions and external validation, and relatively low levels of survivors and selfless behavior.

The contentious political landscape of Greece, coupled with relatively free political and press systems, made blame or responsibility a theme in 47% of the stories. Stories often featured opposition parties blaming the Alexis Tsipras government, the federal government blaming local officials, and people affected by the fires blaming a wide range of authorities. The Greek press system has historically been party oriented and EuroTopics (Kathimerini report, nd) classifies *Kathimerini*'s political orientation as conservative. Tsipras was leader of the left-wing party Coalition of the Radical Left (Syriza), which ruled until they were forced out in 2019. Perhaps the conservative orientation of *Kathimerini* made the newspaper less likely to withhold blame of the socialist ruling party. That's in line with predictions from Papathanassopoulos (2001) of journalists adopting the political position of their news organization, but contrary to assertions from Iosifidis and Boucas (2015) of a journalistic culture cautious about reporting news embarrassing to state officials. Additionally, Dimitrakopoulou (2017) found that Greek journalists emphasized current affairs and information people need to make political decisions, along with limited faith in public institutions, which fit into stories focused on blame or responsibility involving governmental and political matters.

Wildfires that still needed to be doused, along with sources of concerns (including illegal construction and alleged incompetence of officials), triggered a constant flow of needs for action. This offers parallel evidence to the political emphasis of blame or responsibility stories, as the actions provide answers to the causes and inform political choices that Greek journalists prefer (Dimitrakopoulou, 2017). The local publication in Greece readily turned to government officials to explain ongoing and anticipated actions to deal with wildfires.

High levels of death stories were likely due to the centralized nature of the disaster, as family and friends of victims, including those who were with the deceased during the wildfires, were relatively easy for journalists to locate. Stories in *Kathimerini* provided several anecdotes of fire victims from their friends and relatives, bringing a personal touch to stories that turned the deceased into well-rounded people.

High levels of external validation may be tied to Greece's status as one of the poorer countries in the European Union, with more than half of the examples of sympathy or aid coming from other countries in Europe. Perhaps this reflected a cultural affinity in more support from fellow EU members and/or similar social identities between Greek journalists and other European countries.

The relatively low levels of survivor and selfless behavior stories were partially a product of the large volume of stories about the Greek disaster, as coverage did include a fair amount of such stories (fourteen survivor, twelve selfless). Journalists did not avoid those story themes—instead, it may have been a product of editorial choices. Although the frequency of survivor stories was relatively low among the eight disasters, the Greek wildfire stories had the second-most paragraphs about survivors. The anecdotes about survivors and selfless behaviors came mostly from witnesses and survivors rather than government or other official sources.

GUATEMALA'S VOLCANIC ERUPTION

About 10% of the stories were drawn from the volcanic eruption in Guatemala, with 80% of those in *La Hora*, the local publication. As a small country with little wealth and surrounded by even smaller and poorer countries, the limited worldwide attention toward the disaster in Guatemala may reflect a lack of baseline awareness toward Central America overall. That is, a worldview that has largely ignored the region has less interest in a disaster that seems so remote. Another obstacle was difficulties reaching the mountainous terrain around the volcano. The country's status on the low end of political freedom may have further limited attention; consider the tale of volunteers from Mexico who did not readily gain entry to help the disaster in Guatemala (Gamez, 2018).

By theme, news coverage about Guatemala's disaster was relatively high in three themes—selfless behavior; community, cohesion, and intimacy; and faith, belief, and salvation, and relatively low in actions and blame or responsibility.

Selfless behavior was a product of the suddenness of the disaster and the response in a country that depends on individual help to deal with inequalities. The volcanic eruption triggered lahars that engulfed entire villages with little warning, leaving people at the scene to help each other escape. Stories from Guatemala often highlighted churches and organizations helping others, using those nongovernmental sources in stories. Although previous published work did not specifically address motivations or characteristics of journalists in Guatemala, the story themes painted a picture of news workers who readily sought out stories about selfless behavior by people hit by the volcanic eruption.

Guatemala's disasters triggered the most examples of collectivity and solidarity, a theme within community, cohesion, and intimacy, among all of the disasters. This fits with Hofstede (2001), whose analysis placed Guatemala as the most collective among seventy-one countries analyzed. Solidarity was primarily a response to the emergency, as people gathered together, both physically and virtually, to aid their survival. Perhaps the small population and lack of wealth leads to people building stronger personal relationships to thrive. Additionally, journalists may have identified with the psychological distress that the volcanic eruption unleashed, such that they felt solidarity with fellow Guatemalans. Columnists with *La Hora* offered most of the profound examples of collectivity and solidarity, suggesting they saw a critical journalistic role to remind people of their shared fate and responsibilities as part of healing and recovery.

Faith, belief, and salvation content may be a product of the religiosity of Guatemala, in which 89% of the population identifies with a religion, mostly Christians (Guatemala-religion, nd). This points to socialization of journalists who likely grew up with fellow Christians and may have also been Christians. Writers and survivors were common sources of faith, belief, and salvation in Guatemala.

News about Guatemala's disaster was relatively low in actions, perhaps due to the nature of the disaster, in which no obvious actions were needed to cope with the disaster beyond aiding those who lost homes. For similar reasons, blame or responsibility stories were low since there was little that officials could have done to mitigate the disaster other than more quickly evacuate people from the threat. Perhaps the relatively low levels of press freedom and political freedom played a role, although some blame was leveled toward national leaders for a delayed response to the disaster.

INDONESIA'S EARTHQUAKE AND TSUNAMI

With the second-most volume of stories in this analysis (20.6%), Indonesia's twin disasters of an earthquake and tsunami received heavy coverage in the local news organization (76% of the coverage about Indonesia's tragedies). Indonesia's disaster caused the most deaths and widespread destruction, suggesting both short- and long-term impact on the country, one reason for the heavy coverage. The breadth of the disaster area in a large country with a vibrant media ecology may have made it convenient for journalists to reach affected areas and victims.

Coverage about Indonesia was in the middle in frequency of most themes, with two significant exceptions: first in external validation and last in blame or responsibility. Both characteristics fall in line with the country's political environment, in which media are evaluated as partially free, but sometimes obstructed by government or private actors (Indonesia report, 2017). Certainly there is room to argue that government could do little to prevent or mitigate an earthquake and tsunami, thus not a target of blame, but the only critique about malfunctioning tsunami warning buoys appeared in just a BBC story (Indonesia earthquake and tsunami: How warning system failed the victims, 2018).

In turn, the high frequency of stories about external validation demonstrates support for the ruling government. Several stories specifically mentioned President Joko Widodo receiving sympathy or aid, or praised his response to the disasters. External validation came from countries around the world and nongovernmental organizations, demonstrating breadth of recognition to the plight of Indonesians and the role of their leaders. The most common sources were Indonesia's leaders, especially the president, and leaders from other countries, typically expressing sympathy toward their plight and confidence in Indonesia's leaders to deal with the problems.

JAPAN'S FLOODS

Stories from flooding in Japan represented just 6% of the sample (79% of those in the local publication), perhaps due to the widespread flooding and the publications analyzed. Heavy rain affected large portions of the country, making no geographic focal point for news attention. While Japan has several of the largest newspapers in the world, the publication used in this study (*Japan Times*) is much smaller and published in English, making it targeted to a specialized segment of the audience inside the country and people outside of Japan.

By theme, coverage from Japan was relatively high in recovery efforts and low in death stories; community, cohesion, and intimacy; and reassurance, purpose, or meaning. Journalists in Japan face few political barriers to reporting, as the country has high levels of press and political freedom.

The emphasis on recovery efforts may reflect the nature of the news organizations and the country's wealth. One common theme was officials and volunteers digging mud and debris out of people's homes, sending a message to readers of the country's current and future needs in establishing shelters, rebuilding and reestablishing normalcy. Stories depended heavily on government and business officials to articulate recovery efforts, along with victims left homeless by flooding.

Death stories were completely absent from the coverage, fitting an Asian culture within journalism that emphasizes the group over the individual (Winfield et al., 2000). Explanations for the absence of stories in the themes of community, cohesion, and intimacy, and reassurance, purpose, or meaning, may reflect news outlets that are less directly targeted at the average Japanese-speaking person within the country.

NIGERIA'S FLOODS

With just sixteen stories (3%, all but two in the local newspaper), the floods in Nigeria produced the fewest stories among the disasters, although several of those stories were among the longest in the sample. As in Japan, floods affected such a wide area that it was difficult to find a center of the disaster zone. Unlike Japan, however, Nigeria is low in wealth and stories indicated a limited and heavily damaged transportation system, adding logistical barriers to journalists. Some stories highlighted rivers as key transportation corridors, the same rivers that were swollen with rain and debris.

By theme frequency, Nigeria was first in four themes and second in three themes, perhaps due to the stories being longer than those found in other disasters, allowing more themes within a story. Stories from Nigeria were at the top for actions; blame or responsibility; death stories; and community, cohesion, and intimacy.

The widespread impact of flooding led to actions of immediate needs, including goods and supplies, relief items, and rebuilding. The vast majority of sources used in stories about actions were from government officials, including state leaders, flood control managers, and federal legislators. Thus, government was at the center of actions in news portrayal.

Blame or responsibility in Nigeria primarily targeted government and infrastructure, much of it originating from survivors who lost family or goods. Many were personal narratives told in chronological order, matching the preempirical style of oral discourse described by Bourgault (1995) as common in sub-Saharan Africa.

High numbers of death stories and survivor stories further fit the oral discourse (Bourgault, 1995; Schaefer, 2003) of very personal and emotional language from survivors, friends, and family. People who knew the deceased were given space in the news to tell details and motivations of their friends or relatives, giving depth to the dead. Survivors were the main sources in telling about their own dramatic escapes. Emphasis on community, cohesion, and intimacy fits the precolonial values of group orientation, continuity, harmony, and balance identified by Bourgault (1995). Survivors and government officials were the main sources in Nigeria in stories about community, cohesion, and intimacy.

PAKISTAN'S HEAT WAVE

All of the thirty-two articles (6%) about the heat wave in Pakistan came from the local publication, the *News International*, the largest English-language newspaper in the country. The absence of any coverage in BBC perhaps reflects the nature of a heat wave, which killed silently and sporadically, rather than the tight focus and visual elements that typified the other natural disasters. The diffuse nature of the heat wave raised complications for journalists trying to locate a focal point for the event.

Five of the themes were absent from the news coverage—survivor stories; death stories; recovery efforts; reassurance, purpose, and meaning; and external validation. The context certainly plays a role in the lack of recovery—without physical damage to buildings or roads, there's nothing obvious to repair—while there are no obvious survivors of a heat wave with dramatic stories to tell. Journalists certainly could have sought out death stories, but the nature of the audience for an English-language newspaper (as was the case in Japan, which also had no death stories) may make such stories less appealing. Further, the English-language press cater to the urban elite readers (Prakash, 2013), who were less likely to be affected by a heat wave. The lack of external validation raises two possibilities: (1) that a heat wave lacks any obvious target for outside assistance so outside entities did not respond or (2) publicity about external validation may suggest inability of government to handle the disaster in a country offering little press or political freedom.

By contrast, stories from Pakistan were relatively high in stories about actions (second) and blame or responsibility (third), in both cases largely without targeting government. Two types of actions were common, advising caution and planning for the future, the first oriented toward steps for people to take during the heat wave and the second suggestions for preventing problems in the future. Both broadly fit a journalistic culture that listed societal development as a key value (Pintak & Nazir, 2013). Government officials were the primary source used to articulate actions, with those from nongovernmental organizations also frequently used.

Nature (climate change, weather patterns) and infrastructure (too few trees in urban areas) were targets of blame. Government officials and unaffiliated people were the most common sources who blamed nature for the heat wave. Blame toward infrastructure could reflect a societal development value (Pintak & Nazir, 2013) and was typically expressed by experts.

PAPUA NEW GUINEA'S EARTHQUAKE

The earthquake produced thirty-one stories (6%), with twenty-eight appearing in the local publication. Papua New Guinea faced many of the same challenges as journalists in the Nigerian disaster, with a large affected area, limited and damaged transportation systems, and low levels of wealth, plus it has a small population and is mostly rural.

News about Papua New Guinea was relatively high in frequency of faith, belief, and salvation themes, fitting the context of the country. Religious themes of Word of God and fate or destiny were especially common in coverage of Papua New Guinea, where 98% of citizens identify as Christians and many integrate Christian faith with some indigenous beliefs and practices (Papua New Guinea—Religion, nd). The most common sources were religious leaders and unaffiliated citizens.

Papua New Guinea had no death stories and relatively low levels of actions and blame or responsibility themes. The diffuse nature of the disaster and transportation limits may have prevented journalists trying to reach affected areas for stories about the deceased and ongoing actions. The limited amount of blame stories likely reflected dynamics of the disaster, which could not have been prevented, but the response did draw criticism of government, fitting within the largely free press and political systems.

U.S. WILDFIRES

With fifty stories (10%), the wildfires in the United States were the only natural disaster analyzed in which the majority of stories were in the BBC (66%). Like in Greece, the centralized nature of wildfires aided reporting, but the main burned area in Northern California was more rural than in Greece and transportation in the mountainous area was difficult, making access a challenge. Additionally, the target audience of the local publication (the *New York Times International Edition*) was less focused on the needs of audiences in the burned areas, helping to explain the lack of stories.

Coverage of the U.S. wildfires had the highest frequency of stories about survivors; selfless behavior; and reassurance, purpose, or meaning, along with no external validation stories. The centralized nature of the Camp Fire made it fairly easy for reporters to find survivors and other witnesses who could tell tales of harrowing escapes during the fires and examples of selfless behavior both during and after the fires. The vast majority of sources used were from survivors and witnesses, giving them ample opportunity to articulate their stories about survival and selflessness. The centralized nature of the Camp Fire scene also allowed opportunities to find people in a reflective mood after losing homes, such as those living in a parking lot. This broadly fits themes that emerged from surveys of journalists (Vos & Craft, 2016) favoring educating the audience and reporting things as they are.

The absence of external validation stories may be due to outside countries and other entities not offering assistance for such a wealthy country.

DISCUSSION OF COUNTRY ANALYSIS

Overall, the country analysis found unique patterns within news coverage of each natural disaster, with likely explanations arising in characteristics of each disaster and unique elements within each journalistic culture. Each natural disaster occurred in a space that either made reporting easier or more difficult, with access to victims, survivors, and heirs varying considerably. For instance, the centralized nature of the Greek wildfires and their proximity to a major city made it easier for journalists to track down witnesses. By contrast, the flooding in Nigeria occurred over a wide area with compromised transportation corridors, making it more difficult for reporters. The sudden nature of the disasters thrust average people into extraordinary conditions, leading to selfless behavior in disasters like the volcanic eruption in Guatemala and the wildfires in the United States. The nature of Pakistan's heat wave—which killed silently and without drama—helped explain the absence of several themes.

Journalistic culture influenced reporting patterns in different ways. This could help explain the emphasis on blame or responsibility within the contentious political nature of Greece and the external validation in Indonesia's twin disasters offering praise (sometimes direct, sometimes indirect) to the country's leader. Guatemala and Papua New Guinea had high levels of faith, belief, and salvation, fitting countries with high levels of religiosity. Death stories were absent from Japan, a country with a primarily collectivist culture.

Based upon statistical analysis, any evidence of a common journalistic culture was largely missing from the news about these eight natural disasters. Chi-square analysis (see table 4.1) showed significant differences on each theme of healing, hope, coping, and recovery across the countries. But a closer look shows an outlier country or two on several variables, with the other countries mostly grouped together. For instance, frequency of survivor stories shows two outliers (Pakistan low and the United States high); recovery efforts had two outliers (Japan high and Pakistan low); faith, belief, and salvation with two outliers (Papua New Guinea high and Nigeria low); and reassurance, purpose, and meaning with one outlier (United States high). Considering the many contextual differences across the eight natural disasters, finding even modest levels of similarity provides some support for a common journalistic culture. Depending upon evidence from just eight countries blunts any argument for a worldwide journalistic culture, but future studies that increase the number of countries and decrease the contextual differences could help better tease out the influences on news content.

Chapter 16

Conclusions

The goal of this book was to evaluate themes of healing, coping, hope, and recovery in news coverage following significant traumas, as represented by eight natural disasters in 2018. By selecting disasters in diverse countries around the world, the design allowed comparisons based upon structural and cultural differences, including journalistic practices. Additionally, contextual characteristics by the type of disaster and a range in human toll, allowed for further understanding of the ways in which journalists responded to a natural disaster.

Additionally, the evaluation of news about eight natural disasters was designed to illustrate a broader phenomenon—a news practice of aiding a community in the aftermath of a significant trauma. While the evidence from this book cannot establish that themes of healing, coping, hope, and recovery appear in news following each major trauma, this chapter provides additional evidence of this news practice as historic and routine.

THEMES OF HEALING, COPING, HOPE, AND RECOVERY

Themes of healing, coping, hope, and recovery were undoubtedly part of the news coverage following the eight natural disasters evaluated. The study was designed to identify relevant themes and each of the ten themes was part of the coverage across the disasters. The frequency of the themes varied across the sample and within each disaster. The study did not typify everything within the coverage—many stories focused on the extent of damage and statistics about the human toll. While those were common elements within the news content, each was outside the purpose of this book.

However, one indicator of the importance of healing, coping, hope, and recovery themes was analysis that looked exclusively at the first paragraph of stories, which often includes the most important element. Most of the 528 stories in the sample (52.1%) included one or more theme related to the study's focus in the opening paragraph. This suggests that elements of healing, coping, hope, and recovery were prominent within the news discourse and a signal that such elements were important to journalists.

As noted above, each of the ten themes was mentioned in the news coverage. In order of frequency (see table 4.1 for details), the themes were actions; blame and responsibility; external validation; recovery efforts; community, cohesion, and intimacy; survivor stories; selfless behavior; death stories; faith, belief, and salvation; and reassurance, purpose, and meaning. Each delivered a unique message that potentially allowed readers, including those physically or psychologically affected by the disaster, opportunities for healing, coping, hope, and recovery.

Rather than heavy dependence on government officials and other authorities (e.g., Livingston & Bennett, 2003; Sigal, 1973), source usage within each theme showed ample opportunities for victims, survivors, and other unaffiliated people to contribute toward the focus of stories. For instance, unaffiliated people accounted for the majority of sources used on four themes (survivors; death stories; recovery; and reassurance, purpose, and meaning), while the most institutional sources, government, led source usage on just two themes (actions and community, cohesion, and intimacy). This demonstrates a journalistic commitment to let people tell their own stories and those anecdotes provided the building blocks to effective articulation of healing, coping, hope, and recovery. It also fits a constructive journalism perspective to seek out people to broaden sources used in stories (e.g., Hermans & Gyldensted, 2019; Hermans & Drok, 2018).

As noted in chapter 2, a natural disaster not only affects people directly, but it can affect people with social, cultural, or emotional ties to the damaged area. Terms such as collective trauma (Erikson, 1976; Ostertag & Ortiz, 2013), cultural trauma (Alexander, 2004; Sztompka, 2000), vicarious traumatization (McCann & Pearlman, 1990), secondary traumatic stress (Creamer & Liddle, 2005), and compassion fatigue (Backholm & Björkqvist, 2010) explain diffusion of emotional distress to those not directly affected by the trauma. News content serves as the primary source of information about the tragedy and it can also serve as a critical source of healing by giving readers hope that leads to recovery. Themes of healing, coping, hope, and recovery in the news serve as a bridge to help people move forward.

How might each of those themes bring elements of healing, coping, hope, and recovery to an audience? Each offers both physical and virtual examples of efforts articulated within the news content to aid the audience, often by showing efforts to deal with the ongoing disaster. Such examples can be explicit or implicit. While each theme could fit within the four elements of healing, coping, hope, and recovery, some themes were more prominent within a specific element.

HEALING

Healing in the news represented ways in which physical wounds and psychological needs could become sound or healthy again. Healing was most prominently found in themes of blame and responsibility; recovery; faith, belief, and salvation; reassurance, purpose, and meaning; and community, cohesion, and intimacy.

Blame and responsibility provided a virtual sense of healing, allowing people to manage tension through their grievances being aired in the news content. This potentially gave people a sense of control and helped relieve anxiety from the natural disaster by giving them a focal point to articulate their worries. For instance, stories about the wildfires in Greece contained criticism of the government's response to the fire, demonstrating to the audience that someone was being held accountable. Themes of recovery were also closely related to healing, especially through examples that dealt with psychological needs such as establishing normalcy and expressions of grief or emotions. Physical types of recovery, like providing goods or assistance, included concrete examples to aid in healing by demonstrating that improvements were under way. This included efforts in Indonesia to rebuild.

Faith, belief, and salvation themes offered a valuable mix of healing and hope. The most common subtheme was fate or destiny, especially tied to religion, as people sought a spiritual explanation for the disaster and a path to the future. This provided a source of comfort and healing. In Papua New Guinea, this was typified by stories in which people turned to their faith for perspective in moving forward with their lives.

The latter two themes were most clearly mentioned in the Greek wildfires, through memorial events in which people gathered. Reassurance, purpose, and meaning offered profound perspectives tied to healing. Remembrance and sacrifice brought depth of understanding about the disaster that aided healing. Themes of community, cohesion, and intimacy created a virtual sense of togetherness that can aid healing, such as through mourning and sorrow within stories about gatherings to honor victims.

COPING

News helped people deal effectively with the trauma, including perspectives that gave them insights. Most frequent themes that aided coping were actions; selfless behavior; blame and responsibility; community, cohesion, and intimacy; and faith, belief, and salvation.

Actions provided tangible evidence that authorities were addressing both the ongoing and future needs. This helped people deal with the trauma by giving them a path forward through both physical acts (like rescues and rebuilding) and verbal acts (such as advice). News about the floods in Nigeria and Japan each featured numerous examples of both physical and verbal actions. Examples of selfless behavior, such as volunteerism and donations, gave readers a tangible way to cope with the disaster, such as contributing to aid others. For instance, some stories provided specific websites and physical locations for readers to contribute money or goods, like clothing or bedding. This included volunteers cleaning up mud and debris in Japan, including non-Japanese residents and a prominent athlete.

Blame and responsibility served as a proxy to readers' own sense of justice or need to blame an entity like government, helping them cope. Often this was for a perceived inadequate response to the crisis or poor planning that could have mitigated the tragedy, such as the Greece wildfires. Examples of community, cohesion, and intimacy enhanced coping through remembrance of disaster victims and expressions of emotions, helping people deal with the trauma. Nigeria's flooding brought several poignant examples of remembrance and emotions. Readers gained insights that helped them cope with the disaster by turning to themes of faith, belief, and salvation, including prayer and other spirituality, especially in Papua New Guinea and in a prayer for rain to ease Pakistan's heat wave.

HOPE

Hope in the news gave readers reasons to believe that something good may happen, such as a return to normalcy in their personal and community lives. Hope was especially found in themes of selfless behavior, survivor stories, and external validation. In addition, it was prominent within themes of recovery; actions; death stories; faith, belief, and salvation; and reassurance, purpose, and meaning.

Selfless behavior provided wonderful anecdotes of people demonstrating the best of humanity, raising hope. An Indonesian air traffic controller was portrayed heroically sacrificing his life for others and stories included details of people volunteering to aid others, suggesting compassion and caring, serving as aspirational models. Other types of selfless behavior delivered hope as well, including assistance, donations, and rescues. Survivor stories, by offering dramatic anecdotes of people escaping wildfires and other disasters, brought camaraderie and empathy toward the people who made it out alive, raising hope. From harrowing escapes in Greece and the United States, readers gained hope and perspective that life goes on. External validation offered hope through messages of sympathy or solidarity toward those afflicted, demonstrating that the area was not alone and that others empathized with them. These messages mostly came from other governments, businesses, and nongovernmental organizations, mostly prominently after the twin disasters in Indonesia.

Physical acts of recovery provided tangible evidence that the immediate needs of disaster victims and survivors were being addressed and that work was under way on long-term needs, bringing hope to the area by restoring normalcy. Actions provided evidence of a return to normalcy, especially through physical acts like rebuilding, cleanup, providing supplies, and relief aid. The depth of people's lives revealed through death stories signaled hope to the audience by suggesting that, even in death, life can be part of a record for eternity. The most detailed example was a tribute to a fire victim in the United States. Religious expressions within theme of faith, belief, and salvation provided reassurance and hope that could help people through the trauma. Themes of reassurance, purpose, and meaning provided hope through calmness, safety, and assurance, often in philosophical expressions from columnists. This was mostly clearly demonstrated within the news content of Guatemala's local publication.

RECOVERY

A return to a normal state of mind or health, recovery included examples of acts designed to address physical and psychological needs. Not surprisingly, this was directly supported through the theme of recovery, plus was prominent within themes of actions; community, cohesion, and intimacy; external validation; and blame or responsibility.

Recovery efforts were obviously a tight fit with the overarching theme, providing tangible evidence of support. This included physical elements like providing shelter and dealing with homelessness; providing goods and assistance; examples of escape, rescue, and search; and construction. Floods in Japan and Nigeria led to stories fitting each of those physical elements. Actions by government and other entities offered physical evidence of recovery through reconstruction and promises of future acts. Most of examples of actions demonstrated a clear and concrete way to address the problem and/or recognition of the suffering that others have faced, such as tearing down buildings and planning new regulations after the Greek wildfires.

Articulating themes of community, cohesion, and intimacy aided recovery by helping people deal with internal anxiety, allowing them to move on in life by demonstrating they are not alone. External validation aided recovery through tangible support in the form of donations or promises to provide goods and/or money. Blame or responsibility offered recovery from anxiety by providing a path forward to deal with grievances shared with others.

STRUCTURAL AND CONTEXTUAL INFLUENCES

News responses to trauma, by providing content classified as healing, coping, hope, and recovery, have been touched upon previously by scholars. That includes this author (McCluskey, 2017), whose analysis of news following eleven school shootings in the United States found overlap with several themes covered in this book. Other scholarly analyses of news content addressed traumas in the United States, including the 9/11 terror attack (Hume, 2003; Kitch, 2003), a mine disaster (Kitch & Hume, 2007), and a shooting at Virginia Tech University (Berkowitz, 2010). From Europe, studies analyzed six man-made disasters in the United Kingdom (Pantti & Wahl-Jorgensen, 2007) and the murder of a Dutch politician (Pantti & Wieten, 2005).

Many of the prior studies were based upon a single case and were drawn from one Western country. By contrast, this study analyzed eight separate traumas and utilized a multination comparative approach that drew from diverse countries around the world. Analyzing news content from eight countries allowed for comparisons to tease out differences in coverage, taking into account contextual factors unique to each disaster and structural factors within each country. It offers guidance for theory to build upon scholarly understanding of influences on news content (chapter 2), usually characterized as news values or values of journalists. Additionally, it offered parallel characteristics to constructive journalism and humanitarian journalism. Further, the journalism culture of each country (chapter 3) was introduced as another potential contributor to news about healing, coping, hope, and recovery.

Statistical analysis (chapter 4) found significant differences across the eight countries on each theme of healing, coping, hope, and recovery. This points to more variety across countries rather than uniformity. Relatively more similarity was found across the countries on two themes, survivor stories and faith, belief, and salvation, in which news about six of the disasters was mostly alike. The other themes showed more spread in news frequencies, perhaps due to unique characteristics tied to the disaster and location.

From each event, news coverage had its own points of emphasis, perhaps driven by elements of the natural disaster, characteristics of the country, and/ or that country's journalism culture. Analysis by country (see chapter 15 for more details) showed a range of potential influences. Emphasis in stories from Greece was on blame or responsibility, death stories, actions, and external validation, perhaps driven by the political ideology of the local publication and elements of the wildfire, along with the country's vibrant journalism culture. In Guatemala, news coverage featured more attention toward selfless behavior; community, cohesion, and intimacy; and faith, belief, and salvation. The high collective nature of Guatemala (e.g., Hofstede, 2001) helps explain themes related to solidarity and themes of faith fit the high level of religiosity in the country (Guatemala-religion, nd).

Indonesia's only significant points of emphasis were to be high in external validation and low in blame or responsibility, both of which fit the country's historic political climate of deference to government. In Japan, recovery efforts were more prominent in the news, reflecting the country's relatively high level of wealth, allowing officials and volunteers to begin rebuilding. By contrast, Japan was relatively low in death stories, fitting the communal nature of Asian journalistic culture that favors the group over individuals. Nigeria news areas of emphasis were actions; blame or responsibility; death stories; and community, cohesion, and intimacy, partly reflecting a tradition of oral discourse common in sub-Saharan Africa (Bourgault, 1995), especially the narratives that fit many death stories and community, cohesion, and intimacy themes. The widespread nature of the flooding also contributed to news emphasis in Nigeria, especially actions and blame or responsibility.

In Pakistan, the nature of the tragic heat wave and characteristics of the local news organization explained why themes like recovery efforts, death stories, and survivor stories were absent from the news coverage. For instance, a heat wave does not cause any obvious physical damage to be repaired nor anyone who can clearly be identified as a survivor. News about the Papua New Guinea earthquake was relatively high in frequency of faith, belief, and salvation, matching the country's high level of religious belief (Papua New Guinea—Religion, nd). By contrast, the low economic status, rural population, and widespread damage to roads contributed to a limited focus on death stories and actions. The wildfires in the United States led to story emphasis on survivors; selfless behavior; and reassurance, purpose, or meaning, as to the centralized nature of the wildfire made reporting easier in finding witnesses.

Analysis of structural and contextual factors identified several distinctions in coverage patterns. Among the contextual factors, statistical analysis revealed significant differences by natural disaster (see chapter 4 for details). Breaking the eight natural disasters into four types of disasters showed that the two floods featured more emphasis on recovery, action, and blame/responsibility stories; the two wildfires had more blame or responsibility, death, and action stories; and the heat wave and volcanic eruption had more emphasis on community, cohesion, and intimacy stories. The geographic spread of the disaster made a difference as well; in centralized disasters, external validation and blame or responsibility stories were more common, while widespread disasters had more action stories. The amount of time since the disaster influenced the frequency of three types of stories, with survivor stories earlier in the four-week period, blame/responsibility in week 2, and recovery efforts later in the time period studied. A higher number of casualties correlated with more external validation stories and lower casualties with more death; community, cohesion, and intimacy; and blame or responsibility stories.

Structural conditions within each country were less connected with coverage trends. High levels of press freedom were linked with more survivor; recovery; and reassurance, purpose, and meaning stories, and fewer external validation stories. High levels of political freedom were linked to more blame or responsibility stories. High wealth was tied to more survivor and blame or responsibility stories, and fewer external validation stories. High population correlated with more survivor and reassurance, purpose, and meaning stories, and fewer death; community, cohesion, and intimacy; and blame or responsibility stories. Another distinction was between stories written by an in-country publication as compared with the worldwide focus of the BBC. Statistical analysis showed significantly more emphasis in BBC articles on survivor stories and selfless behavior; the eight local publications were not higher than BBC on any theme.

The flip side is that other themes showed no statistical relationships with contextual and structural factors. So broad characteristics had some influence on several themes and little influence on the remaining themes of healing, coping, hope, and recovery.

Lessons for News Coverage of Traumas

As mentioned in Chapter One, news about the COVID-19 pandemic in the first half of 2020 reflects patterns of healing, coping, hope, and recovery. Additionally, this author's analysis of a trauma from 1865 also revealed evidence of healing, coping, hope, and recovery in news content. Other significant traumas mentioned in chapter 2 included elements of healing, coping, hope, and recovery, including school shootings, terrorist attacks, a politician's murder, a hurricane, an earthquake, and a concert shooting.

While COVID-19 news coverage was not systematically analyzed, news during the winter and spring of 2020 (when this book was being completed) shows evidence of the ten themes of healing, hope, coping, and recovery analyzed in this book. The balance and frequency appear to be different from the 2018 natural disasters that formed the context of this book. One prominent theme of COVID-19 news attention in the United States was selfless behavior—such disparate professions as nurses, transit workers, trash collectors, and grocery store employees have been explicitly called heroes and praised for their willingness to put personal safety aside to help others. News about COVID-19 had regular attention to death and survivor stories, especially in early days of the pandemic's spread. Themes of community, cohesion, and intimacy abounded during conditions of social distancing in the United States, Italy, and other countries, including significant new roles of video connections for those isolated by quarantines. Community, cohesion, and intimacy was also a theme as areas of the United States reopened from stay-in-place orders in the early spring.

Actions by government were a daily presence in the news around the world, especially declarations to close public facilities and efforts to provide health responses. Expressions of blame or responsibility were constant news themes as experts and others singled out government for what it did or failed to do. Recovery stories were common as well, including efforts in the spring to reopen businesses and public facilities. While the global nature of the pandemic has made external validation less prominent, there has still been attention and sympathy toward emerging pandemic hot spots throughout the first six months of 2020.

This journalistic practice may be historic as well. This author (McCluskey, 2018) used a similar mix of news themes related to healing, coping, hope, and recovery from a significant trauma in 1865. That study examined the social and cultural trauma that engulfed the United States upon the assassination of President Abraham Lincoln. The focus of that study was on the fourteen-day, 1,600-mile series of funeral events as Lincoln's corpse was transported by train from Washington, DC, to his burial site in Illinois. While the balance of news themes was different from the 2018 natural disasters, it featured many examples that reflected themes that could aid the healing and recovery of the nation. Pantti and Wahl-Jorgensen (2007) went back to 1929 in their analysis of disasters to trace the historic nature of disaster journalism as therapy news.

The range of news contexts includes man-made tragedies and natural disasters, occurring at local to national to global events, across time. This breadth suggests that news patterns of healing, coping, hope, and recovery are generalizable to a range of traumas. It opens a new avenue in sociological evaluation of news, broadly within the range of news values and values held by journalists. News values typically explain which events become news and what points are emphasized in that coverage; by establishing themes of healing, coping, hope, and recovery as regular parts of news coverage during and after significant traumas, it deserves mention in textbooks that train journalists, topics for journalism courses, and scholarly understanding of influences on news. Placing this within values held by journalists is implicit rather than explicit. Essentially, it argues that since those themes are absent from the training of journalists (such as in textbooks), those trends emerge elsewhere. This could emerge within the individuals who create news stories and/or the organizations that guide those decisions. This point will be explored further in the next section.

Additionally, themes explored in this book loosely fit within newer models of positive journalism within labels of constructive journalism and humanitarian journalism. While these positive journalism concepts are described as a conscious goal, this book cannot place news about the eight natural disasters as intentional efforts to promote positive themes. By relying upon content alone, this analysis cannot state whether those parallels were intentional or unintentional.

Looking Ahead

Analysis of news content about eight natural disasters supports expectations of healing, coping, hope, and recovery as part of the news coverage. This news practice crosses nations and cultures, plus a study of nineteenth-century news content suggests it has historic roots. Anecdotal evidence from other traumatic events, including natural disasters and man-made traumas, further indicates this is a common news practice. This is not to suggest that themes of healing, coping, hope, and recovery constitute a majority of the news content about traumas, merely that such themes are present and can be the focus of some stories. The ten themes analyzed in this study may not be the only relevant themes; for instance, in the spring of 2020 in the United States, news about the COVID-19 pandemic included acts of kindness that may constitute another theme.

First, some pieces of this journalistic practice are still missing. As noted above, the evidence from this book leaves open the question of how these trends may fit into values held by journalists or intentional efforts to focus on positive news. Where does this emphasis on healing, hope, coping, and recovery originate? Is it an inherent trait (do some or all journalists possess high levels of empathy) or a learned behavior? In other words, do journalists hold fundamentally different values about the world than nonjournalists? Do inherent traits lead people into journalism? Alternately, this trend could occur within news organizations. Do journalists learn on the job, consciously or unconsciously, that themes like healing, coping, hope, and recovery should be part of stories? Another possibility is formal learning—although absent from most journalism textbooks, prospective journalists could be taught to explore such themes. Surveys and interviews could tease out some of these answers.

Second, evidence of media content about traumas bringing hope and relief to the audience is mostly conjecture. Experimental work taking a constructive journalism perspective offers limited evidence of effects broadly connected to themes in this book. Experiments by McIntyre (2015) found stories with positive emotions and stories that contained solutions made participants feel better. Experimental work by Meier (2018) offered a mixed verdict, with constructive stories counteracting a negative view of the world. Interviews, surveys, or experiments could help determine whether people feel an increased sense of hope or relief when exposed to media content focused on themes of healing and recovery. It could clarify which themes are most helpful in helping people. Additionally, it could help determine whether individual audience characteristics mediate or moderate the influences of news content on attitudes.

Third, the text-only evidence in this book leaves out a wide range of visual and audio resources common in contemporary news that could further support themes of healing, coping, hope, and recovery. Of the nine news sources analyzed in this book, just two included photographs in its archives, so visuals were left out of the analysis. Zelizer (2002) articulated a profound role of photography in bearing personal witness to trauma, as photos stand for a larger event and aids recall. Video and audio content could further affect the audience either separated or together.

Fourth, the focus of this book on news content is incomplete. Any understanding of the modern media environment cannot ignore user-generated content, which may contain deep understandings of contemporary society. While outside the scope of this study, user-generated content is an important realm for understanding. A handful of stories in this book mentioned Twitter, Facebook, and other social media delivering themes of healing, coping, hope, or recovery. Stories from 2017 traumas mentioned survivors using social media to aid their healing (Las Vegas survivor, 2017). Stories from 2017 also mentioned celebrities, including athletes, using social media to raise money for trauma victims. For instance, American professional football player J. J. Watt raised $37 million for Houston-area flood victims through the website You Giving, assisted through his Twitter account and other social media. Mixing an investigation of social media into an understanding of healing, coping, hope, and recovery could be valuable.

Finally, recognition of this media role to aid the public following a trauma should broaden perspectives on how people heal and the purposes of journalism. Trauma is such a common human experience that indications of media content helping people to heal or recover could be of therapeutic value. For journalists and journalism, such trends can be more explicitly incorporated into education and made a conscious part of their professional goals. Considering low levels of trust in the news (noted in chapter 1), it can provide a new perspective on how to think about journalism. Rather than being a pariah that picks upon the traumatized from the latest disaster, journalism instead can be seen as helping solve a difficult problem. Perhaps this could turn public opinion and bring a new appreciation of journalism's value to society.

References

12 states may experience flooding 2018 – NIHSA (2018, Sept. 14). *The Nation*.
2018 California wildfires (2019, June). *The American Red Cross*. Accessed Sept. 10, 2019 at https://www.redcross.org/content/dam/redcross/about-us/disaster-relief/ca-wildfires-2018-6-month-update.pdf
2018 Indonesia quakes and tsunamis: Facts, FAQs, and how to help (2018, Dec. 27). *World Vision*. Accessed Sept. 6, 2019 at https://www.worldvision.org/disaster-relief-news-stories/2018-indonesia-earthquake-facts
Adeyemi, K., Asishana, J., & Rufai, A. (2018, Sept. 18). Water, water everywhere. *The Nation*.
Agboke, A. (2019, May 28). 10 leading Nigerian newspapers. *Hintng.com*. Accessed Oct. 14, 2019 at https://hintng.com/10-leading-newspapers-in-nigeria/
Aguilar, D. (2018a, June 5). Search efforts for eruption of the volcano of fire continue. *La Hora*.
Aguilar, D. (2018b, June 7). More donations are added to attend emergency for the Volcán de Fuego. *La Hora*.
AHEPA announces post-fire aid program (2018, July 28). *Kathimerini*.
AHI calls for donations to help Greece's wildfire victims (2018, July 25). *Kathimerini*.
Air Force aircraft evacuate quake, tsunami victims (2018, Sept. 29). *Antara News*.
Akhavan-Majid, R. (1990). The press as an elite power group in Japan. *Journalism Quarterly, 67*(4), 1006–1014.
Akinrinade, K. (2018, Oct. 6). Rubble after the RAINS. *The Nation*.
Alexander, J. (2004). Toward a theory of cultural trauma. In J. Alexander (Ed.), *Cultural trauma and collective identity* (pp. 1–30). Berkeley, CA: University of California Press.
Andrew, L. (2018, March 14). Lae Snax Tigers assist earthquake victims with container of biscuits. *The National*.
Ano, G. G., & Vasconcelles, E. B. (2005). Religious coping and psychological adjustment to stress: A meta-analysis. *Journal of Clinical Psychology, 61*(4), 461–480.
Antara News (Indonesia). https://en.antaranews.com/

Antoniou, D. (2018a, July 28). PM heralds crackdown on illegal building but no blame for fires. *Kathimerini*.
Antoniou, D. (2018b, Aug. 9). Greek PM heralds new agency to tackle emergencies. *Kathimerini*.
Applications for wildfire aid reach 1,761 in three days (2018, Aug. 3). *Kathimerini*.
Arango, T. (2018, Nov. 16). A 'perfectly imperfect' life: The victims of the California wildfires. *New York Times International Edition*.
Archbishop slams 'wrath of God' comments (2018, July 25). *Kathimerini*.
As fire victims named, their stories emerge (2018, Aug. 10). *Kathimerini*.
As sea breeze resumes, Karachi gets some respite—for now (2018, May 25). *The News International*.
Assegaf, F. (2018, Oct. 2). News focus: World leaders extend sympathies over deadly Sulawesi earthquake by Fardah. *Antara News*.
'Atheist PM' to blame for deadly fires, says Greek bishop (2018, July 25). *Kathimerini*.
Athens festival to donate proceeds to fire victims (2018, July 26). *Kathimerini*.
Athens wildfires: Death toll rises to 24 as huge fire sweeps through holiday resorts (2018, July 24). *Kathimerini*.
Attica regional governor declares state of emergency (2018, July 23). *Kathimerini*.
Australia PM: 'A tragedy that affects Greece also affects Australia' (2018, July 25). *Kathimerini*.
Avila, R., & Gutiérrez, A. (2013). *Mapping digital media: Guatemala country report*. London: Open Society Foundations.
Azly, E. (2018, Sept. 29). News focus—Indonesian government moves swiftly in handling Gonggala quake victims. *Antara News*.
Babalola, E. T. (2002). Newspapers as Instruments for building literate communities. *Nordic Journal of African Studies*, *11*(3), 403–410.
Backholm, K., & Björkqvist, K. (2010). The effects of exposure to crisis on well-being of journalists: A study of crisis-related factors predicting psychological health in a sample of Finnish journalists. *Media, War & Conflict*, *3*(2), 138–151.
Barrick's power facility damaged by earthquake (2018, Feb. 28). *The National*.
Barthel, M. (2019, July 23). 5 key takeaways about the state of the news media in 2018. *Pew Research Center*. Accessed Oct. 20, 2019 at https://www.pewresearch.org/fact-tank/2019/07/23/key-takeaways-state-of-the-news-media-2018/
Batchelor, A. (2018, Feb. 26). 'I'm so grateful to be here,' Parkland school shooting survivor says. *WPLG Local 10 News*. Accessed March 29, 2018 at https://www.local10.com/news/parkland-school-shooting/parkland-school-shooting-survivor-speaks-about-multiple-surgeries
Becatoros, E., & Gatopoulos, D. (2018, July 30). Divers recover body offshore of where wildfire raged. *Kathimerini*.
Bell, C. (2018, Nov. 13). No, these photos are not from the California wildfires. *BBC*.
Ben-Zur, H., Gil, S., & Shamshins, Y. (2012). The relationship between exposure to terror through the media, coping strategies and resources, and distress and secondary traumatization. *International Journal of Stress Management*, *19*(2), 132–150.
Bender, J. R., Davenport, L. D., Drager, M. W., & Fedler, F. (2016). *Writing and reporting for the media*, 11th edition. New York: Oxford University Press.

Berkowitz, D. (2010). The ironic hero of Virginia Tech: Healing trauma through mythical narrative and collective memory. *Journalism, 11*(6), 643–659.

Berkowitz, D. (2011). Telling the unknown through the familiar: Collective memory as journalistic device in a changing media environment. In M. Neiger, O. Meyers, & E. Zandberg (Eds.), *On media memory* (pp. 201–212). New York: Palgrave Macmillan UK.

Berlinger, J. (2018, July 12). Japan floods: Death toll rises to 200 as UN offers assistance. *CNN*. Accessed Sept. 11, 2019 at https://www.cnn.com/2018/07/10/asia/japan-floods-intl/index.html

Bhatti, M. W. (2018a, May 20). Karachi heatwave: City braves a hotter day as mercury hits 42°C. *The News International*.

Bhatti, M. W. (2018b, May 31). At 46°C, city suffers hottest day in May since 1981. *The News International*.

Blau, P. M. (1960). Structural effects. *American Sociological Review, 25*(2), 178–193.

Blistering heatwave continues to grip country (2018, May 28). *The News International*.

BMKG should clarify lifting of tsunami early warning (2018, Oct. 1). *Antara News*.

Bourgault, L. M. (1995). *Mass media in Sub-Saharan Africa*. Bloomington and Indianapolis: Indiana University Press.

Bowles, S. (1997, Dec. 3). Shattered school days: Even those closest to teen cannot answer why. *USA Today*, 1A.

Bro, P. (2019). Constructive journalism: Proponents, precedents, and principles. *Journalism, 20*(4), 504–519.

Brooks, B. S., Kennedy, G., Moen, D. R., & Ranly, D. (2005). *News reporting and writing*, 8th edition. Boston: Bedford/St. Martin's.

Bunce, M., Scott, M., & Wright, K. (2019). Humanitarian Journalism. *Oxford Research Encyclopedia*. Accessed June 18, 2020 at https://oxfordre.com/communication/view/10.1093/acrefore/9780190228613.001.0001/acrefore-9780190228613-e-821

Burials of Greece's wildfire victims begin (2018, July 28). *Kathimerini*.

California fires: At least 42 die in state's deadliest wildfire (2018, Nov. 13). *BBC*.

California fires: Firefighters hold containment lines in north (2018, Nov. 13). *BBC*.

California fires: Winds propel fires as death toll rises (2018, Nov. 13). *BBC*.

California wildfires: 250,000 flee monster flames ravaging state (2018, Nov. 10). *BBC*.

California wildfires: Air quality rated 'world's worst' (2018, Nov. 16). *BBC*.

California wildfires: Concern over rain in search efforts (2018, Nov. 19). *BBC*.

California wildfires: Death toll reaches grim milestone (2018, Nov. 12). *BBC*.

California wildfires: Death toll rises to 25 (2018, Nov. 11). *BBC*.

California wildfires: Fears of further damage as winds strengthen (2018, Nov. 11). *BBC*.

California wildfires: Finland bemused by Trump raking comment (2018, Nov. 19). *BBC*.

California wildfires: 'I saw cars become metal and bones' (2018, Nov. 12). *BBC*.

California wildfires: Is smoke toxic to the East Coast? (2018, Nov. 15). *BBC*.

California wildfires: Is Trump right when he blames forest managers? (2018, Nov. 15). *BBC*.
California wildfires: 'More than 1,000 missing' in Camp Fire (2018, Nov. 17). *BBC*.
California wildfires: Nine dead and more than 150,000 evacuated (2018, Nov. 19). *BBC*.
California wildfires: Number of missing leaps to 631 (2018, Nov. 16). *BBC*.
California wildfires: Rain brings threat of mudslides (2018, Nov. 22). *BBC*.
California wildfires: Survivors share stories of heroic rescues (2018, Nov. 16). *BBC*.
California wildfires: Thanksgiving hope from ashes of Paradise (2018, Nov. 22). *BBC*.
California wildfires: Town of Paradise will need 'total rebuild' (2018, Nov. 15). *BBC*.
California wildfires: Trump visits state's deadliest blaze (2018, Nov. 18). *BBC*.
Carcamo, C., Tchekmedyian, A., Mather, K., & Winton, R. (2017, Oct. 4). Survivors from California recount their terrifying escape from danger in Las Vegas. *Los Angeles Times*. http://www.latimes.com/local/lanow/la-me-california-survivors-las-vegas-20171004-story.html
Castanon, M. (2018, June 7). MP will investigate ex-officio tragedy of Volcán de Fuego. *La Hora*.
Central Sulawesi earthquake response plan (2018, Oct. 5). *ReliefWeb*. Accessed Sept. 6, 2019 at https://reliefweb.int/report/indonesia/central-sulawesi-earthquake-response-plan-oct-2018-dec-2018
Chaudhary, A. G. (2001). International news selection: A comparative analysis of negative news in the Washington Post and the Daily Times of Nigeria. *Howard Journal of Communications*, 12(4), 241–254.
Chavez, N. (2018, Feb. 17). These are the heroes of the Florida school shooting. *CNN*. Accessed March 30, 2018 at https://www.cnn.com/2018/02/17/us/florida-school-shooting-heroes/index.html
Chouliaraki, L. (2006). *The spectatorship of suffering*. London: Sage.
Climate Change minister says provinces warned of heatwave (2018, May 22). *The News International*.
Commission chief writes to Greek PM to express condolences over deadly fires (2018, July 24). *Kathimerini*.
Condolences pour in over Greek fires (2018, July 26). *Kathimerini*.
Creamer, T. L., & Liddle, B. J. (2005). Secondary traumatic stress among disaster mental health workers responding to the September 11 attacks. *Journal of Traumatic Stress*, 18(1), 89–96.
Damage control without accountability (2018, July 28). *Kathimerini*.
Dayan, D., & Katz, E. (1993). *Media events: The live broadcasting of history*. Cambridge, MA and London: Harvard University Press.
Death toll from Greek wildfire reaches 91 as village grieves (2018, July 30). *Kathimerini*.
Deaths, destruction as floods ravage states (2018, Sept. 14). *The Nation*.
Del Real, J. A., & Nicas, J. (2018, Nov. 13). California fire death toll now at 44 with discovery of 13 more bodies. *New York Times International Edition*.

Depression cases surface at hospitals following earthquake, tsunami (2018, Oct. 9). *Antara News.*
Desperate Greeks search for missing after fires (2018, July 25). *Kathimerini.*
Deuze, M. (2002). National news cultures: A comparison of Dutch, German, British, Australian, and US journalists. *Journalism & Mass Communication Quarterly, 79*(1), 134–149.
Deuze, M. (2005). What is journalism? Professional identity and ideology of journalists reconsidered. *Journalism, 6*(4), 442–464.
Dickinson, R., & Memon, B. (2012). Press clubs, the journalistic field and the practice of journalism in Pakistan. *Journalism Studies, 13*(4), 616–632.
Digicel to provide free calls to earthquake-affected areas (2018, March 1). *The National.*
Dimitrakopoulou, D. (2017). Journalists in Greece. *Worlds of Journalism.* Accessed June 23, 2020 at https://epub.ub.uni-muenchen.de/35064/1/Country_report_Greece.pdf
Diocese of Escuintla sympathizes with those affected by eruption of Fuego volcano and offers alternative aid (2018, June 4). *La Hora.*
Doss, E. (2002). Death, art and memory in the public sphere: The visual and material culture of grief in contemporary America. *Mortality, 7*(1), 63–82.
Dummit, R. (1999, April 26). Service here stresses talking about problems: A time to share grief, ideas. *St. Louis Post Dispatch*, A1.
Earthquake is not punishment (2018, March 7). *The National.*
Earthquake suffering (2018, March 6). *The National.*
Earthquake victims receive K20,000 worth of clothes (2018, March 23). *The National.*
Economic activities begin to recover in tsunami devastated Donggala (2018, Oct. 5). *Antara News.*
Edwards, A. (2012, Dec. 16). After Connecticut shooting massacre, Newtown seeks comfort in churches and congregations. *San Jose Mercury News*, np.
Ela Motors gives K50,000 to earthquake victims (2018, March 19). *The National.*
Elafros, Y. (2018, July 28). Experts warn of pollution in areas hit by Attica wildfires. *Kathimerini.*
Elekwa, E. (2018, Oct. 4). Flooded, displaced, hungry in Anambra. *The Nation.*
Ellis, T. (2018, July 27). Chronic problems, responsibilities and resignations. *Kathimerini.*
Empresarial, R. (2018a, June 5). Cervecería CA and Fundación Castillo Córdova provide support in response to the tragedy caused by the Volcán de Fuego. *La Hora.*
Empresarial, R. (2018b, June 9). Banrural and TECHO Guatemala stand in solidarity with those affected by the tragedy of the Volcán de Fuego. *La Hora.*
Erikson, K. (1976). *Everything in its path: Destruction of community in the buffalo creek flood.* New York: Simon and Schuster.
Everything is wrong (2018, Aug. 4). *Kathimerini.*
Eze, D. (2019, Feb. 1). Trace the history of newspaper in Nigeria. *Legit.* Accessed Sept. 17, 2019 at https://www.legit.ng/1219230-trace-history-newspaper-nigeria.html

Farinas, Y. (2018, Feb. 17). Community mourns loss of those killed in Parkland school shooting. *WPEC CBS 12*. Accessed March 30, 2018 at http://cbs12.com/news/local/community-mourns-loss-of-those-killed-in-parkland-school-shooting

Fast, J. (2003). After Columbine: How people mourn sudden death. *Social Work*, *48*(4), 484–491.

Fatir, M. D. (2018, Sept. 30). President Jokowi scheduled to visit tsunami-hit Palu. *Antara News*.

Feeling the heat of climate change (2018, July 31). *Japan Times*.

Figueroa, S. (2018, June 12). Volcán de Fuego: There are still 100 thousand people at risk. *La Hora*.

Find and fix the weak points in disaster defenses (2018, July 13). *Japan Times*.

Fire survivor sues officials (2018, Aug. 18). *Kathimerini*.

Firefighter's wife, baby among 93 victims of Greece blaze (2018, Aug. 9). *Kathimerini*.

First 18 Attica fire victims receive aid (2018, Aug. 2). *Kathimerini*.

Fiske, A. P. (2002). Using individualism and collectivism to compare cultures—A critique of the validity and measurement of the constructs: Comment on Oyserman et al. (2002). *Psychological Bulletin*, *128*(1), 78–88.

Fitriyanti, A. (2018, Oct. 4). German Ambassador leads moment of silence for C Sulawesi. *Antara News*.

Flood: Ogbeh predicts rice shortage in 2019 (2018, Oct. 4). *The Nation*.

Flooding: Edo distributes relief materials to victims (2018, Sept. 19). *The Nation*.

Flooding: Edo, ECOWAS re-strategise on disaster management (2018, Sept. 17). *The Nation*.

Foreign NGOs should have local partners: BNPB (2018, Oct. 12). *Antara News*.

Forest rangers see operational failures in tackling deadly blaze (2018, Aug. 1). *Kathimerini*.

Fotiadi, I. (2018a, July 25). Group helping place fire-stricken pets with foster families. *Kathimerini*.

Fotiadi, I. (2018b, Aug. 5). How should we respond to children's questions after the deadly wildfires? *Kathimerini*.

Freedom House. (2017). Freedom of the press 2017. Accessed March 21, 2019 at https://freedomhouse.org/report/freedom-press/freedom-press-2017

Freedom House. (2019). Freedom in the world 2019. Accessed March 21, 2019 at https://freedomhouse.org/report/freedom-world/freedom-world-2019/map

Frey, E., Rhaman, M., & El Bour, H. (Eds.). (2017). *Negotiating journalism: Core values and culture diversities*. Gothenburg: Nordicom.

Friedman, M. (2018, Feb. 20). These are some of the heroes of the Marjory Stoneman Douglas school shooting. *Redbook*. Accessed March 30, 2018 at https://www.redbookmag.com/life/a18371040/parkland-school-shooting-heroes-stories/

Galtung, J., & Holmboe Ruge, M. (1965). The structure of foreign news. *Journal of Peace Research*, *2*(1), 64–91.

Gamez, D. (2018, June 9). Come feeling of helplessness, after tragedy of the Volcano of Fire. *La Hora*.

Gans, H. J. (1979). *Deciding what's news: A study of CBS Evening News, NBC Nightly News, Newsweek and Time*. Vintage Books: New York.

Gatopoulos, D. (2018, July 24). Friends flee into sea, battle waves, as Greek wildfires rage. *Kathimerini*.

Georgiopoulos, G., & Kambas, M. (2018, July 25). Death toll from Greek fire rises to 81, Irishman confirmed dead. *Kathimerini*.

Germany offers help to combat Greece fires (2018, July 24). *Kathimerini*.

Goldstein, A. (1999, April 27). In Colorado, questions about accomplices, 'martyrs': Deaths seen in Christian context. *Washington Post*, A3.

Gonzales, R. (2019, Jan. 28). California wildfire insurance claims total $11.4 billion for November 2018. *National Public Radio*. Accessed Sept. 10, 2019 at https://www.npr.org/2019/01/28/689494921/california-wildfire-insurance-claims-total-11-4-billion-for-november-2018

Goodstein, L. (2006, Oct. 4). Strong faith and community may help Amish cope with loss. *New York Times*, A20.

Government says it will knock down illegal properties (2018, Aug. 1). *Kathimerini*.

Government to build new Palu city after earthquake (2018, Oct. 15). *Antara News*.

Government to deliver food aid in large quantities: President (2018, Oct. 1). *Antara News*.

Government urged to propose new spatial arrangements for Palu (2018, Oct. 10). *Antara News*.

Gov't issues decree for demolition of illegal construction (2018, Aug. 11). *Kathimerini*.

Grant, W. (2018, June 6). Guatemala volcano: Stories of grief in a village wiped off the map. *BBC*.

Greece reporet (2015). *Freedom House*. Accessed Oct. 19, 2019 at https://freedomhouse.org/report/freedom-press/2015/greece

Greece report (2017). *Freedom House*. Accessed Oct. 4, 2019 at https://freedomhouse.org/report/freedom-press/2017/greece

Greece thanks 'friends and partners' for support with deadly wildfires (2018, July 25). *Kathimerini*.

Greece to demolish 'illegal buildings' after wildfire (2018, Aug. 7). *BBC*.

Greece to start burying wildfire victims, government facing criticism (2018, July 27). *Kathimerini*.

Greece wildfires: At least 74 dead as blaze 'struck like flamethrower' (2018, July 24). *BBC*.

Greece wildfires: British man in hospital with burns (2018, July 25). *BBC*.

Greece wildfires: Dozens dead in Attica region (2018, July 24). *BBC*.

Greece wildfires: Emergency chiefs replaced (2018, Aug. 5). *Kathimerini*.

Greece wildfires: 'Hundreds went into the sea' (2018, July 25). *BBC*.

Greece: Wildfires information bulletin (2018, July 24). *ReliefWeb*. Accessed Sept. 9, 2019 at https://reliefweb.int/report/greece/greece-wildfires-information-bulletin-24-july-2018

Greece wildfires: Search for missing family members after 80 people die (2018, July 25). *BBC*.

Greek central bank pledges financial assistance to fire victims (2018, July 26). *Kathimerini*.
Greek fires: 'Hearts empty' over death of Irishman Brian O'Callaghan-Westropp (2018, July 27). *BBC*.
Greek fire victims sue authorities over deaths in Mati (2018, Aug. 1). *Kathimerini*.
Greek government sent out spin guidelines after lethal wildfires, report says (2018, Aug. 12). *Kathimerini*.
Greek gov't shrugs off blame in handling of deadly fire (2018, July 29). *Kathimerini*.
Greek officials see 'serious indications' arson led to fire (2018, July 26). *Kathimerini*.
Greek PM to unveil new plan for civil protection (2018, Aug. 9). *Kathimerini*.
Greek wildfires death toll rises to 79 (2018, July 25). *Kathimerini*.
Green, E. G., Deschamps, J. C., & Páez, D. (2005). Variation of individualism and collectivism within and between 20 countries: A typological analysis. *Journal of Cross-Cultural Psychology, 36*(3), 321–339.
Guatemala-religion (nd). *GlobalSecurity.org*. Accessed April 1, 2020 at https://www.globalsecurity.org/military/world/centam/gt-religion.htm
Guatemala report (2015). *Freedom House*. Accessed Oct. 19, 2019 at https://freedomhouse.org/report/freedom-press/2015/guatemala
Guatemala report (2017). *Freedom House*. Accessed Oct. 4, 2019 at https://freedomhouse.org/report/freedom-press/2017/guatemala
Guatemala volcano aftermath—In pictures (2018, June 6). *BBC*.
Guatemala volcano: Almost 200 missing and 75 dead (2018, June 6). *BBC*.
Guatemala volcano: Dozens die as Fuego volcano erupts. (2018, June 4). *BBC*.
Guatemala volcano: Emergency agency 'failed to heed warnings' (2018, June 7). *BBC*.
Guatemala volcano: Helping communities recover (2018, Aug. 20). *ReliefWeb*. Accessed Sept. 9, 2019 at https://reliefweb.int/report/guatemala/guatemala-volcano-helping-communities-recover
Guatemala volcano: Lava ash like 'black rain'. (2018, June 5). *BBC*.
Guatemala volcano: 'These families are our priority' (2018, July 23). *ReliefWeb*. Accessed Sept. 9, 2019 at https://reliefweb.int/report/guatemala/guatemala-volcano-these-families-are-our-priority
Gyldensted, C. (2011). *Innovating news journalism through positive psychology*. Thesis, University of Pennsylvania.
Hanitzsch, T. (2005). Journalists in Indonesia: Educated but timid watchdogs. *Journalism Studies, 6*(4), 493–508.
Hanitzsch, T., Ahva, L., Oller, M., Arroyave, A. J., Hermans, L., Hovden, J. F., Hughes, S., Josephi, B., Ramaprasad, J., Shapiro, I., & Vos, T. (2019). Journalistic culture in a global context: A conceptual roadmap. In T. Hanitzsch, F. Hanusch, J. Ramaprasad, & A. S. De Beer (Eds.), *Worlds of journalism: Journalistic cultures around the globe* (pp. 23–45). New York: Columbia University Press.
Hanitzsch, T., Hanusch, F., Mellado Ruiz, C., Anikina, M., Berganza, R., Cangoz, I., Coman, M., Hamada, B., Elena Hernández, M., Karadjov, C. D., & Virginia Moreira, S. (2011). Mapping journalism cultures across nations: A comparative study of 18 countries. *Journalism Studies, 12*(3), 273–293.

Hanitzsch, T., Hanusch, F., Ramaprasad, J., & De Beer, A. S. (Eds.). (2019a). *Worlds of journalism: Journalistic cultures around the globe.* New York: Columbia University Press.

Hanitzsch, T., Hanusch, F., Ramaprasad, J., & De Beer, A. S. (2019b). Exploring the worlds of journalism: An introduction. In T. Hanitzsch, F. Hanusch, J. Ramaprasad, & A. S. De Beer (Eds.), *Worlds of journalism: Journalistic cultures around the globe* (pp. 1–21). New York: Columbia University Press.

Hanitzsch, T., Vos, T., Standaert, O., Hanusch, F., Hovden, J. F., Hermans, L., & Ramaprasad, J. (2019). Role orientations: Journalists' views on their place in society. In T. Hanitzsch, F. Hanusch, J. Ramaprasad, & A. S. De Beer (Eds.) *Worlds of journalism: Journalistic cultures around the globe* (pp. 161–197). New York: Columbia University Press.

Harcup, T., & O'Neill, D. (2001). What is news? Galtung and Ruge revisited. *Journalism Studies, 2*(2), 261–280.

Harcup, T., & O'Neill, D. (2017). What is news? News values revisited (again). *Journalism Studies, 18*(12), 1470–1488.

Hayashi, K., & Kopper, G. G. (2014). Multi-layer research design for analyses of journalism and media systems in the global age: Test case Japan. *Media, Culture & Society, 36*(8), 1134–1150.

Head, J. (2018, Oct. 2). A volley of shots and tear gas. *BBC.*

Heatwave in Karachi (2018, May 27). *The News International.*

Heatwave woes to worsen further as temperature spikes steadily (2018, May 21). *The News International.*

Hendrick, B. (1999, April 22). Colorado school massacre; special report; search for answers; solace when life seems senseless; tragedy can teach sanctity of life, love. *Atlanta Journal Constitution*, 8B.

Henschke, R. (2018a, Oct. 1). Patients and corpses side by side. *BBC.*

Henschke, R. (2018b, Oct. 3). No drinks since yesterday. *BBC.*

Hermans, L., & Drok, N. (2018). Placing constructive journalism in context. *Journalism Practice, 12*(6), 679–694.

Hermans, L., & Gyldensted, C. (2019). Elements of constructive journalism: Characteristics, practical application and audience valuation. *Journalism, 20*(4), 535–551.

Herrera, C. H., & Pinto, L. (2018, June 23). Guatemalans in Barcelona join in favor of those affected by the Volcán de Fuego. *La Hora.*

Herrscher, R. (2002). A universal code of journalism ethics: Problems, limitations, and proposals. *Journal of Mass Media Ethics, 17*(4), 277–289.

Herscovitz, H. G. (2004). Brazilian journalists' perceptions of media roles, ethics and
foreign influences on Brazilian journalism. *Journalism Studies, 5*(1): 71–86.

Hertz, R. (1960/1907). A contribution to the study of the collective representation of death. In R. Hertz (Ed.), *Death and the right hand* (pp. 27–86). London: Cohen and West.

History of Journalism in Indonesia. (nd). *Facts of Indonesia.* Accessed Sept. 17, 2019 at https://factsofindonesia.com/history-journalism-indonesia

Hofstede, G. (1980). *Culture consequences: International differences in work-related values.* Beverly Hills, CA: Sage.
Hofstede, G. (2001). *Culture's consequences: Comparing values, behaviors, institutions and organizations across nations.* Thousand Oaks, CA: Sage Publications.
Holy Synod calls for prayers after deadly wildfires (2018, July 27). *Kathimerini.*
Hovardas, T. (2014). "Playing with fire" in a pre-election period: Newspaper coverage of 2007 wildfires in Greece. *Society & Natural Resources, 27*(7), 689–705.
Hua, M., & Tan, A. (2012). Media reports of Olympic success by Chinese and American gold medalists: Cultural differences in causal attribution. *Mass Communication and Society, 15*(4), 546–558.
Hughes, R. (2018, Nov.16). California wildfires: The day Paradise burned down. *BBC.*
Hume, J. (2003). "Portraits of grief," reflectors of values: The New York Times remembers victims of September 11. *Journalism & Mass Communication Quarterly, 80*(1), 166–182.
Hundreds of temporary housing units planned for rain-hit Ehime Prefecture and city of Kurashiki (2018, July 24). *Japan Times.*
Hunter, J., & Harris, H. R. (2012, Dec. 17). National Cathedral dean challenges people of faith to take on gun lobby. *Washington Post,* A13.
ICAO honors Anthonius Agung for saving air passengers during earthquake (2018, Oct. 24). *Antara News.*
Identified wildfire victims reach 76, eight remain missing (2018, Aug. 1). *Kathimerini.*
IMF managing director visits victims of Lombok earthquake (2018, Oct. 8). *Antara News.*
Indonesia. (2019, April 5). *United Nations office for the coordination of humanitarian affairs.* Accessed Sept. 9, 2019 at https://www.unocha.org/asia-and-pacific-roap-indonesia/indonesia
Indonesia earthquake and tsunami: Dead buried in mass grave (2018, Oct. 1). *BBC.*
Indonesia earthquake and tsunami: Desperate search for survivors (2018, Oct. 1). *BBC.*
Indonesia earthquake and tsunami: How warning system failed the victims (2018, Oct. 1). *BBC.*
Indonesia earthquake and tsunami response (2018, Oct. 23). *Australia Council for International Development.* Accessed Sept. 6, 2019 at https://acfid.asn.au/content/indonesia-earthquake-and-tsunami-response
Indonesia earthquake: Huge surge in death toll (2018, Sept. 30). *BBC.*
Indonesia needs more tents, fogging for earthquake-hit area (2018, Oct. 2). *Antara News.*
Indonesia report (2017). *Freedom House.* Accessed Oct. 4, 2019 at https://freedomhouse.org/report/freedom-press/2017/indonesia
Indonesia tsunami: Authorities fight hoaxes (2018, Oct. 3). *BBC.*
Indonesia tsunami: Frustration in remote areas waiting for aid (2018, Oct. 3). *BBC.*
Indonesia tsunami: Palu hit by 'worst case scenario' (2018, Oct. 2). *BBC.*
Indonesia tsunami: Pilot calls air traffic controller his 'guardian angel' (2018, Oct. 2). *Antara News.*

Indonesia tsunami: Search for victims to end, though hundreds still missing (2018, Oct. 7). *BBC*.

International Monetary Fund. (2018). *GDP per capita*. Accessed March 25, 2019 at https://www.imf.org/external/datamapper/PPPPC@WEO/OEMDC/ADVEC/WEOWORLD

Iordanidis, C. (2018, July 26). Respecting the victims. *Kathimerini*.

Iosifidis, P., & Boucas, D. (2015, May 1). Media policy and independent journalism in Greece. *Open Society Foundations*. Accessed Sept. 17, 2019 at https://www.opensocietyfoundations.org/uploads/7aa33e1e-6d0a-4739-94da-42eef04c316f/media-policy-independent-journalism-greece-20150511.pdf

Irishman on honeymoon dies in Greek fire, family confirms (2018, July 26). *BBC*.

Iskandar, M. A. (2018, Sept. 30). Vice President offers condolences to earthquake victims in Donggala. *Antara News*.

Italy, Romania sending more aircraft, minister says (2018, July 25). *Kathimerini*.

Japan faces $2bn price tag for flood rebuilding (2019, July 20). *Nikkei Asian Review*. Accessed Sept. 11, 2019 at https://asia.nikkei.com/Politics/Japan-faces-2bn-price-tag-for-flood-rebuilding

Japan flood: At least 179 dead after worst weather in decades (2018, July 11). *BBC*.

Japan floods: 155 killed after torrential rain and landslides (2018, July 10). *BBC*.

Japan floods and landslides 2018 (2018, July 19). *The Japanese Red Cross Society*. Accessed Sept. 11, 2019 at http://www.jrc.or.jp/english/relief/180719_005356.html

Japan report (2015). *Freedom House*. Accessed Oct. 19, 2019 at https://freedomhouse.org/report/freedom-press/2015/japan

Japan report (2017). *Freedom House*. Accessed Oct. 4, 2019 at https://freedomhouse.org/report/freedom-press/2017/japan

Japan Times. https://www.japantimes.co.jp/

Jeffres, L. W., & Kumar, A. (2014). Community editors look beyond watchdog role. *Newspaper Research Journal, 35*(3), 81–93.

Johnson, J. (2018, July 16). Abe takes to Twitter to thank leaders for condolences over western Japan rain deaths. *Japan Times*.

Johnson, K. (2018, Nov. 16). What started the California fires? Experts track the blazes' origins. *New York Times International Edition*.

Johnston, E. (2018a, July 7). Tourists visiting western Japan stranded amid flood warnings and canceled trains. *Japan Times*.

Johnston, E. (2018b, July 10). In flood-hit area of Okayama, residents shocked by scale of destruction. *Japan Times*.

Johnston, E. (2018c, July 10). After deadly rains, Hiroshima residents try to put lives in order. *Japan Times*.

Joye, S. (2014). Media and disasters: Demarcating an emerging and interdisciplinary area of research. *Sociology Compass, 8*(8), 993–1003.

Kambas, M., & Papadimas, L. (2018, July 28). Greece to tear down illegal buildings after killer blaze. *Kathimerini*.

Kammenos defends government's response to blaze (2018, July 30). *Kathimerini*.

Kantouris, C., & Becatoros, E. (2018, July 27). Greek forensics experts work on identifying dead from fire, put toll at 86. *Kathimerini*.

Karachi heatwave (2018, May 24). *The News International*.
Karachi hit by sweltering heatwave (2018, May 21). *The News International*.
Karachiites gather to offer special prayer for rain (2018, May 26). *The News International*.
Karamanoli, E. (2018, July 26). Many launch initiatives to help survivors. *Kathimerini*.
Kathimerini (Greece). http://www.ekathimerini.com/
Kathimerini report (nd). *Euro Topics*. Accessed Oct. 4, 2019 at https://www.eurotopics.net/en/148651/kathimerini
Katsounaki, M. (2018, Aug. 11). A glimmer of hope. *Kathimerini*.
Khaskheli, J. (2018, June 7). Fishermen fear for survival as heat wave continues to kill crabs. *The News International*.
Khosla, V., & Rowlands, L. (2014). Opportunities for development journalism in Papua New Guinea. *Pacific Journalism Review: Te Koakoa, 20*(2), 96–117.
Kingsley, P. (2018, Nov. 19). Trump says California can learn from Finland on fires. Is he right? *New York Times International Edition*.
Kitch, C. (2000). 'A news of feeling as well as fact' Mourning and memorial in American newsmagazines. *Journalism, 1*(2), 171–195.
Kitch, C. (2003). Mourning in America: Ritual, redemption, and recovery in news narrative after September 11. *Journalism Studies, 4*(2), 213–224.
Kitch, C., & Hume, J. (2007). *Journalism in a culture of grief*. New York: Routledge.
Konstantinidis, A., & Fronista, P. (2018, Aug. 16). Firefighters contain destructive wildfire near Athens. *Kathimerini*.
Koputantou, A. (2018, July 27). No apology, no resignation: Pressure grows on government over fire deaths. *Kathimerini*.
Krugman, P. (2018, Nov. 27). The depravity of climate-change denial. *New York Times International Edition*.
Kyodo, J. (2018a, July 12). Mazda restarts auto plants in flood-hit parts of western Japan. *Japan Times*.
Kyodo, J. (2018b, July 14). About 5,900 flood evacuees still in shelters; Tokyo moves to expedite aid. *Japan Times*.
La Hora (Guatemala). https://lahora.gt/
Lack of early warning, town planning led to high death toll, study finds (2018, Aug. 1). *Kathimerini*.
Laderman, G. (2002). 9/11 on our mind. *Religion in the News*, Fall.
Las Vegas survivor discusses life after shooting (2017, Oct. 21). *National Public Radio*. https://www.npr.org/2017/10/21/559278034/las-vegas-survivor-discusses-life-after-shooting
Lazarus, R. S. (1999). Hope: An emotion and a vital coping resource against despair. *Social Research, 66*(2), 653–678.
Lee, G. (2018, July 24). Greece wildfires: Families left homeless as village of Mati is destroyed. *BBC*.
Lee, J. H. (2009). News values, media coverage, and audience attention: An analysis of direct and mediated causal relationships. *Journalism & Mass Communication Quarterly, 86*(1), 175–190.

Lemert, J. B. (1981). *Does mass communication change public opinion after all?: A new approach to effects analysis.* Chicago: Nelson-Hall.

Let's get earthquake relief aid moving (2018, March 2). *The National.*

Levine, A. S. (2018a, Nov. 28). After a wildfire, rebuilding life can be hardest for the oldest. *New York Times International Edition.*

Levine, A. S. (2018b, Dec. 3). After a California wildfire, new and old homeless populations collide. *New York Times International Edition.*

Lipsher, S., & Finley, B. (1999, April 22). 'I cried and cried ... now I'm dry of tears.' *Denver Post*, A12.

Living condition of Central Sulawesi quake victims gets improved: Mily (2018, Oct. 10). *Antara News.*

Livingston, S., & Bennett, W. L. (2003). Gatekeeping, indexing, and live-event news: Is technology altering the construction of news? *Political Communication, 20*(4), 363–380.

Logistic distribution for earthquake victims needs to be improved: President (2018, Oct. 4). *Antara News.*

Lombard, M., Snyder-Duch, J., & Bracken, C. C. (2002). Content analysis in mass communication: Assessment and reporting of intercoder reliability. *Human Communication Research, 28*(4), 587–604.

Lopez, K. (2018a, June 4). President visited area affected by Volcán de Fuego. *La Hora.*

Lopez, K. (2018b, June 10). They point out shortcomings in acting of authorities before crisis by Volcán de Fuego. *La Hora.*

Loukoumaki the dog recovers from Greek wildfire (2018, July 31). *Kathimerini.*

Lowe, P. (1999, April 27). Kids connect by prayers; Indiana pupils respond. *Denver Post*, AA6.

Maltezou, R. (2018a, July 24). It was all a blur in fire chaos, Greek victim says. *Kathimerini.*

Maltezou, R. (2018b, July 26). Greece searches for survivors after killer wildfire. *Kathimerini.*

Maltezou, R. (2018c, July 26). Greek authorities lost in red tape over fire evacuation drill. *Kathimerini.*

Maltezou, R. (2018d, July 27). Tsipras's words mean little to fire-stricken Greeks standing on ashes. *Kathimerini.*

Maltezou, R., & Konstantinidis, A. (2018, July 26). 'Left at God's mercy': Greeks seek answers as fire toll mounts. *Kathimerini.*

Man arrested for arson in Marathonas (2018, Aug. 1). *Kathimerini.*

Mandiri, BNI to build houses for 400 quake-hit families: Government (2018, Oct. 17). *Antara News.*

Marathon municipal council votes to oust mayor over wildfire tragedy (2018, Aug. 3). *Kathimerini.*

Maroussi municipality accused of indifference after floods (2018, July 31). *Kathimerini.*

Martin, C., & Bingham, J. (1999, April 23). Remembering the slain; Cassie Bernall; Girl's faith a beacon to those she left. *Denver Post*, A6.

Mata, A. (2018, June 26). IDB offers its support to Guatemala after the tragedy of Volcán de Fuego. *La Hora*.

Matbob, P. (2007). The post-courier and media advocacy: A new era for Papua New Guinean journalism? *Pacific Journalism Review, 13*(1), 87.

Matoli, K. (2018, March 2). Can franking cause earthquakes? *The National*.

Matthews-Trigg, N. (2018, May 29). Deadly heat. *The News International*.

Mayer, J. (2019, Nov. 19). Five ways to feel empowered about trust in journalism. *Poynter*. Accessed May 6, 2020 at https://www.poynter.org/from-the-institute/2019/five-ways-to-feel-empowered-about-trust-in-journalism/

McCann, L. I., & Pearlman, L. A. (1990). Vicarious traumatization: A framework for understanding the psychological effects of working with victims. *Journal of Traumatic Stress, 3*(1), 131–149.

McCluskey, M. (2017). *News framing of school shootings: Journalism in times of trauma and violence*. Lanham, MD: Lexington Press.

McCluskey, M. (2018). Lincoln's funeral cortege: The press as instrument of healing, coping and recovery. Presented to the *symposium on the 19th Century Press, the civil war, and free expression*, Chattanooga, TN, Nov. 9.

McGregor, J. (2002). Restating news values: Contemporary criteria for selecting the news. In *Refereed articles from the proceedings of the ANZCA 2002 conference*, Coolangatta. Communication: Reconstructed for the 21st Century.

McIntyre, K. (2015). *Constructive journalism: The effects of positive emotions and solution information in news stories*. Dissertation, University of North Carolina.

McIntyre, K., & Gyldensted, C. (2017). Constructive journalism: An introduction and practical guide for applying positive psychology techniques to news production. *The Journal of Media Innovations, 4*(2), 20–34.

Meier, K. (2018). How does the audience respond to constructive journalism? Two experiments with multifaceted results. *Journalism Practice, 12*(6), 764–780.

Mellado, C., Hanusch, F., Humanes, M. L., Roses, S., Pereira, F., Yez, L., De León, S., Márquez, M., Subervi, F., & Wyss, V. (2013). The pre-socialization of future journalists: An examination of journalism students' professional views in seven countries. *Journalism Studies, 14*(6), 857–874.

Mercury soars to 42 degrees again (2018, May 26). *The News International*.

Michailidou, A. (2012). "Second-order" elections and online journalism: A comparison of the 2009 European Parliament elections' coverage in Greece, Sweden and the United Kingdom. *Journalism Practice, 6*(3), 366–383.

Minister says 'serious indications' of arson behind deadly wildfire (2018, July 26). *Kathimerini*.

Minister Soemarno revisits Palu to review economic recovery efforts (2018, Oct. 10). *Antara News*.

Minyak (2018, Oct. 6). dpr supports pertamina to assist victims of c sulawesi earthquake. *Antara News*.

Missing 13-year-old boy identified among wildfire victims (2018, July 28). *Kathimerini*.

Mitchell, M. (2012, Dec. 16). Test of faiths: 'We are in a world where evil is real.' *Chicago Sun-Times*, 6.

Mitsotakis blasts 'deplorable' government reaction to deadly wildfire (2018, July 31). *Kathimerini*.

Mitsotakis: Government wanted to shift blame for deadly blaze (2018, Aug. 8). *Kathimerini*.

Mitsotakis insists heads must roll (2018, July 31). *Kathimerini*.

Monahan, B., & Ettinger, M. (2018). News media and disasters: Navigating old challenges and new opportunities in the digital age. In *Handbook of disaster research* (pp. 479–495). New York: Springer.

More than 3,100 illegal buildings slated for demolition, after deadly blaze (2018, Aug. 1). *Kathimerini*.

Muchtar, N., & Masduki. (2016). Journalists in Indonesia. *Worlds of Journalism*. Accessed June 23, 2020 at https://epub.ub.uni-muenchen.de/30120/1/Country_report_Indonesia.pdf

Municipal camps evacuated during wildfires to reopen on Sunday (2018, July 27). *Kathimerini*.

Murakami, S. (2018, July 18). Tokyo to offer free housing for evacuees. *Japan Times*.

Mwesige, P. G. (2004). Disseminators, advocates and watchdogs: A profile of Ugandan journalists in the New Millennium. *Journalism*, 5(1), 69–96.

Nalu, M. (2018a, March 1). Hela still trying to come to terms with earthquake. *The National*.

Nalu, M. (2018b, March 7). Helping earthquake-affected areas an obligation for MRDC. *The National*.

Nalu, M. (2018c, March 19). Oil search gives an overview of its earthquake relief effort. *The National*.

Nasution, R. (2018a, Oct. 3). New focus: Keeping good deeds alive amid Central Sulawesi's catastrophe. *Antara News*.

Nasution, R. (2018b, Oct. 7). News focus: Unsung heroes in Central Sulawesi catastrophe. *Antara News*.

Nations Online. (2019). *Population figures by country*. Accessed March 25, 2019 at https://www.nationsonline.org/oneworld/population-by-country.htm

NATO 'in solidarity with the Greek people,' alliance chief says (2018, July 24). *Kathimerini*.

ND slams Tsipras's early Monday visit to Mati as PR stunt (2018, July 30). *Kathimerini*.

Nedos, V. (2018, Aug. 5). SYRIZA metaphysics. *Kathimerini*.

Nedos, V., & Georgiopoulou, T. (2018, Aug. 3). Minister quits over fires amid pressure for more departures. *Kathimerini*.

Nedos, V., Georgiopoulou, T., & Souliotis, Y. (2018, Aug. 3). Pressure grows for apportioning of blame for fires. *Kathimerini*.

News Focus: Indonesian government moves swiftly in handling Gonggala quake victims (2018, Sept. 29). *Antara News*.

Newspaper fact sheet (2019, July 9). *Pew Research Center*. Accessed Oct. 20, 2019 at https://www.journalism.org/fact-sheet/newspapers/

Nicas, J., Fuller, T., & Arango, T. (2018, Nov. 12). Forced out by deadly fires, then trapped in traffic. *New York Times International Edition*.

Nigeria flood response preparedness standard project report 2018 (2018). World Food Programme in Nigeria. *Federal Republic of (NG)*. Accessed Sept. 6, 2019 at https://docs.wfp.org/api/documents/WFP-0000103908/download/?_ga=2.231761623.958862570.1567893524-137589326.1567893524

Nigeria floods 2018: Work report 1 (2018, Oct. 24). *ReliefWeb*. Accessed Sept. 6, 2019 at https://reliefweb.int/report/nigeria/nigeria-floods-2018-work-report-1

Nigeria: Large-scale floods affect close to two million people (2018, Oct. 11). *United Nations office for the coordination of humanitarian affairs*. Accessed Sept. 6, 2019 at https://www.unocha.org/story/nigeria-large-scale-floods-affect-close-two-million-people

Nigeria report (2017). *Freedom House*. Accessed Oct. 4, 2019 at https://freedomhouse.org/report/freedom-press/2017/nigeria

No remorse, no accountability (2018, July 29). *Kathimerini*.

Noelle, M. (2002). The ripple effect of the Matthew Shepard murder impact on the assumptive worlds of members of the targeted group. *American Behavioral Scientist, 46*(1), 27–50.

Norwegian envoy 'shocked' by wildfire deaths in east Attica (2018, July 25). *Kathimerini*.

Odunlami, D. (2014). Journalism and mass communication education in Nigeria: In search of right pedagogy. *Journal of Literature, Language and Linguistics, 3*, 45–49.

Oi, S., & Sako, S. (2017). Journalists in Japan. *Worlds of Journalism*. Accessed June 23, 2020 at https://epub.ub.uni-muenchen.de/36330/1/Country_report_Japan.pdf

Ojewale, B. (2018, Sept. 19). Flooding: Avoiding the fury of nature. *The Nation*.

Okereocha, C. (2018, Sept. 27). Flooding: Fresh threat to investors, rice self-sufficiency. *The Nation*.

Okoro, N., & Chinweobo-Onuoha, B. (2013). Journalists' perceptions of brown envelope syndrome and its implications for journalism practice in Nigeria. *Covenant Journal of Communication, 1*(2), 130–144.

Ololade, O. (2018, Sept. 15). Floods of fury. *The Nation*.

Omenugha, K. A., & Oji, M. (2008). News commercialization, ethics and objectivity in journalism practice in Nigeria: Strange bedfellows? *Revista Estudos em Comunicação/Communication Studies*. http://www.ec.ubi.pt/ec/03/html/omenugha-oji-news-commercialization.html

Ortiz, G. (2018, June 9). Tragedies that generate migration: The somber future of the survivors of the Volcán de Fuego. *La Hora*.

Ostertag, S. F., & Ortiz, D. G. (2013). The battle over meaning: Digitally mediated processes of cultural trauma and repair in the wake of hurricane Katrina. *American Journal of Cultural Sociology, 1*(2), 186–220.

Osumi, M. (2018a, July 14). Volunteers risk slowing west Japan relief efforts. *Japan Times*.

Osumi, M. (2018b, July 24). Foreign residents extend helping hand to Hiroshima amid ongoing disaster-relief efforts. *Japan Times*.

Osumi, M. (2018c, July 26). Flood victims face uncertain future. *Japan Times*.
Our good side (2018, Aug. 10). *Kathimerini*.
Oyserman, D., Coon, H. M., & Kemmelmeier, M. (2002). Rethinking individualism and collectivism: Evaluation of theoretical assumptions and meta-analyses. *Psychological Bulletin, 128*(1), 3–72.
Pakistan report (2017). *Freedom House*. Accessed Oct. 4, 2019 at https://freedomhouse.org/report/freedom-press/2017/pakistan
Pakistan's heatwave woes to worsen further as summer temperatures spike steadily (2018, May 20). *The News International*.
Pakistan's 'shocking' spring heat drives up water use, health risks (2018, May 31). *ReliefWeb*. Accessed Sept. 7, 2019 at https://reliefweb.int/report/pakistan/pakistan-s-shocking-spring-heat-drives-water-use-health-risks
Paletz, D. L., & Entman, R. M. (1981). *Media, power, politics*. New York: Free Press.
Pantti, M., & Wahl-Jorgensen, K. (2007). Disaster journalism as therapy news? The political possibilities of the spectacle of suffering. *International Communication Association*, 1–23.
Pantti, M., & Wahl-Jorgensen, K. (2011). 'Not an act of God': Anger and citizenship in press coverage of British man-made disasters. *Media, Culture and Society, 33*(1), 105–122.
Pantti, M., & Wieten, J. (2005). Mourning becomes the nation: Television coverage of the murder of Pim Fortuyn. *Journalism Studies, 6*(3), 301–313.
Papachelas, A. (2018, July 27). The state we're in. *Kathimerini*.
Papadiochos, C. P. (2018, Aug. 6). After Toskas departure, PM looks to government reshuffle. *Kathimerini*.
Papadopoulos, N. (2018, July 25). Without a captain, without a compass. *Kathimerini*.
Papathanassopoulos, S. (1999). The effects of media commercialization on journalism and politics in Greece. *Communication Review, 3*(4), 379–402.
Papathanassopoulos, S. (2001). Media commercialization and journalism in Greece. *European Journal of Communication, 16*(4), 505–521.
Papua New Guinea earthquake: At least 14 killed amid landslides (2018, Feb. 27). *BBC*.
Papua New Guinea: Humanitarian Situation Report No. 1 (2018, April 13). *ReliefWeb*. Accessed Sept. 10, 2019 at https://reliefweb.int/report/papua-new-guinea/papua-new-guinea-humanitarian-situation-report-no1-13-april-2018
Papua New Guinea quake: An invisible disaster which could change life forever (2018, March 10). *BBC*.
Papua New Guinea-religion (nd). *GlobalSecurity.org*. Accessed April 1, 2020 at https://www.globalsecurity.org/military/world/oceania/png-religion.htm
Papua New Guinea report (2015). *Freedom House*. Accessed Oct. 19, 2019 at https://freedomhouse.org/report/freedom-press/2015/papua-new-guinea
Papua New Guinea report (2017). *Freedom House*. Accessed Oct. 4, 2019 at https://freedomhouse.org/report/freedom-press/2017/papua-new-guinea
Pargament, K. I., Ishler, K., Dubow, E., Stanik, P., Rouiller, R., Crowe, P., Cullman, E. P., Albert, M., & Royster, B. J. (1994). Methods of religious coping with the

Gulf War: Cross-sectional and longitudinal analyses. *Journal for the Scientific Study of Religion, 33*(4), 347–361.

Pargament, K. I., Koenig, H. G., & Perez, L. M. (2000). The many methods of religious coping: Development and initial validation of the RCOPE. *Journal of Clinical Psychology, 56*(4), 519–543.

Park, R. E. (1941). News and the power of the press. *American Journal of Sociology, 47*(1), 1–11.

Park, R. E. (1967/1925). *The city.* Chicago: University of Chicago Press.

Pastor calling on people to focus on God as PNG counts cost of earthquake (2018, March 15). *The National.*

Patterson, S., Cheang, J., Smith, A., & Johnson, A. (2017, Sept. 22). Mexico earthquake survivors rescued after 2 days in Rubble. *NBC News.* https://www.nbcnews.com/news/world/frantic-rescues-continue-mexico-quake-deaths-rise-273-n803641

Peloni, A. (2018, July 30). Number of wildfire victims points to 'gaps' in prevention, says Stylianides). *Kathimerini.*

Pemble, A., & Hadjicostis, M. (2018, July 27). Pets rescued after Greece's devastating fire find new homes. *Kathimerini.*

Pence will visit Guatemala and meet with victims of the Volcán de Fuego (2018, June 14). *La Hora.*

Penn, I., & Eavis, P. (2018, Nov. 15). California utility customers may be on hook for billions in wildfire damage. *New York Times International Edition.*

Perez, S. (2018, June 4). A whole nation mourns the eruption of the Volcano of Fire; millions of affected. *La Hora.*

Perez-Lugo, M. (2004). Media uses in disaster situations. *Sociological Inquiry, 74*(2), 210–225.

Pfefferbaum, B., Seale, T. W., McDonald, N. B., Brandt, E. N., Jr., Rainwater, S. M., Maynard, B. T., Meierhoefer, B., & Miller, P. D. (2000). Posttraumatic stress two years after the Oklahoma City bombing in youths geographically distant from the explosion. *Psychiatry, 63*(4), 358–370.

Pintak, L., & Nazir, S. J. (2013). Pakistani journalism: At the crossroads of Muslim identity, national priorities and journalistic culture. *Media, Culture & Society, 35*(5), 640–665.

Piraeus Port Authority expresses solidarity with wildfire victims (2018, July 28). *Kathimerini.*

Pitas, C., & Maltezou, R. (2018, July 30). Tsipras meets survivors in fire-stricken town as families mourn dead. *Kathimerini.*

Plot where 26 wildfire victims died is encroached state land (2018, Aug. 1). *Kathimerini.*

PM accepts resignation of Citizens' Protection Minister Toskas over Attica fires (2018, Aug. 3). *Kathimerini.*

PM finally takes blame for deadly conflagration after outcry (2018, July 27). *Kathimerini.*

Police, fire chiefs replaced in wake of deadly Attica blazes (2018, Aug. 5). *Kathimerini.*

Pope Francis sends message of support to Greek president after wildfires (2018, July 27). *Kathimerini*.

Pope prays for victims of Greek fires (2018, July 24). *Kathimerini*.

Prakash, A. (2013). Peace or war journalism: Case study of the Balochistan conflict in Pakistan. *Strategic Analysis, 37*(5), 621–636.

President issues orders to repair tsunami detection buoys (2018, Oct. 2). *Antara News*.

President Jokowi again visits quake-hit C Sulawesi (2018, Oct. 3). *Antara News*.

President Jokowi outlines four priorities in Central Sulawesi disaster handling (2018, Oct. 2). *Antara News*.

President Jokowi visits quake, tsunsmi-stricken areas (2018, Sept. 30). *Antara News*.

President orders government agencies to prepare for quake effects (2018, Sept. 29). *Antara News*.

President receives aid offers from various countries (2018, Oct. 2). *Antara News*.

Press reference: Papua New Guinea (nd). Accessed Sept. 17, 2019 at http://www.pressreference.com/No-Sa/Papua-New-Guinea.html

Prihantoro, A. (2018, Oct. 5). LDII helps earthquake-affected victims in Central Sulawesi. *Antara News*.

Protect the socially weak from heat waves (2018, July 26). *Japan Times*.

Purnamawati, D. (2018, Oct. 6). Central Sulawesi's quake victims to receive social aid funds: Ministry. *Antara News*.

Quake, tsunami death toll in Central Sulawesi rises to 420 (2018, Sept. 29). *Antara News*.

Ramaprasad, J. (2001). A profile of journalists in post-independence Tanzania. *Gazette (Leiden, Netherlands), 63*(6), 539–555.

Ramaprasad, J., & Hamdy. N. N. (2006). Functions of Egyptian journalists: Perceived importance and actual performance. *International Communication Gazette, 68*(2), 167–185.

Ramaprasad, J., & Kelly, J. D. (2003). Reporting the news from the world's rooftop: A survey of nepalese journalists. *International Communication Gazette, 65*(3), 291–315.

Red Cross responds to Greece's deadly wildfire disaster (2018, July 25). *ReliefWeb*. Accessed Sept. 9, 2019 at https://reliefweb.int/report/greece/red-cross-responds-greece-s-deadly-wildfire-disaster

Reel, M. (1997, Dec. 3). Kentucky town tries to come to grips with shooting at high school. *St. Louis Post-Dispatch*, A17.

Reforestation to begin without delay, says minister (2018, July 27). *Kathimerini*.

Relief operations ongoing in earthquake affected areas (2018, March 23). *The National*.

Report—The Japanese Red Cross Society's response to the heavy rain event of July 2018 (2019, Sept. 10). *The Japanese Red Cross Society*. Accessed Sept. 11, 2019 at http://www.jrc.or.jp/english/relief/190910_005860.html

Rescuers race against time as death toll in western Japan floods rises to at least 176 (2018, July 10). *Japan Times*.

Residents flee wildfire raging west of Athens (2018, July 23). *Kathimerini*.

Residents in Palu to be relocated to safer regions (2018, Oct. 17). *Antara News*.

Residents to depart from earthquake-hit area aboard Pelni ship (2018, Oct. 1). *Antara News*.

Residents told 'just leave' as wildfire rages near Athens (2018, July 23). *Kathimerini*.

Revival of agriculture fields in rural Karachi can minimise heatwave effects (2018, June 3). *The News International*.

Reyes Lopez, J. F. (2018, June 8). The tragedy of the Volcano of Fire. *La Hora*.

Rich, C. (2005). *Writing and reporting news: A coaching method*, 4th edition. Belmont, CA: Wadsworth Thomson Learning.

Risk of deadly flood in badly hit area of Okayama Prefecture known in advance (2018, July 11). *Japan Times*.

Robbins, K. (1999, April 22). Teens cling to each other—And faith: "Now we've really got to be a light," says Colorado girl. *St. Louis Post Dispatch*, A1.

Robie, D. (1999). Pacific newsrooms and the campus: Some comparisons between Fiji and Papua New Guinea. *Australian Studies in Journalism*, 8, 176–196.

Robie, D. (2008). Changing paradigms in media education aid in the Pacific. In U. Harris & E. Papoutsaki (Eds.), *South Pacific islands communication: Regional perspectives, local issues* (pp. 59–81). Singapore, Auckland, Fiji: NUS, PMC and USP.

Romero, S. (2018, Nov. 20). In a Walmart lot, a rough refuge for California wildfire Evacuees. *New York Times International Edition*.

Rooney, D. (2003). Rethinking the journalism curriculum in PNG. *Asia Pacific Media Educator*, *1*(14), 6.

Rosenblatt, K. (2018, Feb. 27). Parkland school shooting: Stoneman Douglas students prepare to confront memories as they return to classes. *NBC News*. Accessed March 30, 2018 at https://www.nbcnews.com/news/us-news/parkland-school-sh ooting-stoneman-douglas-students-prepare-confront-memories-they-n851656

Saavedra, A. (2018, June 9). Nature calamities, inclement fire volcano. *La Hora*.

Saifi, S., & Yeung, J. (2018, May 22). Heatwave kills at least 65 in Pakistan. *CNN*. Accessed Sept. 7, 2019 at https://cnn.com/2018/05/22/asia/pakistan-heat-wave -wxc-intl/index.html

Saudi King expresses condolences over Central Sulawesi earthquake (2018, Oct. 2). *Antara News*.

Scenes of chaos after floods and landslides wreak havoc in western Japan (2018, July 7). *Japan Times*.

Schaefer, T. M. (2003). Framing the US embassy bombings and September 11 attacks in African and US newspapers. In P. Norris, M. Kern, & M. Just (Eds.), *Framing terrorism: The news media, the government and the public* (pp. 93–112). New York: Routledge.

Schudson, M. (1995). *The power of news*. Cambridge, MA: Harvard University Press.

Schuster, M. A., Stein, B. D., Jaycox, L. H., Collins, R. L., Marshall, G. N., Elliott, M. N., Zhou, A. J., Kanouse, D. E., Morrison, J. L., & Berry, S. H. (2001). A national survey of stress reactions after the September 11, 2001 terrorist attacks. *New England Journal of Medicine*, *345*(20), 1507–1512.

Scott, M., Bunce, M., & Wright, K. (2018). *The state of humanitarian journalism*. Norwich, England: University of East Anglia.

Search continues as wildfires death toll climbs to 80 (2018, July 25). *Kathimerini*.
Seaside town remembers lives lost to fire, children's camp reopens (2018, July 30). *Kathimerini*.
Sheasby, R. E. (nd). *Press reference: Guatemala*. Accessed Sept. 17, 2019 at http://www.pressreference.com/Fa-Gu/Guatemala.html
Siapera, E., Papadopoulou, L., & Archontakis, F. (2015). Post-crisis journalism: Critique and renewal in Greek journalism. *Journalism Studies, 16*(3), 449–465.
Sideridis, D. (2019, July 23). 'Swimming with dead bodies': A year on, Greeks haunted by inferno. *Al Jazeera*. Accessed Sept. 14, 2019 at https://www.aljazeera.com/indepth/inpictures/dead-bodies-1-year-greeks-haunted-inferno-190722193111770.html
Siegler, K. (2019, May 28). Rethinking disaster recovery after a California town is leveled by wildfire. *National Public Radio*. Accessed Sept. 15, 2019 at https://www.npr.org/2019/05/28/724404528/rethinking-disaster-recovery-after-a-california-town-is-leveled-by-wildfire
Sigal, L. V. (1973). *Reporters and officials: The organization and politics of newsmaking*. Lexington, MA: DC Heath.
Siraj, S. A. (2009). Critical analysis of press freedom in Pakistan. *Journal of Media and Communication Studies, 1*(3), 43–47.
Situation of emergency officially extended in Central Sulawesi (2018, Oct. 12). *Antara News*.
Slater, M. D. (2007). Reinforcing spirals: The mutual influence of media selectivity and media effects and their impact on individual behavior and social identity. *Communication Theory, 17*(3), 281–303.
Slone, M., Shoshani, A., & Baumgarten-Katz, I. (2008). The relation between actual exposure to political violence and preparatory intervention for exposure to media coverage of terrorism. *Anxiety, Stress and Coping: An International Journal, 21*(3), 243–261.
SNF to support Greek fire department with 25 mln grant (2018, July 30). *Kathimerini*.
Social Ministry sends logistic assistance for donggala earthquake response (2018, Sept. 29). *Antara News*.
Souliotis, Y. (2018a, July 27). Forensic investigators call on relatives of missing in Attica wildfires to provide DNA samples. *Kathimerini*.
Souliotis, Y. (2018b, Aug. 2). Finger-pointing over fires as police tapes depict alarm. *Kathimerini*.
Souliotis, Y., & Antoniou, D. (2018, July 28). Fire service did not brief police, Kathimerini learns, as more officials are replaced. *Kathimerini*.
Souliotis, Y., & Elafros, Y. (2018, Aug. 14). Relatives testify in Attica fires inquiry. *Kathimerini*.
Souliotis, Y., & Mandrou, I. (2018, Aug. 13). Probe hones in on fire service, regional authority officials. *Kathimerini*.
Sparks, C., & Splichal, S. (1989). Journalistic education and professional socialization. *Gazette, 43*, 31–52.
Steele, J. (2011). Justice and journalism: Islam and journalistic values in Indonesia and Malaysia. *Journalism, 12*(5), 533–549.

Stevenson, M. (2017, Sept. 28). In Mexico, survivors recount amazing escapes from earthquake. *Chicago Tribune*. http://www.chicagotribune.com/news/nationworld/ct-mexico-earthquake-survivors-20170928-story.html

Still on earthquake (2018, March 16). *The National.*

Stories from the aftermath of Hurricane Maria in Puerto Rico (2017, Sept. 28). *Fox News*. http://www.foxnews.com/world/2017/09/28/stories-from-aftermath-hurricane-maria-in-puerto-rico.html

Stovall, J. G. (2006). *Writing for the mass media*, 6th edition. Boston: Pearson Education, Inc.

Struggle for survivors of fire trying to return to normalcy (2018, Aug. 8). *Kathimerini.*

Students give to help earthquake victims (2018, March 19). *The National.*

Suchenwirth, L., & Keeble, R. L. (2011). Oligarchy reloaded and pirate media: The state of peace journalism in Guatemala. In I. S. Shaw, J. Lynch, & R. A. Hackett (Eds.), *Expanding peace journalism: Comparative and critical approaches* (pp. 168–190). Sydney: Sydney University Press.

Suk, S. (2018, July 12). Large-scale evacuation a key concern in the event of a major flood in Tokyo. *Japan Times.*

Suliman, A. (2018, July 26). No charge for Airbnb rooms as victims of Greek wildfires scramble for shelter. *Kathimerini.*

Sylvie, G., & Huang, S. J. (2008). Value systems and decision-making styles of newspaper front-line editors. *Journalism & Mass Communication Quarterly*, *85*(1), 61–82.

Synolakis, C. (2018, July 25). Mistakes and oversights. *Kathimerini.*

Sztompka, P. (2000). Cultural trauma: The other face of social change. *European Journal of Social Theory*, *3*(4), 449–466.

Tagaris, K., & Konstantinidis, A. (2018, July 25). House to house, crews search for missing in wildfire aftermath. *Kathimerini.*

Tajfel, H., & Turner, J. C. (1979). An integrative theory of intergroup conflict. *The Social Psychology of Intergroup Relations*, *33*(47), 74.

Tamindael, O. (2018, Oct. 1). News feature: Nightmare waves wipe out Palu and Gonggala. *Antara News.*

Tanaka, C. (2018, July 11). High horse: Crew rescues miniature mare from rooftop. *Japan Times.*

Tears, grief at memorial service for Greek wildfire victims (2018, July 29). *Kathimerini.*

Tenenboim-Weinblatt, K. (2008). We will get through this together': Journalism, trauma and the Israeli disengagement from the Gaza Strip. *Media, Culture & Society*, *30*(4), 495–513.

Tenenboim-Weinblatt, K., Hanitzsch, T., & Nagar, R. (2016). Beyond peace journalism: Reclassifying conflict narratives in the Israeli news media. *Journal of Peace Research*, *53*(2), 151–165.

Tester, K. (2001). *Compassion, morality and the media*. Buckingham: Open University Press.

The Nation (Nigeria). http://thenationonlineng.net/

The National (Papua New Guinea). https://www.thenational.com.pg/

The News International (Pakistan). https://www.thenews.com.pk/

The survivors of the Fire Volcano safe, but with uncertainty about the future (2018, June 16). *La Hora*.

The World Bank in Guatemala (2019). Accessed April 6, 2020 at https://www.worldbank.org/en/country/guatemala

These are the names of some people who sadly lost their lives by the Volcán de Fuego (2018, June 12). *La Hora*.

They ask resignation of Morales and other officials after the tragedy of Volcán de Fuego (2018, June 9). *La Hora*.

They denounce Secretary of the Conrad, Sergio Cabañas, for the tragedy of the Volcán de Fuego (2018, June 27). *La Hora*.

Three battalions of army troops dispatched to Palu: Mily commander (2018, Oct. 2). *Antara News*.

Tian, Y., & Stewart, C. M. (2005). Framing the SARS crisis: A computer-assisted text analysis of CNN and BBC online news reports of SARS. *Asian Journal of Communication, 15*(3), 289–301.

Too little, too late (2018, July 29). *Kathimerini*.

Touri, M., Theodosiadou, S., & Kostarella, I. (2017). The internet's transformative power on journalism culture in Greece: Looking beyond universal professional values. *Digital Journalism, 5*(2), 233–251.

Triandafllou, V., & Georgiopoulos, G. (2018, July 24). Wildfires kill at least 60 near Athens; three days of mourning called. *Kathimerini*.

Triandafllou, V., & Konstantinidis, A. (2018, July 24). Wildfires kill at least 60 near Athens, EU states respond to appeal for help. *Kathimerini*.

Triandafllou, V., & Maltezou, R. (2018, July 23). Greece battles raging forest fires as homeowners flee to safety. *Kathimerini*.

Trump calls Jokowi, offers US aid for earthquake victims (2018, Oct. 4). *Antara News*.

'Tsunami' of support for Greek fire victims in Cyprus (2018, July 29). *Kathimerini*.

Tsunami waves hit several parts of central Sulawesi: BNPB (2018, Sept. 29). *Antara News*.

Turks express solidarity for Greeks outside consulate in Izmir (2018, July 27). *Kathimerini*.

Turner, V. (1977). *The ritual process: Structure and anti-structure*. Ithaca, NY: Cornell University Press.

Tusk: 'Europe will stand by our Greek friends' (2018, July 25). *Kathimerini*.

Tzembelicos, A. (2018, July 31). Being better prepared for disasters. *Kathimerini*.

UK aid gives emergency medical treatment to world's poorest in deadly heatwave (2018, June 11). *ReliefWeb*. Accessed Sept. 7, 2019 at https://reliefweb.int/report/pakistan/uk-aid-gives-emergency-medical-treatment-world-s-poorest-deadly-heatwave

Ukaha, J. (2018, March 23). Lae earthquake relief appeal raises K26,000. *The National*.

UNICEF Guatemala Humanitarian Situation Report No. 4 (2018, Aug. 17). *ReliefWeb*. Accessed Sept. 9, 2019 at https://reliefweb.int/report/guatemala/unicef-guatemala-humanitarian-situation-report-no-4-17-august-2018

United States report (2017). *Freedom House.* Accessed Oct. 4, 2019 at https://freedomhouse.org/report/freedom-press/2017/united-states

Valys, P. (2018, Feb. 15). Religious leaders try to make sense of Stoneman Douglas school shooting. *South Florida Sun Sentinel.* Accessed March 30, 2018 at http://www.sun-sentinel.com/local/broward/parkland/florida-school-shooting/fl-reg-florida-school-shooting-religious-reactions-20180215-story.html

Van Gennep, A. (1909/1960). *The rites of passage.* Chicago: University of Chicago Press.

Vankwani, R. K. (2018, May 25). Tackling heatwaves. *The News International.*

Velasco, S. (2018, June 4). Volcano of fire and our heroes of truth! *La Hora.*

Vigil held in Athens for wildfire victims (2018, July 30). *Kathimerini.*

Villanueva, E. (2018, June 8). Alternative lessons of the tragedy of the Volcán de Fuego. *La Hora.*

Violence and landslides block aid access to Papua New Guinea quake victims (2018, April 12). *ReliefWeb.* Accessed Sept. 10, 2019 at https://reliefweb.int/report/papua-new-guinea/violence-and-landslides-block-aid-access-papua-new-guinea-quake-victims

Volunteers of Jokowi-Ma'ruf in Malaysia collect tsunami donation (2018, Oct. 2). *Antara News.*

Vos, T. P., & Craft, S. (2016). Journalists in the United States. *Worlds of Journalism.* Accessed June 23, 2020 at https://epub.ub.uni-muenchen.de/34878/1/Country_report_US.pdf

Wahune, T. (2018, March 23). USAid hailed for role in earthquake relief work. *The National.*

Walsh, A. (2001). Good for what ails us. *Religion in the News*, Fall.

Wani, D. (2018a, March 5). Earthquake not caused by humans, says expert. *The National.*

Wani, D. (2018b, March 5). Western confirms 13 deaths in earthquake. *The National.*

Waskita, A. (2018, Sept. 30). President Jokowi calls on public to pray for earthquake victims. *Antara News.*

Water outages continue in flood-hit areas across western Japan, as death toll tops 170 (2018, July 11). *Japan Times.*

Watson, A. (2019, July 1). Trustworthiness of news media worldwide 2019. *Statista.* Accessed May 6, 2020 at https://www.statista.com/statistics/308468/importance-brand-journalist-creating-trust-news/

Weaver, D. H., & Willnat, L. (Eds.). (2012). *The global journalist in the 21st century: News people around the world.* New York: Routledge.

Wehmeyer, P., & Jennings, P. (1999, April 26). Columbine victim Cassie Bernall's story. *ABC World News Tonight.*

Wereh points out roads badly affected by earthquake (2018, March 5). *The National.*

Western Japan struggles to restore water to flood-hit towns as temperatures soar (2018, July 13). *Japan Times.*

What else can trigger an earthquake? That is the question (2018, March 23). *The National.*

WHO works with government agencies to respond to floods across Nigeria (2018, Oct. 3). *World Health Organization*. Accessed Sept. 6, 2019 at https://www.afro.who.int/news/who-works-government-agencies-respond-floods-across-nigeria

Why does Nigeria keep flooding? (2018, Sept. 27). *BBC*.

Williams, M. (1997, Dec. 3). Kentucky school killings; heartbreak unites town as students try to forgive. *Atlanta Journal and Constitution*, 3A.

Wills, K., & Boyle, C. (2012, Dec. 15). Mourners pack church for vigil. *Daily News (New York)*, 13.

Winfield, B. H., Mizuno, T., & Beaudoin, C. E. (2000). Confucianism, collectivism and constitutions: Press systems in China and Japan. *Communication Law and Policy*, 5(3), 323–347.

Wings Air resumes Gorontalo-Palu flights (2018, Oct. 2). *Antara News*.

Woman dies in hospital, raising number of wildfire fatalities to 88 (2018, July 28). *Kathimerini*.

World Bank offers five million dollars of grant for C Sulawesi earthquake reconstruction (2018, Oct. 13). *Antara News*.

World Press trends (2016). *WAN-IFRA*. Accessed Oct. 11, 2019 at http://anp.cl/wp-content/uploads/2017/02/WAN-IFRA_WPT_2016_3.pdf

Wright, J. C., Kunkel, D., Pinon, M., & Huston, A. C. (1989). How children reacted to televised coverage of the space shuttle disaster. *Journal of Communication*, 39(2), 27–45.

Wu, H. D. (2003). Homogeneity around the world? Comparing the systemic determinants of international news flow between developed and developing countries. *Gazette (Leiden, Netherlands)*, 65(1), 9–24.

Yahaya, F. (2018, Sept. 24). WMO chief attributes flooding to poor climatic data. *The Nation*.

Yair, G., Girsh, Y., Alayan, S., Hues, H., & Or, E. (2014). "We don't need another hero": Heroes and role models in Germany and Israel. *Comparative Education Review*, 58(2), 269–295.

Yet another heatwave to hit city in a week (2018, May 24). *The News International*.

Yildiz, A. A., & Verkuyten, M. (2011). Inclusive victimhood: Social identity and the politicization of collective trauma among Turkey's Alevis in Western Europe. *Peace and Conflict: Journal of Peace Psychology*, 17(3), 243–269.

Young, R. (1999, April 21). Services encourage prayer, compassion. *Denver Post*, A19.

Youth begins with sowing 200 neem plants in Karachi (2018, June 3). *The News International*.

Zandberg, E., Meyers, O., & Neiger, M. (2012). Past continuous: Newsworthiness and the shaping of collective memory. *Critical Studies in Media Communication*, 29(1), 65–79.

Zelizer, B. (2002). Finding aids to the past: Bearing personal witness to traumatic public events. *Media, Culture & Society*, 24, 697–714.

Index

Abe, Shinzo, 91, 107, 118, 126, 141, 149, 160
Antara News, 25, 162
Anthonius Gunawan Agung, 77–78, 102, 111
Athens, Greece, 24, 63, 67, 93, 98, 116, 120, 124, 125, 130–32, 142, 145, 155, 160, 165
Attica, Greece, 23, 58, 63, 73, 102, 114, 116, 122, 125, 129, 133, 142–44, 146, 150–51, 155, 160

Banderas, Antonio, 99
BBC, 20–21, 44–45, 47, 51, 53–54, 64–65, 68, 72–73, 100, 168, 170, 172, 182
Brown, Jerry, 100, 153
Butler, Gerard, 65

Camp Fire, United States, 25, 71, 75, 86, 100, 110, 130, 172
Central Sulawesi, Indonesia, 24–25, 79, 87–89, 92–93, 99, 111, 114–15, 117, 123, 125–26, 132, 161–62
community interest function in news, 11
constructive journalism, 11–12, 176, 180, 184–85

coping in journalism, 2–3, 8, 14, 18–19, 54, 68–69, 75, 85, 103, 105, 109, 111–12, 134, 157, 175–78, 183–86
COVID-19, 2, 182–83

Del Toro, Guillermo, 60
Donggala, Indonesia, 24, 88, 92, 101, 121, 123, 161

Facebook, 60, 62, 82, 122, 161–62, 185

Greece wildfires, 24–25, 45, 48, 57–59, 63, 65, 67–68, 73–74, 80, 83, 88, 90, 93–94, 97–102, 105, 107, 110–11, 114, 116, 118–20, 122, 124–26, 128–33, 137–40, 142–53, 155–57, 159–61, 165–67, 177–81
Guatemala volcanic eruption, 22–23, 45, 48, 60–63, 66, 68, 72–73, 78, 80, 82, 87–89, 91, 97–100, 106–7, 109–10, 115, 126–28, 131, 140–47, 149, 156, 160–62, 167–68, 179, 181

Hakuho, 81
healing in journalism, 2–3, 6, 8, 10, 13–14, 16, 19, 54, 85, 96, 105, 108, 163, 175–77, 183–86

Hela, Papua New Guinea, 21, 65, 106
hope in journalism, 2–3, 8, 13–15, 19, 54, 57, 68–69, 75, 84–85, 97, 102, 105, 108–9, 111, 133–34, 163, 175–79, 183–86
humanitarian journalism, 11–12, 180, 184

Indonesia earthquake and tsunami, 24–25, 45, 48, 61, 64–65, 67, 77–79, 81, 87–95, 98–99, 101–2, 106–8, 111, 114–26, 132–33, 141, 143–44, 149, 156, 159–62, 168–69, 178–79, 181
International Monetary Fund, 44, 46, 159, 162

Japan flooding, 23, 45, 48, 66–67, 79, 81–83, 87, 89, 91–93, 107, 114–16, 118, 120–21, 125–26, 139–41, 146–47, 149, 151–52, 154–55, 160, 169, 178–79, 181
Japan Times, 23, 34, 169
Jokowi, 115, 123, 125–26, 162. *See also* Widodo, Joko
Journalism culture, 6, 27–30, 172–73, 180–81; Greece, 30–31, 165–67, 181; Guatemala, 32, 167–68, 181; Indonesia, 32–34, 168–69, 181; Japan, 34–35, 169, 181; Nigeria, 35–36, 169–70, 181; Pakistan, 37–38, 170–71, 181; Papua New Guinea, 38–39, 171–72, 181; United States, 39–40, 172–73, 181
Journalistic healing themes: actions, 19, 45, 48, 50–51, 113–35, 166, 168, 170–72, 176, 178–82; blame or responsibility, 19–20, 45, 48, 50, 52, 137–58, 165, 168, 170–72, 176–77, 178–82; community, cohesion, and intimacy, 16–18, 46, 48, 50, 52–53, 97–103, 167, 170, 176–82; death stories, 14–15, 47–48, 50, 53, 71–75, 166, 169–70, 176, 178–79, 181–82; external validation, 20, 45–46, 48, 50, 52, 159–63, 166, 168–69, 171, 176, 178–82; faith, belief, and salvation, 18, 47–48, 50, 53, 105–8, 168, 171, 176–81; reassurance, purpose and meaning, 18–19, 47–48, 50, 53–54, 109–12, 172, 176–79, 181–82; recovery efforts, 16, 46, 48, 50, 52, 85–96, 169, 171, 176–79, 181–82; selfless behavior, 15–16, 46–48, 50, 53, 77–84, 166–67, 172, 176, 178–79, 181; survivor stories, 14, 46, 48, 50, 53, 57–69, 166–67, 172, 176, 178, 180–82
Journalists' values, 2, 3, 6, 10–11, 27–28, 33, 54, 180, 183–84

Karachi, Pakistan, 21–22, 47, 80, 101, 107, 119–20, 128–29, 139, 143, 150–51, 154
Kardashian, Kim, 64, 107
Kathimerini, 24, 30, 74, 119, 138, 143, 165–66

Lady Gaga, 60
Lae, Papua New Guinea, 80–81, 89, 101, 163
La Hora, 23, 32, 61, 72, 74, 103, 127, 131, 145, 167

Mabicho, Japan, 66, 83, 93, 115
Malibu, United States, 60, 62, 65–66
Mati, Greece, 23, 46, 57–58, 63, 67–68, 73–74, 80, 90, 98, 101, 126, 129, 138, 140, 142, 148, 150–51, 155, 165
media events, 5
mobilizing information, 13
Morales, Jimmy, 80, 97, 126, 141, 149

The Nation, 24, 36, 74
The National, 21, 38, 81, 139
news functions, 6
The News International, 22, 37, 170, 178
news values, 3, 6, 8–10, 27–28, 54, 180, 183–84

Index

New York Times International Edition, 26, 40, 71, 172

Nigeria flooding, 24, 45, 48, 66, 72, 74–75, 82, 86–87, 90, 98, 101, 115, 117–19, 121–23, 126, 128, 130, 133, 140–41, 143, 146, 150, 152–54, 156–57, 163, 169–70, 178–79, 181

Pacific Gas and Electric, 156

Pakistan heat wave, 21–22, 45, 48, 101, 106–7, 119–20, 127–30, 139, 143, 150–51, 154–55, 170–71, 178, 181

Palu, Indonesia, 24, 45, 61, 65, 67, 82, 87, 89–95, 101, 114–15, 117, 119, 122, 124, 126, 133, 141, 149

Papua New Guinea earthquake, 21, 45, 48, 50, 65, 67, 80–81, 89, 93–94, 99, 101, 105–8, 110, 115, 118, 120, 132, 138–39, 143, 147, 151, 162–63, 171–72, 177–78, 181

Paradise, United States, 25, 45, 59–64, 68, 72, 74, 78, 81–83, 86, 88–89, 92–93, 100, 110, 114, 116, 124, 126, 144–45, 151–52, 156

peace journalism, 11, 15, 19–20, 75, 134, 157

political freedom, 29–30, 32–35, 38–39, 44, 51–52, 54, 165, 167, 169, 171, 182

Pope Francis, 47, 107, 159, 161

press freedom, 28–30, 32–35, 37–39, 43–44, 50, 52–54, 165, 168–69, 171, 182

Prince Charles, 159–60

recovery in journalism, 2–3, 8, 10, 13–14, 16, 19, 54, 84–85, 95, 102, 105, 108–9, 163, 175–77, 179–80, 183–86

Red Cross, 22–25, 73, 79, 81, 122–123, 131

El Rodeo, Guatemala, 22, 62, 66, 72, 88

school shooting, 2, 14–20, 75, 84, 96, 102, 108, 180, 182

sources in news, 3, 39, 43, 57, 61, 63, 67–69, 71, 73, 75, 77–78, 81–82, 84–85, 88, 90–95, 97, 99, 102–3, 105, 109, 113, 125, 134, 137, 142, 147, 152–53, 157, 159, 163, 167–72, 176

terrorism, 7–8, 14, 16–17, 36, 75, 102, 180, 182

Toskas, Nikos, 100, 129, 143–44, 153, 155

trauma: collective, 7–8, 12–13, 68; cultural, 7–8; impact of, 1–8, 12, 102, 124, 175–76, 183–84; individual, 6–8; in news, 2, 5–8, 12, 14–20, 41–42, 45, 54, 63–65, 68–69, 178–80, 182, 185; vicarious, 7

Trump, Donald, 97, 100, 111, 126, 128, 144–45, 149, 151–53, 155–57, 160, 162

trust in journalism, 3, 186

Tsipras, Alexis, 46, 97, 118, 125–26, 129, 132, 143–44, 147–48, 150–53, 160, 165–66

United States wildfires, 25–26, 45, 48, 59–61, 63–66, 68, 71–72, 74–75, 78, 80–83, 85–86, 88–89, 93–95, 97, 100–101, 107, 110–11, 114, 116, 124, 126, 128, 130, 133, 144–45, 149, 151–53, 155–56, 172–73, 179, 181

values, collective, 28–29, 35–36, 55, 170

values, individualistic, 29, 53, 55

Widodo, Joko, 89, 107, 110, 114, 117, 120–21, 123, 125–26, 149, 161–62, 168. *See also* Jokowi

Woods, James, 81

World Bank, 32, 46, 111, 159, 161

Young, Neil, 65–66

About the Author

Dr. Michael McCluskey is a professor in the Department of Communication at the University of Tennessee, Chattanooga. His previous book, *News Framing of School Shootings: Journalism in Times of Trauma and Violence*, was also published by Lexington Books. His research, focused primarily on journalism and political communication, has been published in a wide variety of academic journals. Dr. McCluskey is an editorial board member of two journals, *Mass Communication & Society* and *Newspaper Research Journal*, and serves as book review editor of *Mass Communication & Society*. His previous academic appointments were at California State University at Fresno, the Ohio State University, and American University. After completing his bachelor's degree at the University of Washington, he worked as a newspaper journalist for seventeen years in Washington State, including news editor of the *Snoqualmie Valley Record* and reporter at the *Wenatchee World*. Dr. McCluskey earned his master's degree at the University of Washington and doctorate at the University of Wisconsin.

www.ingramcontent.com/pod-product-compliance
Lightning Source LLC
Chambersburg PA
CBHW050904300426
44111CB00010B/1376